Fairhope, 1894-1954

Fairhope, 1894-1954

THE STORY OF

A single tax COLONY

PAUL E. AND BLANCHE R. ALYEA

UNIVERSITY OF ALABAMA PRESS 1956

Preface

*T*HE decision to write the story of Fairhope was not made on the spur of any moment. The authors have been acquainted with the community for many years. To one, the place is the scene of some of his happiest boyhood recollections; the other has visited Fairhope with increasing frequency for almost twenty-five years. Both have had training in economics and some previous acquaintance with single tax doctrine, although neither claims to be a singletaxer. However, we do admit to a degree of fascination with Henry George and his doctrines, and we admire most of the singletaxers we have known for their individualism and liberalism in the older sense of the terms. We suspect that a large proportion of thinking individuals share our worry over some of the current social and political forces directed toward an achievement of social aims. Some of the means employed appear to threaten certain individual freedoms and tend to relegate our local governments to the status of dependents upon the largess and control of federal and state legislatures. On the one hand, we have come to believe that absolute poverty has been diminished, that gross inequalities in the distribution of wealth have been reduced, and that the economy as a whole has been made somewhat more stable. On the other hand, we recognize that these desirable social objectives have been attained, in part, by an ever-increasing positive role played by government, and we wonder whether even free men are capable of controlling such a public concentration of economic power without either making fatal errors, or without drifting into too much reliance on government paternalism. We are therefore interested in the results of any social experiment made to learn whether there might not be a better and safer way of accomplishing these social objectives.

This is not a study of the single tax; rather it is a study of a small and limited experiment, which is based upon the hypothesis that a local community would be more prosperous and more stable, if it limited itself to those public facilities and services which could be financed solely out of land rents. Real live social experiments are understandably few, and they are never completely controlled in a laboratory sense. It is our conviction that all social experiments are precious however imperfectly they are conducted. Certainly it would appear that an experiment which has survived for sixty years—even one which is based upon an idea which Robert L. Heilbroner, in his *Worldly Philosophers*, categorized as belonging to "the underworld of economics"—has earned the dignity of being evaluated and reported. This study is an independent analysis of an experiment made by outside observers, who believe there is a hypothesis to be tested rather than an eternal verity to be demonstrated.

The task has not been an easy one. Under the best of conditions people and their social groupings are complex almost to the point of defying understanding. The inherent imperfections in the manner of conducting the Fairhope demonstration have been so diverse as to magnify the tasks of describing what actually took place and of isolating the resulting effects.

For the most part we chose to rely on the historical method with occasional departures in order to look more deeply into particular local institutions, controversies or events, without strict regard to chronology. In addition to the sources of information generally available with respect either to the single tax or to the Fairhope colony, we examined the official minutes of every colony meeting, and every issue of the Fairhope *Courier* up to the time it became more of a community weekly and less exclusively a colony organ. In addition we read hundreds of letters in the files of E. B. Gaston, James Bellangee, and Anne B. Call, and many in the files of the Fairhope Single Tax Corporation. We examined several scrapbooks of newspaper clippings and other fugitive materials, and talked with a large number of individuals living in Fairhope. We held several score conferences with the present secretary, Dr. C. A. Gaston, in an effort to clarify or to document certain points. We have examined many of the books, records, forms and materials which either are or have been used by the corporation and some of its offshoots.

Unfortunately, we could not fully examine all facets and were forced to make choices as to which areas would be relatively untreated. Four of the important gaps in this study are:

1. There are no biographical sketches of colony leaders. Our desire was to minimize personal influences and to concentrate on the policies and procedures of the colony as an entity. In a few instances, however, we chose to present the activities and points of view of certain individuals, primarily to achieve an effect of greater authoritativeness, but partly to enliven an otherwise dull but important episode. We hope we have struck a reasonable balance in this respect. Certainly our objective in bringing personalities into the story even in a limited fashion was neither to glorify nor to vilify any individual.

2. We did not undertake a detailed and highly technical analysis of the Somers System of land valuation as practiced by the Fairhope Single Tax Corporation.

3. We did not make a systematic personal opinion and social psychological analysis of the impact of the colony on the several groups within the municipality of Fairhope.

4. We did not make a financial study of the municipality to determine the precise extent to which the single tax corporation has affected local choices among revenues or public serv-

ices. Nor did we look with precision into the extent to which
the municipality might be financed exclusively from land rents
assuming it should obtain local option in taxation. However,
one of the authors did prepare, at the invitation of the city
council of Fairhope, a comparative analysis of the revenue
patterns of Fairhope and twenty-six other small Alabama
municipalities. The study showed that the revenue pattern of
Fairhope definitely is atypical within Alabama, and doubtless
the presence of the single tax corporation is largely responsible.
(Cf. *Revenues of Small Alabama Cities,* published jointly by
the University of Alabama Bureaus of Business Research and
Public Administration, 1952.) With respect to local ownership
of utilities and the consequent effects on the disbursement
patterns and city indebtedness, the municipality of Fairhope
differs markedly in degree from most cities of its population
group. This, too, is largely the outgrowth of earlier colony
influence.

We mention these gaps in the hope that they may be filled
by others. Clearly a comprehensive knowledge of the Fairhope
venture requires that more attention be paid to the areas mentioned than we have given to them.

The reader should be forewarned that the authors did not
write the usual final chapter of detailed recapitulation of find-
ings, conclusions and recommendations. However, they did not
hesitate to draw conclusions in connection with the treatment
of special stages in the development of the colony or with
reference to special controversies and problems. The concluding chapter is wholly one of opinion as to the nature of the
survival value of the demonstration together with certain suggestions as to future policies and procedures.

Readers who have had little personal experience with
Fairhope will find some of the sections dealing both with history and with special problems somewhat detailed—indeed
much of the text might be scanned by the general reader. To a
degree, however, we have attempted to write to the interest of
a large group who have known Fairhope intimately. Whether

they be 'phobe or 'phile, we trust that a bit of detailed chronology will awaken in them some feeling of nostalgia for the "good old days" when everybody in the vicinity, and many from a distance, got into the fray. The last bitter controversy of any consequence took place over two decades ago. Certainly time must have healed most wounds; at least we trust that perspective and a sense of humor will have softened any recollections which might be unpleasant. Certainly we do not want to be the instrumentality of renewing old internecine struggles. Nor do we want to start new ones with our recommendations.

This study would not have been possible without the interest, encouragement and assistance of many, an indebtedness we wish to acknowledge publicly, with the understanding that none other than the authors are to be held responsible for any errors of fact or judgment contained herein. To the Research Committee of the University of Alabama, we acknowledge a great material indebtedness; the study would have been delayed for an indefinite period except for the financial assistance granted from its limited budget. The Fairhope Single Tax Corporation, and its secretary, Dr. C. A. Gaston, made available all of its official papers, and an unlimited amount of Dr. Gaston's time, without making any request or reservation of any kind. Dr. Gaston made available the invaluable personal files of his father, E. B. Gaston. Such co-operation seldom is encountered. The Fairhope *Courier* staff took considerable pains to make available for our use all of the files of past issues. We acknowledge an indebtedness to the late Mrs. Anne B. Call and to her daughter, Miss Helen Bellangee Call, for the hours given in a discussion of the history of the colony. In addition, Mrs. Call furnished us letters and materials from her own files as well as those contained in the files of her husband, William Call, and her father, James Bellangee. We appreciate the courtesy of the Robert Schalkenbach Foundation in lending us scarce issues of the *Single Tax Review*. Miss Alice Kingery of the University of Alabama Library made many efforts to assist us in obtaining scarce materials, a service for which we are grateful. The kindness and services rendered to us by citizens of Fairhope were legion, but we wish to thank Mr. Elof M. Tuveson and Mr. Henry George Coleman for answering our inquiries; Mr. Arthur Mershon and Mayor E. B. Overton for sharing with us their knowledge of the history of Fairhope and its people, and Miss Anna Braun of the Fairhope Public Library. To Claude Bagge, of Elberta, Alabama, we are indebted for permission to make certain uses of his copyrighted map of Baldwin County.

PAUL E. ALYEA

BLANCHE R. ALYEA

Tuscaloosa, Alabama

Contents

Fairhope, 1894-1954

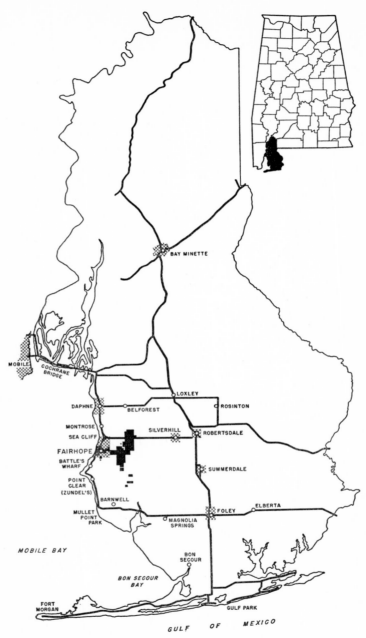

BALDWIN COUNTY, ALABAMA
Location of Fairhope Single Tax Corporation land in solid black.

i

THE FAIRHOPE SINGLE TAX THEORY

FAIRHOPE is the name of the oldest and largest single tax colony in America. It is also the name of an Alabama municipality with a 1954 population of about 4,200. Fairhope is located on the bluffs of the eastern shore of Mobile Bay, midway between the communities of Montrose and Battles Wharf, and about twenty-five miles by highway from Mobile. Its location very well could have been somewhere in Tennessee, or in any of five states visited by the location committee, but Baldwin County, Alabama, was chosen by the Fairhope Industrial Association because of its climate, its beauty and the cheapness of its land in 1894. The first colonists occupied their chosen site in the winter of 1894-1895; the municipality of Fairhope was incorporated in 1908. The original implementing agent, the Fairhope Industrial Association, was incorporated under the laws of Iowa in 1894, and gave way in 1904 to the Fairhope Single Tax Corporation, incorporated under Alabama law.

In its beginning the Fairhope colony contained a considerable admixture of socialism; but the core of the colony plan, and the features which survived, were contained in those provisions of the constitution that permitted it to experiment with a simulated single tax.

The term single tax as used in Fairhope refers to the suggestion made by Henry George in *Progress and Poverty* that the ageless and universal problem of poverty and other economic and social evils might be cured by a simple fiscal reform. The remedy urged by Mr. George was simply that government would tax away the full annual use value of land and would refrain from any other mode of taxation. Under his plan there would be no taxes on the value of or income from buildings, industrial equipment, household furniture, jewels, stocks of goods or other intangible personal property. There would be no customs duties, no income taxes and no sales, excise or business license taxation. To the maximum extent practicable, however, all economic rent would be taken for community purposes.

Singletaxers offer a two-fold justification for this simple fiscal program, and they maintain this justification is based on natural law. Morally, they argue, economic rent belongs to the community for the simple reason that it is a product solely of community demand for land. The supply of land is fixed by nature, thus providing a basis for differentiating land from labor and capital. Since the supply of land cannot be increased there is no cost of reproduction, hence no basis for any individual or private claim to its income. In taxing away economic rent the community is merely taking that which it has created independent of any action by the landowner. Taxation of the products either of capital or of labor would be robbery; singletaxers recognize no ethical justification for the community *compelling* individuals to contribute to its support any part of incomes individually earned.

The second justification for this fiscal program is rooted in several adverse economic consequences which singletaxers believe follow from the private appropriation of economic rent. The most serious ill effect of such appropriation is that it encourages speculation in land. Singletaxers maintain that land speculation is wholly evil; that no useful purpose is served comparable to that served by speculation in commodities. Land speculation causes better endowed and better located land either to be wholly withheld from use, or grossly under-used. As a consequence, they reason, the community income is lower than it would otherwise be, it is maldistributed, and the economy is much more vulnerable to cycles of boom and bust.

If, they maintain, government would simply tax away all income from land, as differentiated from capital, this would be sufficient to destroy the most basic and wholly evil monopoly, *i.e.,* the land monopoly. If all economic rent were taken in taxation no profit would remain for the land speculator; hence, there would be no reason why land would not be made available for its highest use. Wages and interest would tend to be higher in any community using the single tax. If the plan were used internationally, *general* industrial booms and depressions would be greatly mitigated, and one fundamental cause for war would be eliminated. Society would become more stable and more wholesome. More of the benefits of progress in technology, in the growth of capital, in improvements in government and in the spread of educational opportunities, would redound to the general benefit; the landlord, who contributes nothing in this capacity, would not be able, under the single tax, to forestall such general sharing of the benefits of progress by pre-empting economic rent.

The single tax doctrine is more than a fiscal reform and a logical argument for its support; it is a blueprint for a free society. There are alternative means of accomplishing some of the benefits singletaxers hope for. For example, land might be nationalized or periodically redistributed. Poverty might be mitigated by private charity and governmental largess. Other kinds of taxation might be used primarily to redistribute income. The economic system might be made somewhat more secure by means of social insurance, market supports and monetary and fiscal policies. Or the economy might be planned in detail and operated through some sort of corporate state, *i.e.,* fascism, communism, or a middle course of more democratic collectivism. Singletaxers reject most of these alternative reme-

dies because of the social compulsion involved. The essence of
the single tax philosophy is a profound belief in freedom, in
individualism under institutions compatible with natural law.
Henry George is said to have replied to a sneering question by
a heckler, who asked whether he thought that the single tax was
a panacea: "No, but freedom is!"

Whether a fair trial of the single tax on a world-wide basis
would demonstrate the benefits hoped for by ardent singletaxers must remain conjectural. At the time the Fairhope plan
was conceived and placed in operation, most literate people
either had read or were somewhat familiar with Henry George's
Progress and Poverty. Countless throngs had heard Mr. George
speak from the lecture platform. There were several flourish-
ing periodicals dedicated to explaining and spreading the single
tax gospel. As a consequence, many individuals professed an
understanding of, and a belief in, the single tax "in principle."
In 1894 it must have been easy to hope that the world just
might adopt George's remedy and thus pursue political, social
and economic individualism within his frame of reference. At
any rate, in 1894 the projection of a single tax enclave did not
seem incongruous, although neither Henry George, nor many
of his followers, believed in a colony as a proper device for
propagating the "true course of reform."

Among singletaxers the Fairhope pioneers were a relatively
lonely group. As colonists, however, they were filled with
courage and optimism. It was a period characterized by social
experimentation through colonies, the great bulk of which were
short-lived. The abortive experience of most colonies did not
discourage the Fairhope group because they were certain that
they had the soundest of all possible bases for a successful
colony. They were convinced that their venture would be so
successful in its single tax aspects that countless local communities would come to see the light, and would demand the legal
right to inaugurate discriminatory land taxation through local
option.

As everyone knows, most of the competing social, political
and economic philosophies of the twentieth century exclude

almost entirely any serious consideration of the one closely identified with Henry George. Indeed, the world seems destined for the indefinite future to adopt policies leading to extreme collectivism—a destination diametrically opposed to the degree of individualism so devoutly sought by the single-taxer. When the Fairhope single tax colony was founded the single tax was a living issue, large numbers were actively interested in the theory, either as ardent and dedicated advocates, or as bitter opponents. Within a few years there was a marked change in the fashions of economic, social and political doctrines. To a considerable extent both public opinion and political actions relegated George's doctrine almost to the status of an anachronism. Not that the consensus with respect to the single tax turned markedly antagonistic; worse still, public opinion became indifferent toward it.

The Fairhope colony survived this and many other handicaps and shortcomings. It not only has survived but has grown increasingly strong in a material or financial sense. And a curious thing has occurred: instead of shedding its single tax characteristics as the general public lost interest in the doctrine, the colony gradually purged itself of non-single tax impurities in its functions, its policies and its procedures. The Fairhope Single Tax Corporation of 1954 is very much a going concern. At least from the point of view of its small membership it is anything but an anachronism; rather it is viewed as one of the more realistic and soundly rooted reform organizations in existence.

The Fairhope story is one of the origin, early experiences, struggles and conflicts, adjustments and adaptations, material growth, shortcomings and accomplishments of the Fairhope colony. The intent of this study is to present the history of the first sixty years of the colony, together with a critical analysis of the substantive issues, both past and present. Some conclusions and recommendations are drawn by the authors but it is their hope that sufficient documented data are offered the reader to enable him to draw his own conclusions and make his own evaluation. The authors would be pleased if any reader should become sufficiently interested in Fairhope to search out the information necessary to fill the many lacunae left by this chronicle; or for that matter to offer alternative interpretations to the data included herein. An institution such as the Fairhope colony experimenting with fundamental social, governmental and economic problems for a period of sixty years, and still going strong, deserves a more intensive critical attention than it has received in recent decades.

The following paragraphs are offered purely in the interest of orienting the reader who has no previous knowledge of Fairhope. They contain a brief description of the essential nature and functioning of the Fairhope Single Tax Corporation. All of the points made in the remainder of this chapter are covered in much more detail either in the body of the study or in the appendices.

The Fairhope Single Tax Corporation is a non-profit, private corporation organized under an Alabama statute passed with its requirements specifically in view. Fundamentally, it is a private land owning corporation organized to demonstrate the efficacy of the single tax theory. Despite its title, *the corporation has no power of taxation.* The colony, its lessees and the lessees' tenants, are subject to the same tax system as residents of Fairhope living on deeded land. It is therefore obvious that the single tax is not, and never has been, in operation in Fairhope in a technical sense.

The Fairhope colony attempts to operate its version of the single tax through a system of land tenure intended to shift the incidence of some of the state and local taxes from capital and labor to land. The *modus operandi* involves: first, the leasing of land under contractual provisions that permit the colony to levy whatever annual rental is necessary to capture the whole of economic rent from the land under lease; and second, the refunding of certain taxes paid by lessees, and in other ways disbursing the rents collected for the benefit of the lessees. The plan is designed to demonstrate two benefits of the Georgian doctrine. First, the colony hopes to prove that land will be more accessible, and more fully utilized, under a complete collection of the annual use value, than it is under the prevailing system. Second, the colonists hope to show that a given community can have more public facilities and services, with less burden on private initiative, enterprise and effort, if it diverts the income it creates to its own purposes and leaves with individuals the incomes which they create.

Like all private organizations, membership is both voluntary and selective. The conditions for membership are two: the possession of $100, and a decision on the part of the executive council that the applicant both understands and believes in the Fairhope plan of applying the single tax. Except to the dedicated singletaxer there are few advantages or reasons for joining the colony. No member could gain materially save in connection with the dissolution of the colony—a contingency that is quite remote since the colony is now quite well off materially and has survived a court test of its legality. Nonetheless, the existing membership ever must remain on guard against admitting as members, persons who might be motivated to seek private enrichment through the dissolution of the corporation.

In addition to exercising supreme authority in controlling the Single Tax Corporation, the members do have a technical advantage in obtaining possession of colony land. This advantage lies in the fact that a member does not have to bid against a non-member for the privilege of leasing a colony site. This may be made clearer upon outlining the lease-granting procedures.

Whenever the colony opens up land for use it publishes a notice of availability. Any person, member or non-member, may apply for the land by signing an application and by tendering an amount equal to the value of any colony-owned improvements on the land (usually trees), plus not more than six months' rent. Notice that a colony site has been applied for is pasted in the window of the colony office for a period of one week. Any other individual interested in this same leasehold might apply and compete with the applicant by an offer of a bonus to the colony. If a bonus is offered by another the initial applicant is notified and given an opportunity to bid against his competitor. Members are not required to bid against non-members. As a matter of practice bonuses have been relatively rare; in a few cases, however, they have amounted to quite sizable sums.

Leases are for a period of ninety-nine years although they are not valid under Alabama law for a period exceeding twenty years unless recorded. A charge of $1.00 is made for the making of any lease. At any time a lessee chooses, he may extend the period of his leasehold to the full ninety-nine years upon the payment of $1.00. The colony imposes no restrictions on the use of its lands by its lessees. Although the colony reserves the legal right of making leaseholds non-transferable except to members, in practice the conditions imposed on transfers to non-members usually have not been unduly difficult.

ii

BACKGROUND, ORGANIZATION AND LOCATION OF THE FAIRHOPE INDUSTRIAL ASSOCIATION

THE last three decades of the nineteenth century were characterized by monetary panics and widespread economic depressions which broke records in the extent of unemployment, poverty and attendant violence. Farmers, industrial workers and many industries were in a generally unhappy condition. City slums and farm tenancy were growing rapidly. To Henry George these conditions and trends pointed to a continuous decay in American civilization unless the underlying economic causes were diagnosed and removed. George wrote: What has destroyed every previous civilization has been the tendency to the unequal distribution of wealth and power. This same tendency, operating with increasing force, is observable in our civilization today, showing itself in every progressive community, and with greater intensity the more progressive the community. Wages and interest tend constantly to fall, rent to rise, the rich to become very much richer, the poor to become more helpless and hopeless and the middle class to be swept away.[1]

Whatever the truth with respect to the ultimate destiny of America, conditions were excellent for the propagation of many types of reform movements. The remedies sought included

[1] Henry George, *Progress and Poverty*, 50th Anniversary Edition (New York, 1953, Robert Schalkenbach Foundation) p. 528.

new political alignments, proposals to alter such institutions as money and credit, the tariff, taxation (particularly agitation for personal income and inheritance taxation), and regulation of railroads and trusts. The period likewise was characterized by the formation of many strongly socialistic "co-operative" colonies, most of which survived only a few months.

The Fairhope Industrial Association, which evolved into the first single tax colony in America, was a product of this period of social and economic unrest.[2] Papers of incorporation were filed February 7, 1894. The stated purpose was to establish and conduct ". . . a model community or colony, free from all forms of private monopoly, and to secure to its members therein equality of opportunity, the full reward of individual efforts, and the benefits of co-operation in matters of general concern." (Constitution)

The predominant characteristic of Fairhope long has been that of a single tax colony with the ostensible purpose of conducting a laboratory test of Henry George's doctrine. The colony, however, did not begin as a pure single tax project, although certain singletaxers of the period were most influential in determining the key provisions of the "plan to solve the problem of practical co-operation." Nonetheless, the constitution of the Fairhope Industrial Association contained many provisions looking to the reform of economic institutions other than those relating to taxation and land tenure. Likewise it is true that some of the more influential leaders of the colony remained something less than simon-pure singletaxers (in the sense that the single tax is viewed as an exclusive reform) for a considerable period of time after the Fairhope association was organized.

Many strong and dedicated personalities have contributed to the Fairhope community. It would be wholly gratuitous to

[2] E. B. Gaston, Fairhope *Courier,* January 8, 1915, credited Alf Wooster, one of the charter members, with the happy selection of Fairhope as the name for the proposed colony. The late Mrs. Anne B. Call, in an interview with the authors, related that the question of who had named Fairhope came up at a colony social years ago, and that at that time someone stated that Dr. Clara Atkinson had suggested the name to her brother, E. B. Gaston.

single out any small number of these for exclusive credit or blame for the accomplishments and shortcomings of the colony. On the other hand, strong personalities do influence the course of events and institutions, and it would be equally unrealistic to overlook entirely the influence of key individuals in any attempt to interpret and evaluate Fairhope as a single tax institution. In the formative stages of the colony, and through much of its early history, three personalities tended to dominate. These were, in order of their appearance, Ernest B. Gaston, James Bellangee and Joseph Fels.

Initially, Mr. Gaston was much more interested in establishing a co-operative colony than he was in conducting a demonstration of the single tax. For several years prior to the incorporation of the Fairhope Industrial Association he maintained an intermittent interest in attempts to achieve economic reform through the device of a separate colony of a socialistic nature. He came close to achieving this in 1890, when he was quite active in promoting a colony to be located in Louisiana, and modeled along lines suggested by Edward Bellamy in *Looking Backward*. The details of his plan for the "National Co-operative Company Limited, A Joint Stock Company" are not relevant to the Fairhope story. However, questions asked of those applying for membership do serve to help in the understanding of this remarkable man: "Do you understand the co-operative spirit?" "Are you willing, if elected a member, to honestly, truly and persistently endeavor to harmonize others, to correct your own faults, to try and discover and do your duty, rather than wholly rely on your Right?" "Do you use intoxicating liquors as a Beverage?"[3]

In the course of his attempt to promote the Bellamy-type colony Mr. Gaston sought the co-operation of Mr. James Bellangee, who suggested, as an alternative, a colony which would serve as a working model of the single tax *"to educate the*

[3] The membership fee was set at $500 with $250 to be paid before taking up residence on company ground. The sketchy data on this project are contained in the files of the late E. B. Gaston. It appears that at least one membership was sold.

public to demand local option in taxation."[4] Mr. Bellangee recently had come under the influence of Mr. William Morphy, one of the early followers of Henry George and the organizer and leading spirit of the Des Moines Single Tax Club. Thus the single tax features of the Fairhope plan flowed from Morphy to Bellangee to Gaston. Since both Gaston and Bellangee were active and influential members of the newly organized Populist party, neither could be characterized at that time as having a conviction that the single tax would serve as an exclusive reform. However, both were active members of the Des Moines Single Tax Club; Mr. Bellangee served as its president.

Gaston and Bellangee joined forces in collaborating with others in the organization of the Fairhope plan and placing it before the public. The proximate chronology of the Fairhope Industrial Association begins with a meeting on Thursday, January 4, 1894, in Mr. Gaston's office, Room 8 over 312 Sixth Street, Des Moines, Iowa. Present were: Alf Wooster, J. Bellangee, J. P. Hunnel, Robert Elder, J. R. Sovereign, W. H. Sanders, L. R. Clements, H. C. Bishop, E. B. Gaston, R. G. Scott, John Swayne, B. G. Dyer, and C. W. Enyard. This initial meeting resulted in agreement on the form of organization for a colony, and the appointment of Alf Wooster, J. Bellangee, J. P. Hunnel, L. R. Clements and E. B. Gaston as a committee to draft a constitution and by-laws. (Minutes)

A second meeting of this group was held January 31, 1894, at which time the constitution was adopted and officers were elected.[5] The first officers of the Fairhope Industrial Association were: President, L. R. Clements; Vice-president, E. A. Ott; Secretary, Ernest B. Gaston; Trustees, S. S. Mann, W. H. Sanders, and H. C. Bishop; Treasurer and Superintendent of the Department of Finance and Insurance, Alf Wooster; Superintendent of Lands and Highways, J. Bellangee; Superintend-

---

4 James Bellangee, *Single Tax Review*, XII, Spring Issue (March 15, 1913), 18.
5 The constitution of the Fairhope Industrial Association is reproduced in full in Appendix A. The paragraphs immediately following are paraphrases of some of its essential features.

ent of Public Services, T. E. Mann; Superintendent of Merchandising, George B. Lang; Superintendent of Industries, J. P. Hunnel; and Superintendent of Public Health, Andrew Engle. The executive council was composed of the six superintendents of departments.

Any person over eighteen subscribing to at least one share of capital stock with a par value of $200 might apply for membership. Applicants for membership had to be approved by the executive council. Ten per cent of the membership might reject any applicant by filing with the secretary a written protest within thirty days after the council had approved the application. The spouse of a member also was considered a member and was entitled to vote upon signing the constitution. Should any member violate the spirit and purpose of the association, or invade the rights of any of its members, he or she might be expelled by the executive council. Such expulsion would be contingent upon charges filed by ten per cent of the members and only after a full public investigation at which the accused might be represented by counsel.

The constitution vested supreme authority in the membership to be exercised through the initiative and referendum. Any member not in arrears was entitled to one vote only, irrespective of the number of shares owned or subscribed to.

The constitution provided that any matter set forth in a petition of ten per cent of the membership must be submitted to a vote of the membership. Further, the executive council could not place in force any measure of general legislation until thirty days following its passage unless it had filed a petition for its submission to the membership. Upon petition of twenty per cent of the members the issue of a dismissal of any officer had to be submitted to popular vote. In all matters except amendment of the constitution a majority vote of those voting would suffice. Amendment of the constitution required a three-fourths affirmative vote of the entire membership.

The constitution forbade any individual ownership of land within the jurisdiction of the association. Land owned by the association was to be held in trust for the entire membership.

Association lands were to be equitably divided and ". . . leased to members at an annually appraised rental which shall equalize the varying advantages of location and natural qualities of different tracts, and convert into the treasury of the association for the common benefit of its members, all values attaching to such lands not arising from the efforts and expenditures thereon of the lessees." The constitution provided that lessees should have full and absolute right to the use and control of the lands under lease, and to the ownership and disposition of all improvements made or products produced thereon, so long as the annually appraised rentals were paid. Lessees, however, might terminate the lease upon six months' notice.

Leaseholds were made assignable *but only to members* of the association.

The association would hold a prior lien on all improvements for any arrearages of rent.

The constitution further provided that if any lessee should exact from another a greater value for the use of land, exclusive of improvements, than the rent paid to the association, the executive council should increase the rental charge to the amount so charged.

Land not desired for use by members might be leased to non-members. The executive council was granted discretion to perform equivalent services for non-members, on such terms as it might choose.

The right of eminent domain was reserved to the association.

The constitution clearly prohibited the association from levying any other tax or charge upon the property or persons of its members. It provided that the revenues of the association were to be used to pay all taxes levied by the state, county or township on the property of the association or of any of its members held within its jurisdiction, money and credits excepted. The constitution provided that in platting association land, "ample provision" must be made to assure land for parks and all other public purposes. The intention was expressed that public lands should be improved as rapidly as possible and schools, libraries, public halls and natatoriums were specifically mentioned.

Under the constitution the "overhead" of the association was to be kept within reasonable limits. An office-holding aristocracy was discouraged by the provision that salaries could not be larger than the average earnings (locally) for like energies and abilities.

The foregoing constitutional provisions made the Fairhope Industrial Association unique among co-operative colonies. The provisions governing land usage and the disposition of revenues were designed to permit the colony to approximate the operation of the single tax as it would work in a community choosing this system of taxation. Private speculation in land would be discouraged by the annually adjusted rental charges which would tend to encourage either the highest use of the lands or their forfeiture by lessees; lessees were granted absolute freedom in their use of land; and the "unearned increment" must be collected by the colony and expended for public purposes.

The constitution, however, contained other provisions of a decidedly different nature; provisions which indicate that not all of the founders were willing to place all of their reform eggs in the one basket of land tenure.

Under the constitution the association might issue association scrip, which would be non-interest-bearing and receivable by the association from bearer in full payment of all association demands. The purpose of such a medium was to provide members with ". . . a safe, adequate, and independent medium for effecting exchanges . . ." Scrip was to be issued for the purchase and handling of all merchandise; for advances on goods stored in the association's warehouse; and for all expenses of public services. The issue in any one year was to be limited to ". . . the estimated revenue available during said year for such purposes."

The constitution prohibited the association from granting any private franchise for public necessities. As soon as practicable, however, the association itself was to erect and maintain such facilities. The constitution did not limit the charges for the services of association-owned utilities but provided that any revenues therefrom should be covered into the general treasury.

Under the original constitution it was mandatory that the association establish a store or stores for the sale of all merchandise for which there might be sufficient demand. The purpose was "To effect in distribution the efficiency and economy demanded in the interests alike of producers and consumers."[6] The indicated pricing policy would be one of following prices prevailing in the neighboring community. Profits would be disposed at the discretion of the executive council in three ways: a portion paid into the general treasury; a portion to provide additional store capital; and the remainder divided among the members trading at the stores in proportion to their purchases. Members were not required to patronize the store (s).

To stock the store (s) the constitution provided that each member contribute a sum not exceeding $100 before taking up residence on colony lands. In exchange the member would receive an equal amount of the association's non-interest-bearing obligations.

Originally it was required that the association should operate a department to assist members in disposing of their surplus products. The management of this department might purchase such products at the market price or handle them on commission as desired. The association was required to provide convenient and safe storage for the products of its members.

The framers of the original colony plan attempted to draw a sharp distinction between production and distribution (marketing), *e.g.*, ". . . the declared general policy . . . to leave production free to individual enterprise." The basis for such a policy as set forth in the constitution was the belief that ". . . the free competition of free men in productive industry is natural and beneficent, and that therefrom will arise a natural and just cooperation in enterprises requiring the associated labor and capital of individuals . . . ." Despite this declaration of faith the association reserved a constitutional right to establish and con-

---

6 This quotation and the several similar ones following reflect general ideas stressed many times in the *Liberty Bell* and in the early issues of the Fairhope *Courier*.

duct manufactories and industries of any kind. The constitution, however, specifically denies to any department of distribution or production the authority to establish a monopoly except for public utilities.

The following rules were adopted governing the subscription and payment of capital stock.

1. Capital stock may be paid for in monthly installments of not less than $5.00, the same to be due on the first of the month and becomes delinquent on the 15th; but must be paid in full before a member shall be entitled to lease lands of the association.

2. A penalty of ten cents per month shall be charged on all installments due and unpaid after the fifteenth day of each month until such delinquent payments are paid together with all penalties accrued.

3. Where the penalties charged against a member for delinquency on installments shall equal the amount already paid by him on his stock, the executive council may declare his membership forfeited and apply the amount before paid on capital stock to the payment of such penalties.

4. Any member may withdraw at any time by filing with the secretary written notice of his desire to do so and paying all installments and penalties due upon his stock, and shall be entitled to receive a certificate showing the total amount paid by him on stock (exclusive of penalties), which certificate shall be transferable, and receivable by the association from any member in payment on stock.

5. Subscriptions for capital stock shall not be held to make the subscribers legally liable for anything beyond the amount actually paid upon such stock.

The above rules represented in part an extension of a resolution unanimously adopted at a meeting of the executive council on February 6, 1894. This resolution also provided that the first payment was due as of February 1 and that all who became members on or before May 15, 1894 would receive the $200 share for $175, but ". . . must make all payments due from February 1."

The following form of application for membership was adopted by the executive council on February 6, 1894:

FIRST APPLICATION FOR MEMBERSHIP

I hereby make formal application for membership in the Fairhope Industrial Association.

I have carefully read your constitution, fully approve of the principles therein set forth and will abide by it and such regulations in accord with it as may from time to time be made.

I hereby subscribe for_____share (s) of stock of the association of the par value of $200 each and agree to pay on the same at least $5 per month in advance until the whole is paid or until I desire to locate in the association lands when I understand that all must be paid.

I also agree to pay to the association the further sums to be fixed by the executive council but not to exceed $100, to be applied to the purchase of stock for the association's merchandise department and to accept in lieu thereof the non-interest bearing obligations of the association described in Article X, Sec. 1, of the Constitution.

Herewith find my correct answers to inquiries made by you and $_____ for first payment on my stock to be returned if my application is not accepted.

(Applicant must answer the following questions)
Where Born?_____ In What Year?_____ Nationality of Father?_____ Mother?_____ Regular Occupation _____ Occupation preferred in this Colony?_____ What (if any) trade or reform organization are you or have you been a member of?_____ What works of sociology or economics have you read?_____ Are you married?_____ Number of Children?_____ Sexes and ages? _____ When would you like to go to the Colony?_____ Do you expect to take your family with you?_____ Would you expect to build at once?_____ How much capital would you probably invest in the Colony?_____. Give references as to your character and standing in your community.

At the meeting of February 16, 1894, Mr. Gaston was retained as secretary on an allowance of $40 per month. The *Liberty Bell* was selected as the official organ of the association. The secretary was instructed to take two and one-half thousand copies of the second number of the *Liberty Bell,* at $4.00 per thousand payable in stock of the association. These copies were requisitioned because the issue contained the full text of the constitution and the details of the organization of the association, all of which would be needed in promotion.

The first seven issues of this paper were published in Des Moines, after which it was moved to Oskaloosa, Iowa. Alf Wooster was persuaded to perform the role of publisher. The paper, however, was not self-supporting and its coverage was extended to general news and political articles. The executive council was not happy over this development and after some attempt to salvage the *Liberty Bell* as its official organ, called a meeting of the committee of the whole on August 10. The membership resolved that the time had arrived for the Fairhope Industrial Association to publish its own paper from its headquarters—a paper devoted exclusively to Fairhope interests. A committee was appointed to arrange as soon as possible for the publication of such a paper on a budget not to exceed $300 per year. Thus was conceived the Fairhope *Courier,* the first issue of which was published in Des Moines, Iowa, August 15, 1894, with Mr. E. B. Gaston as editor.[7] Mr. Wooster was advised of this action and allowed $5.00 per month in stock for the remainder of 1894 provided he would publish in the *Liberty Bell* not less than four columns of Fairhope matter each month.

The greater part of the task of writing articles, preparing leaflets and making speeches in behalf of Fairhope was performed by Mr. Bellangee and Mr. Gaston. While there were no substantial contradictions in the various utterances of these two, there is much evidence of decided differences as to which

[7] Mr. Gaston continued to serve as editor of the Fairhope *Courier,* with the exception of a few months in 1895, as long as the colony owned the paper. In 1899 he made a proposal to the executive council which was accepted. The proposal involved both Gaston's salary as secretary of the colony and the status of the Fairhope *Courier.* He asked to take over the paper as his personal venture and agreed to accept $100, as secretary's salary for the current year, "payable half in scrip and the other half to apply on the purchase of printing material until same was paid and then upon stock." He further agreed to do all the ordinary printing of the association without further charge. (Minutes, February 20, 1899).

As owner and publisher of the *Courier,* Gaston gave space generously for the colony's publicity. However, several years later, at the urging of Joseph Fels, the colony agreed to pay the *Courier* $100 a year for Fairhope Single Tax Corporation publicity. (Fairhope *Courier,* March 23, 1906.)

features of the plan should be given greatest emphasis. Bellangee consistently and almost exclusively stressed the land question, and Gaston (while accepting the projected programs of land tenure as fundamental) appeared to place equal stress upon the commercial and financial provisions of the constitution.

Mr. Bellangee's concern as a singletaxer may be demonstrated by two illustrations. In the leading article of the *Liberty Bell* (April 28, 1894) he stressed that the "Fairhope Industrial Association proposes to correct the evils of our present land system so far as it can be done in a country governed by bad laws concerning land and taxation." He neglected even to mention the non-single tax provisions of the constitution. Of utmost significance is an observation contained in a letter he wrote Gaston from Citronelle, Alabama, July 16, 1894 (Gaston files): "Gaston, I am more than ever convinced that we must take great pains to get *singletaxers only* into it, otherwise we will wreck the thing by dissension. Mr. Mann [S. S. Mann, who with Mr. Bellangee constituted the location committee] professes to be a singletaxer but he mortified me greatly by his talk with Norton, bringing up the same old chestnut of the rich man and his palace, side by side with the poor man and his hovel. You would have thought he never heard of the single tax . . . ."

However, Mr. Gaston, as secretary, necessarily carried the larger load of promotion and his earlier writings covered all phases of the projected plan. Typical of his points of view on different aspects of the proposed colony is his article, "True Co-operative Individualism," in the April 28, 1894, issue of the *Liberty Bell:*

Why a colony? The present social and economic order is doomed, but ". . . we who now recognize and denounce its evils and are striving to unite a majority of its victims for its overthrow, may go before it goes—in waiting the slow movements of majorities." Therefore, ". . . what more reasonable, more practical than for those who understand the devices by which the labor of the many is taken for the profit of the few to unite for the elimination of the land speculator, the usurer, the monopolist of public service and all other parasites who fatten upon industry compelling the producer to gnaw the bone while they eat the meat."

In his promotional writings Gaston emphasized that Fairhope was seeking to build for humanity as it is—for average humanity seeking its own interest. "We have not been carried away by dreams of an ideal society from which selfishness was banished . . . ." Those who framed the Fairhope Industrial Association kept two principles in mind: (1) "All men seek to satisfy their desires with the least exertion," and (2) "Every man has freedom to do all that he wills, provided he not infringe the equal freedom of any other man." Gaston sought to win colonists for Fairhope by stressing that Fairhope had sounder principles than other social experiments which failed because they did not follow these principles.

Ignoring the first, experimenters in community building have utterly failed to measure the dominant forces of human nature. Failing to recognize the second, they have substituted the tyranny of the community for the tyranny of individuals, and the last state has been almost if not quite as bad as the first.

We believe that one of the most common and most grievous errors cherished by social reformers is that Society (with a big S) is possessed of rights and powers superior to those of its individual components. While vehemently denying the right of one individual to the control of the persons or products of another, they as vehemently assert the right of "Society" to direct the action of all individuals and determine the share of each in the joint product.[8]

The fundamental difference between Fairhope and other planned communities frequently was stated in the form of contrasting mottoes. A four-page leaflet edited by Mr. Gaston expressed this difference as follows:

Our mottoes are not "from each according to his ability and to each according to his needs" but "EQUAL OPPORTUNITY TO ALL, AND TO THE LABORER THE FULL PRODUCT OF HIS LABOR." Not "each for all and all for each," but "EVERYONE FOR HIMSELF—UNDER THE LAW OF EQUAL FREEDOM."

From the outset Mr. Gaston evidenced that he was in full

8 Ibid.

accord with the constitutional provisions governing the tenure of corporation lands. He continually pointed out that these provisions were designed to secure the equal rights of all members to the use of natural resources. He recognized that equal rights could not be permanently secured by any apportionment of equal areas because of great variations in site values and also because values would not remain in any given equilibrium. The only way to maintain equal rights to land is ". . . to ascertain annually the relative value of all tracts (exclusive of improvements) and to collect from each the amount required to equalize all land holdings." Also, ". . . the fund thus provided will be ample for all common purposes . . . increasing as the needs of the community increase and doing away with all necessity for levy of taxes upon the personal or labor created property of members."

Bellangee and Gaston were in agreement as to the views above stated. In his enthusiasm to obtain members, however, Mr. Gaston's earlier writings evidence that he retained some of the influence of Bellamy. For example, in outlining the Fairhope plan with respect to public utilities, he wrote: "Lights, power, water . . . will be supplied from a central plant located at an advantageous point and will be under one management, and as the land, freed from private speculators, will be so plotted as to group the population, without crowding, around a common center, the saving to be effected in these departments can hardly be estimated . . . ." (*Liberty Bell*, April 28, 1894). He rationalized the commercial features of the colony plan as follows:

If distribution can be so organized that one man can perform the work of two or four without organization, common sense dictates organization. Experience and observation must convince every one that such a result can be effected by organized co-operative distribution . . . .

There are often in a single block a half dozen places for the sale of the same lines of merchandise, occupying a half dozen store rooms; paying rent or taxes thereon, and for light, heat, water, fire and police protection, street paving, clearing and lighting, insurance, clerks, bookkeepers and interest on capital invested in duplicate stocks, etc. where any one of the six with slight increase in space occupied, capital invested and help employed would serve the trade now divided among all with equal convenience, and, if the savings thus made were divided among the patrons, to their far greater satisfaction.[9]

Thus were the commercial features of the plan elaborated and used to help sell memberships. Nor did Gaston deprecate the other non-single tax provisions. He appealed to all views. For example, he characterized the provisions designed to supply the members with a "safe, adequate and independent medium of exchange" as one of the "most valuable features of our enterprise."[10]

Mr. Gaston clearly viewed the Fairhope plan as a multi-sided planned community. On the one hand, he never wavered in his conviction that a destruction of the monopolization of land was imperative. On the other hand, it is a nice question whether he ever completely accepted the single tax as the exclusive condition needed by organized society to develop maximum productivity, stability and justice in the economy. Let it be emphasized that the impurities in the Fairhope plan and in Gaston's thinking, from the point of view of a singletaxer, were of the nature of voluntary, not compulsory, co-operation. With the single exception of public utilities, the Fairhope community as an organized entity would aspire to no social monopoly and the individual would retain "absolute" freedom. There remained, nonetheless, that undercurrent of conviction that co-operation, voluntary though it might be, was essential to the future of the community.

The presence of these impurities was one of the reasons the more doctrinaire singletaxers refrained from lending their support to the proposed colony. Mr. George White (of New York) wrote Gaston on November 9, 1894: "What singletaxers here seem to be afraid of is the liability of the association amending its constitution and undertaking to make its control of members more and more paternal. In order words, that

9 Ibid.
10 Ibid.

socialism will prevail and resulting dissensions break up the colony." (Letter in E. B. Gaston's files)

Following the adoption of the constitution, the founders agreed that a location should be provided as soon as possible. On May 11, 1894, the executive council unanimously chose Mr. J. Bellangee and Mr. S. S. Mann to act as a committee to seek a location. At the meeting of May 18 the council directed the committee to investigate proposed localities in Arkansas, Texas, Louisiana, Alabama and Tennessee. The reasons for thus narrowing the search were two-fold: the desire to locate in a climate where the winters generally were mild and the necessity for locating on inexpensive land.

The location committee spent about two months investigating various sites in the five states and sending back periodic reports. Many of these reports were published in the *Liberty Bell* and undoubtedly influenced the vote subsequently taken to select the location. From the relatively small number of available letters written by Bellangee while on his location trip, it is clear that he was fascinated by the eastern shore of Mobile Bay. On July 16, 1894, he wrote Gaston: "We viewed the land and country over the hills and along the shore. It is lovely indeed. High banks and sandy beach with every here and there a spring gushing out of the bank with sufficient fall to raise the water by means of rams to the table lands above. . . . Along the beach on the east side of the bay there are old houses formerly. owned by rich people and kept for homes. Now they are in a delapidated condition many of them, and occupied in many instances by colored people. There has been recently a tendency to rehabilitate them and make them summer homes for the wealthy. . . . I believe it is the healthiest region we have struck yet." He noted there was no railroad and products would have to be shipped by water twenty-five miles across the bay to Mobile. Despite this drawback, Bellangee wrote with enthusiasm: "Henry George was at Norton's place and was delighted with it. Norton thinks that if we go there we will be able to get George's endorsement and make it a big single tax enterprise." This last, of course, was pure wishful thinking as Henry George was negative toward the enclave idea.

In another letter Bellangee expressed himself as not being quite sure that making a living would be as good in Baldwin County as in some of the other places visited, but he was quite certain a living would be more worth the making there. In the final report of the location committee the argument was used that "There is probably no other place that we could secure where so many friends from the north would be interested in visiting us and in spending the winters for pleasure and health. Of the healthfulness of the situation there can be no doubt as it has all the advantages of the Gulf Breeze in its purity and the high altitude and perfect drainage and the health giving aroma of the pine trees."

A site in western Tennessee held some attractions for the location committee. This was a place characterized as a "country more closely resembling our northern lands so far as products of agriculture are concerned." The soil was naturally good but more or less exhausted. The committee found the climate good and the rainfall sufficient. Two crops a year were usual and Memphis would be the principal market.

On August 10, 1894, the executive council instructed the secretary to transmit to each member a copy of the report of the locating committee, together with supplementary articles by the committee previously published in the *Liberty Bell*. The members were asked to indicate first, second and third choices confined among these locations: on Bayou Shere, Southwest Louisiana; on the eastern shore of Mobile Bay, Baldwin County, Alabama; and a location, to be chosen after further investigation, in Western Tennessee. The results of this first Fairhope referendum were:

First choice: Baldwin County, Alabama, 26; Western Tennessee, 8.

Second choice: Baldwin County, 4; Western Tennessee, 15.

The vote was announced in the Fairhope *Courier*, October 1, 1894, together with the statement that the association already had favorable options on several suitable tracts. Negotiating for the association in Baldwin County was Mr. Edward Quincy Norton (of Daphne).[11]

---

[11] Attention of the founders of Fairhope and of Mr. Norton was first called to Baldwin County by W. E. Brokaw, editor of the *Single Tax Courier*, St. Louis.

AN INAUSPICIOUS BEGINNING

W*ITH* the selection of "somewhere in Baldwin County" as the site of the Fairhope colony, the *Courier* conducted an intensive campaign to increase the membership of the association. The colony organ reiterated three principles: (1) land values are created by and consequently belong to the community: (2) that which the individual produces belongs to the individual; (3) voluntary co-operation is the preferred plan of distribution.

Two different groups of prospective members were thus sought. Welcome were those whose primary interest was in the establishment of a co-operative or socialistic community. Most welcome, however, were those who believed in individual freedom as an indispensable condition of equality of opportunity. The colony was to attract many who were not strictly singletaxers but who tentatively accepted exclusive land value taxation as one of several needed reforms. From its inception the colony and the community of Fairhope has had to contend with the somewhat unnatural affinity of essentially conflicting schools of economic and political reform. Logically the only thing singletaxers and socialists should have in common is a conviction that the prevailing order is demonstrably imperfect and should be altered. Singletaxers would rest content if the community would break up the monopolization of land, use community-created values for public purposes, but otherwise leave individuals completely free to work out their own destinies. A true singletaxer possesses almost complete faith in the efficacy of freedom provided individuals have effective access to land or nature. To them such a condition would be most moral, in complete harmony with natural law, and any extension of governmental activities beyond this, whether in taxation of wages or interest or in regulation or government ownership, probably would be unwarranted, unwise and immoral. The socialist, on the other hand, fundamentally is a collectivist rather than an individualist. The two types of reform movements are so diametrically opposed as to make it almost inexplicable that any planned community containing both groups could survive the inevitable conflict.

Along with the enlistment of members, the executive council was concerned with the adoption of measures designed to convert the paper organization into a working model. Among the actions taken was the scheduling of a special election for November 26, 1894, "at such place in Baldwin County as may hereafter be announced by the secretary to fill such vacancies as may at that time exist in the association." Next, the council appointed and empowered James P. Hunnel and Ernest B. Gaston to act in conjunction with three others (to be selected by them from the members actually on colony grounds at the time) to select and purchase land on which the Fairhope colony would be established. This committee was prohibited from incurring any indebtedness on behalf of the association. Finally, the committee was instructed to perform such preliminary duties as might be required to conduct the scheduled election. (Minutes, October 26, 1894.)

The executive council set the round-up date at the chosen site for November 15, 1894. As this date approached it became evident that the number of colonists would be much smaller than had been anticipated. Several conditions accounted for this disappointment. Not one publication devoted to land tax reform, not one single tax organization, and few individual singletaxers of national reputation had endorsed the proposed

enclave. The prevailing view among knowledgeable singletaxers was that a small and isolated experiment, carried out under
adverse state and federal laws, could prove nothing as to the
advantages of a generally adopted single tax program, and
might, in case of failure, do the movement much harm. Instead
of supporting the projected colony, singletaxers were encouraged to work within their own communities for the adoption
of local option in tax reform measures.

Prospective reformers other than pure singletaxers did not
oppose the plan but were cautious with respect to casting their
individual lots with that of the colony. They wanted it to become a going concern before moving to the colony—a view easy
to understand in a period when many planned co-operative
communities were short-lived.

A third reason for the small membership was the relatively
high cost of the membership fee and the required contribution
to the mercantile department—a total of $250. The prolonged
depression may have stimulated interest in various reforms but
it also prevented many would-be colonists from joining Fairhope because of difficulties encountered in disposing of their
properties—something many would have to do to raise the
money necessary to join.

As the November 15 round-up date approached, a few groups,
in several cases single families, from various parts of the United
States, departed their homes for Baldwin County, Alabama.

Among this first group of pioneers were: Mr. and Mrs. E. B.
Gaston and four children; Mr. and Mrs. John Hunnel, parents
of J. P. Hunnel who had preceded the party by a few days to
serve as an advance courier. The Gastons and the Hunnels
were from Des Moines. These two families were joined in St.
Louis by a delegation from Minneapolis who made themselves
known by their Fairhope badges. From Minnesota were: Rev-
erend and Mrs. August Dellgren and Mr. and Mrs. Tuveson
and three children. St. Louis singletaxers entertained the
colonists "between trains" but none joined the party. (Fairhope
Courier, December 1, 1894.)

On arrival in Mobile, the colonists were met by Mr. and

Mrs. George Pollay of Vancouver, B. C., and by James P.
Hunnel, the advance courier. The group then boarded the
Carney for the trip across Mobile Bay.

Arrangements had been made for the colonists to stop at
Battles Wharf while negotiations for the first purchase of land
were being completed. The party was met at Battles Wharf by
Mr. and Mrs. C. P. Powers of Dunbar, Pennsylvania, and Mr.
and Mrs. E. Smith and two children of Findlay, Ohio. The
Smiths had made the trip in a covered wagon. They had driven
all night on the fourteenth in order to keep the appointment
for the round-up on the fifteenth.

Mr. C. L. Coleman, of St. Paul, soon joined the group and
has always been considered one of the initial colonists although
he missed the deadline by a few days.

Out of this initial group of twenty-five, including children,
four were not members of the Fairhope Industrial Association
and most of the members had made but one payment of $5.00
on their membership stock. Only two officers were represented
in the group: Mr. E. B. Gaston, secretary; and Mr. J. P. Hunnel, superintendent of industries. Of this group of eight families, only the Gaston family and Mr. Coleman were to remain
active in the colony, although two more continued their memberships in the association and the others became residents of
Baldwin County. (Fairhope *Courier*, February 1, 1898.)

At best the group possessed only modest means. As individuals they had varying degrees of understanding of, and faith
in the principles underlying their undertaking. They had one
important thing in common—a name for their new home—
Fairhope!

The association had attempted to keep its search for land in
Baldwin County as quiet as possible to avoid speculative increases in its price. As late as October 17, less than one month
before round-up date, the association had not purchased any
land and had allowed an option previously obtained to lapse.
The owner of the land optioned pointed out that the association had not "put up any deposit or forfeit as was usual in such

negotiations." (Letter from Mrs. Sarah I. Tatum to E. B. Gaston, Montrose, October 18, 1894.)

The Fairhope *Courier* frequently implied that the association would buy a large tract of land, *e.g.*, ". . . the 15,000 acre tract for which Mr. Edward Q. Norton is negotiating for the colony," but it soon became evident that the paucity of members and the consequent lack of money would reduce the land purchase to a modest acreage. The expenses of location, organization and promotion had absorbed most of the funds received from the first memberships. As one of the members wrote to the secretary: "I do not see how we can buy a great amount of land without going into debt, for if our membership is only twenty-two and the shares are being paid for at the rate of $5.00 per month, this will not form any fund sufficient to strike a big bargain with." (Gilbert Anderson, St. Louis, Missouri, June 14, 1894.)

The first land purchase was small—a modest one hundred thirty-two acres. The exact acreage was subject to correction upon survey and the title to a portion of the land was in litigation. This purchase, however, proved to be very important. It consisted of twenty-eight hundred feet along Mobile Bay, about half the distance between Montrose and Battles Warf. The purchase price was $6.00 per acre.[1] Partly because of the uncertainty over the title, when the negotiation for this first purchase of land was concluded, Mrs. Tatum, the owner, accompanied the colonists to the site and admonished them: "I now put you in peaceable possession of this land; see that you maintain it."

Volunteers among the colonists spent the first few nights in the covered wagon in which the Smiths had driven through from Ohio. Within a few days the "seat of government" was transferred to a shack nearby. Most of the colonists continued for a few weeks to camp out at Battles Wharf until they could build their homes on colony land.

[1] Shortly thereafter the association purchased two hundred acres of land in the interior for $1.25 per acre.

The colonists agreed that the bay shore should be the site of the first settlement. Old settlers of the neighborhood alternatively referred to this location as "New City Hill" or "Stapleton's pasture." The site was one where, fifty years previously, promoters had attempted to found "Alabama City." This earlier attempt to locate a town had been erased by nature. But this time, after many conflicts over principles and policies as well as bouts with nature, a small band of men were to succeed in building an enduring community.

The obstacles to be overcome by these first Fairhopers must have seemed formidable indeed. Consider: the colonists were few—indeed, most of the first arrivals never took up residence upon colony lands. Mostly they were strangers to one another having met for the first time in Fairhope. All were aliens, hence subject to some degree of suspicion and occasionally to threats of violence on the part of a small minority of the native population. All were wholly unfamiliar with local agriculture, and few had had any previous experience with farming of any type. They were poor; few if any of the early arrivals possessed more than $500 per family including furniture and livestock. They professed a non-conventional doctrine, therefore were accounted different in belief as well as in origin and social customs.

The land purchased was poor in quality and located at a considerable distance from any market considering the lack of a railroad or improved highways. There were no essential physical facilities which are indispensable to a civilized community, such as houses, schools, streets and roads, water or wharf. Without the latter it was impossible to make an economical use of water transportation.

Finally, the early arrivals had to organize the association from members on the ground and to discover by trial and error constitutional changes and by-laws needed before their paper plan could become a working model of a planned community dedicated to the elimination of monopoly, especially monopoly in land.

The problems facing the first Fairhopers were not of equal

difficulty. The fact that the colonists came from other sections of the United States and were strangers in the community and to one another, proved relatively unimportant. Almost without exception the newcomers to Baldwin County were individuals of considerable intelligence and good will. They were sensitive to differences in the cultures of the "Old South" and the Midwest, and were determined to adapt themselves to their new environment without losing sight of their own traditions. As a result, local suspicions, occasional acts of violence, and local attitudes of amusement or derision toward certain colony institutions soon receded and ultimately disappeared.

An example of this determination to adapt is the fact that the colonists followed the local custom of segregation of the races. The colony never has had a Negro tenant or lessee. This is not to deny that individual members, almost all of whom were non-resident, did not hold contrary views. From time to time a friend of the colony would voice an objection to the exclusion of Negroes from colony land and upon occasion someone would refuse material assistance unless Negroes were admitted. A typical official position or answer was that no one has the right to insist that ". . . we follow the naked principle of equality unreservedly, regardless of conditions existing, to defy which might simply mean self-destruction." (Fairhope *Courier,* April 1, 1898.)

If the colonists quickly adjusted both to one another and to their new neighbors they had a much more difficult task in adjusting to basic economic realities and to certain of the original features of their plan.

The Fairhope pioneers settled in a very old community on land which had practically no market value. They did not migrate to a new country providing access to virgin prairie soil. The soil of the Fairhope hinterland was poor and the topography irregular. Economists would have no difficulty in agreeing that Fairhope land was marginal, if not sub-marginal, for agricultural purposes.

An important difference between the early settlers in the Fairhope community and the pioneers or migrants to new lands lay in their motivation. The pioneer, as such, traditionally is pictured as an individual seeking to satisfy a hunger for land. He underwent material hardship for the sake of security and ultimate enrichment as the newer communities grew in density of population. He may or may not have had an urge for adventure. Fundamentally the migrant to new lands *wanted to own land in fee simple* without any appreciable outlay of money. Most pioneers had little other than their own work and personal hardship invested in the land. Any capital possessed by them could be invested in improvements or was available for living expenses pending establishment in the new location.

By the time Fairhope was organized, there were no remaining large areas of free fertile land. Landless newcomers to the economic scene had to accumulate sufficient capital both to acquire the land and to finance improvements. Well-located and otherwise inherently productive lands were comparatively expensive whether in use or held idle by speculators. A natural consequence of the prevailing system of private property in land was to force non-landholding individuals to pay owners of land for the privilege of using it for any human purpose. A further difficulty in the way of the landless was the system of property taxation, which at that time included in the base all improvements, and almost all types of personal property, in addition to land as such.

Those who planned and organized Fairhope agreed with Henry George that the prevailing system of taxation and private ownership of land denied individuals an equal opportunity in the use of land, adversely affected the productivity of the country, and was fundamentally unjust. To them, as to George, government should tax the values created by the community before confiscating values created by individuals as workers, savers or investors.

To a singletaxer the essence of the Fairhope plan is: to acquire control over land by purchase or donation; to lease association-owned lands to individuals for their exclusive use on a permanent basis; to levy an annual rental charge against each leaseholder equal to the rental or use value of the land; to use the proceeds to relieve lessees of taxes paid by them on the results of their individual efforts; and to spend the balance for the benefits of the lessees.

From the point of view of the singletaxer, the purpose of Fairhope was to demonstrate that such a program would prevent land speculation, create more jobs at higher real wages, and promote economic progress with justice in the distribution of income and wealth, greater than would be the case under the prevailing system of laws governing ownership of land and taxation. Assuming the success of the demonstration, the Fairhope singletaxers hoped that other localities would be encouraged in their efforts to obtain local option in taxation, and that they would use this privilege to tax only the annual use value of land, thus both destroying land speculation and permitting individuals to retain tax-free all results from their labor and investments.

In many respects those who wrote the constitution of the Fairhope Industrial Association did a superb job; many fundamental features of this document have been altered relatively little in the sixty years of the colony's existence. To a degree, however, the promoters of the colony failed to think out, and to implement, policies and procedures capable of demonstrating the efficacy of the single tax features of the constitution.

In retrospect it appears unfortunate that the colony plan was placed in operation before the association was properly financed and without benefit of a larger number of bona fide singletaxers as members.

Inadequate financing forced the colony to locate on lands largely sub-marginal and with control over a grossly inadequate acreage. All available information indicates that it had been many decades since anyone had made any sort of a living (scarcely more than an existence) off "Stapleton's pasture." Prevailing wages throughout that section of Baldwin County were extremely low. For years after settlement, people were warned not to come to Fairhope unless they possessed some unusual and needed skill, or unless they had a competence which would sustain them for an indefinite period. The reason for

this intelligence was that native labor existed in great quanti-
ties and was available at seventy-five cents or less a day. Add to
this the fact that the land had to be cleared of trees having little
stumpage value, and it becomes clear that the low prices paid
for the original purchases represented speculative possibilities
rather than current use values. The more than four hundred
per cent differential in price paid for bay front property, as
compared with the price paid for inland acreage, again reflects
the speculator's instinct. At one time the bay front had served
wealthy families and there was some stirring of a renewed interest on the part of Mobile families in eastern shore property for
summer homes. This interest was manifestly feeble; it did not
extend for any distance inland.

Assuming the sub-marginal character of the land on which
Fairhope was located, it is difficult to understand how the
founders expected to demonstrate the efficacies of the single
tax theory, unless they were assuming that the low productivity
of the region was due almost wholly to land and tax policies,
rather than to the poor location and low qualities of the land.
There is, however, no evidence that the founders faced this
question, that is, that they debated the issue whether a workable
program based on single tax principles possibly could be developed on land so cheap that its low market value was *entirely
speculative*. Manifestly the early years of the colony were fore-
doomed to be years of relative poverty for the bulk of Fairhope
residents unless or until material assistance was forthcoming
from non-resident friends of means. There could be no other
source of material relief until the colony had established a
sound economic basis for its existence, after which economic
rent would appear, and taxes and other community facilities
could be financed, as planned, without driving wages and
interest below competitive levels. This economic justification
or basis for the existence of the community did not appear for
several years. Repeated efforts to establish itself agriculturally
met with very little success. The community was destined to
become primarily a health and vacation resort and ultimately,
with the coming of the modern highway system, an important

middle class income suburb of Mobile. Sixty years later its agriculture and its industry remain comparatively unimportant as sources of income.

From still another point of view the location selected was inferior. Fairhope proper was located on comparatively high bluffs which made it more difficult and expensive to construct streets to the bay. Further, the shelving from the shore to a water depth sufficient to float the typical Mobile Bay ferry was unusually gradual, making necessary a wharf of extraordinary length. Many other sites on the eastern shore were superior in these respects.

If the founders of Fairhope erred in buying sub-marginal lands they made another mistake in purchasing too little land in solid blocks having bay frontage. Others located on adjoining deeded lands almost at the same time that the colonists appeared. The result was the introduction of many problems of practical co-operation among neighbors living under distinct systems of land tenure. Not only did this limit the financial success of the colony, it served to confuse the actual effects of the demonstration. Individuals who would not have located in Fairhope or invested money there except on terms of complete private property rights in land may have contributed to the colony's subsequent growth, but it is impossible to determine the extent of their contribution. Subsequent developments, however, indicate that the community might have grown even more rapidly if deeded, or privately-owned land, were not available within urban Fairhope. The greater bulk of the improvements and the most intensive land utilization has occurred on colony land. One small tract of land with a nice bay frontage and a small acreage within a few hundred feet of the bay was acquired by an individual just previous to the initial colony purchases. Today, sixty years later, only the bay front of this deeded property is used; while the surrounding colony lands have been intensively, and for the most part, attractively developed.

Unquestionably the presence of deeded land within the colony vicinity, and interspersed among colony holdings, weakened the association in a material sense. Assuming that the population would have grown equally had the colony owned all the land now incorporated in the Town of Fairhope, plus a reasonable surrounding buffer acreage, then it follows that that portion of the community-created increment funneled into the pockets of individual land owners would otherwise have gone to the colony.

Another problem which had to be resolved before a successful experiment in the single tax could be conducted was to obtain an adequate number of members thoroughly indoctrinated in the single tax philosophy. The point has been made that the constitution contained several provisions which made the colony a mixture of reforms. Such provisions attracted the favorable attention of socialists and other reformers. A considerable proportion of the early members were persons who, while perfectly willing to have the community expropriate income from land, did not believe in this fiscal device as an exclusive reform. On the other hand, many clear thinking singletaxers disapproved the socialistic features of the plan. The initial handicaps suffered by the colony from this situation are incalculable.

The early colonists faced truly fundamental difficulties. The land was sub-marginal; the acreage of contiguous land controlled by the association was much too small; well-grounded singletaxers made up too small a proportion of the membership; small as the original acreage was it was too large to be immediately taken up in leaseholds; two few of the original settlers were endowed either with sufficient physical stamina or financial resources to hold out until the community could be firmly established; and the socialistic features embodied in the plan repelled many singletaxers and probably attracted too many socialists for the good of a single tax demonstration.

The prognosis in 1894-1895 was not favorable.

iv

CONSTITUTIONAL AMENDMENTS AND THE FIRST DIVISION AMONG THE COLONISTS

THE constitution of the Fairhope Industrial Association could not be amended except by a three-fourths affirmative vote of the entire membership. This provision remained in effect until 1932 when a "gateway amendment" to the constitution of the Fairhope Single Tax Corporation was passed permitting constitutional amendments on an affirmative vote of three-fourths of those voting. The amending provision contained in the original constitution, and incorporated in the constitution of the Fairhope Single Tax Corporation, proved effective in safeguarding the basic integrity of the Fairhope plan. At the same time it did not prevent needed adjustments in the constitution designed to perfect certain procedures and more clearly to define the individual rights of members. During the very early years, the constitution was amendable in practice because of keen interest and close contact with colony affairs on the part of the small membership. Within a few years it became extremely difficult to locate non-resident members or to persuade them to vote on constitutional questions.

Only a fraction of the membership actually resided in the colony during the first years. After a few weeks, the colonists discovered that if they were to have an executive council re-

sponsive to local needs, the council should be elected from
local members only. Accordingly, ten per cent of the membership initiated an amendment providing that only those on the
grounds on the day of election could vote for officers or on
matters of local concern. This amendment carried unanimously at the election of January 22, 1895. Out of forty members in good standing (including spouses) thirty-seven voted
"yes," while three failed to cast their ballots.[1]

The small membership of the colony handicapped it particularly in the acquisition of land. Funds remaining after
initial expenses permitted the purchase of less than four hundred acres of land, whereas many believed that a successful
demonstration of the single tax would require several thousands of acres. It would have been to the advantage of the
colony to have secured the needed acreage while land was relatively inexpensive, thus both conserving capital funds and conserving all unearned increments for public services. Time was
short because the condition of low market prices for land was
disappearing rapidly. The *Courier* took cognizance of this in
its issue of April 1, 1895:

The stiffening of land values in this section after the decision to
locate Fairhope here was announced, was already marked before an
axe was struck or a sod turned on the ground, and every furrow
that is turned, every nail that is driven is making the land, that
we must have in the future, harder to get, and giving an unearned
advantage to the present holder.

The colony could acquire land only through direct purchase
or through donations by friends. One method favored by
colony management was for members or friends to acquire
control of contiguous acreage, then to option it to the colony
for a consideration of the purchase price, plus six per cent
interest. Of course the colony did not discourage outright
donations of land, and in at least one instance, an attractive
private holding was turned over to it in exchange for two mem-

1 The total membership as of January 9, 1895, was forty-seven, not including
spouses who had signed the constitution. Of these only five were paid in full;
fourteen were paid to date; fourteen were paid ahead; and fourteen were
delinquent.

berships, the value of which in no wise equaled the market value of the land.[2] In too many instances, however, members purchased land, presumably for later transfer to the colony, only to refuse such a transfer except as they received the material benefit from the enhanced value of the lands. The colony management quite consistently rebelled against the policy of a single tax colony paying an unearned increment to its own members.[3]

The problem faced by the early management was two-fold: to sell more memberships and to entice more donations of money or land from singletaxers of means who were interested in advancing the cause, but not necessarily interested in becoming resident colonists. This posed a nice dilemma because the motivations of the two groups tended to be divergent—in some instances extremely so. Only a few of the early colonists were dedicated singletaxers, and many were actually antagonistic to some of the basic principles of the Fairhope plan. On the other hand, the non-resident, dedicated singletaxer of means, who might make a considerable material contribution, was fearful of the non-single tax features of the plan. Under these conditions the colony simply could not grow in land holdings and in population, without experiencing a series of internecine strug-

2 "R. F. Powell deeds his valuable tract of land to the corporation asking in return only credit for the balance due on his membership and a membership for his daughter." (Fairhope *Courier,* March 17, 1905.)

3 Two instances of this were:

A. President Bancroft made "a strenuous effort" to secure C. L. Coleman's land at cost plus six per cent interest. This offer was declined and Coleman refused to sell at less than $10.00 per acre. "Sense of the council that it could not pay a member speculative advance on land purchased by him and enhanced in value because of the colony's presence, and that the president so notify Mr. Coleman, when matter was again brought up." (Minutes, November 16, 1903.)

B. See Fairhope *Courier,* May 5, 1905: "The Doctor's [Dr. Clara Atkinson] many friends will hear with regret that she has parted with her membership, but she felt that while she was holding land adjacent outside the colony and which she did not feel willing, under the circumstances, to turn in, that she should not continue as a member. This action, while it will be regretted by many —for no one is more generally beloved by the community than Dr. Atkinson— does her great credit. It was fully concurred in by the writer—her brother. It will not in the least lessen her interest in Fairhope, nor her helpfulness in its every public undertaking."

gles and without some further modifications of procedure and policy.

Two provisions, one incorporated in a by-law and one in the constitution, unquestionably discouraged migration to the colony. An initial by-law provided that capital stock must be paid in full before a member might lease association land. No record of any discussion leading to this rule was discovered. Hence it can only be surmised that it was invoked as a pressure designed to force members to complete payments on their stocks. The rule was fully and frequently publicized in the *Liberty Bell* and in the Fairhope *Courier*, and there is evidence (*e.g.*, in correspondence from members) that this rule was accepted quite literally by some installment paying members. Such an acceptance was both unfortunate and unnecessary. Official records disclose that the association, in many instances, leased land to members who were not fully paid up. For the most part, the exceptions were handled informally. In a few cases official action was taken and recorded. One such instance occurred at the meeting of the executive council of April 8, 1895, when the council formally accepted the proposition of Mr. H. C. Schakel to pay the remainder of his stock ($70) in one year, he taking residence on the colony grounds at once and going ahead to improve his leasehold.[4]

The other condition which discouraged migration to the

[4] There were other special arrangements which were officially recorded or were reported in the *Courier*. For example, on March 25, 1895, the council accepted a special proposition by Mr. A. J. Cullen, a cigar manufacturer. In applying for membership Mr. Cullen proposed to pay $50 to the merchandise fund and $50 on a stock certificate, but that the balance on his stock would be paid in cigars at current wholesale prices at the rate of one thousand per month. (His cigars bore the brands of "Fairhope" and "Single Tax.") A few months later the secretary was instructed to inquire if Mr. Cullen would be willing to pay the balance of his account $5.00 weekly instead of in cigars. Later it was made known that Mr. Cullen preferred to pay the balance of his membership in cigars whereupon the council demanded a portion of the cigars due. It appears the colony did not know how to market the cigars once it had them. A few months later Mr. Cullen made a deal with a printer to take the colony cigars in exchange for job printing. A human interest footnote to this footnote is that the first child born in Fairhope was born to the Cullens—a daughter christened with a middle name "Fairhope." The first boy baby was born to the Gastons and christened Arthur Fairhope Gaston.

colony was the constitutional requirement that a member must contribute up to $100 to the merchandise department before he could take up residence on colony grounds. Actually, the executive council had set this amount at $50. The thinking behind this constitutional provision was that it was necessary to finance an initial stock of merchandise for the colony store. The scrip received in exchange for this contribution would be used by members to obtain necessities from the store and to provide ". . . the security that members coming to the colony will not be without means of support and a burden on other members." (Fairhope *Courier,* February 1, 1895.)

The comparatively large membership fee and the mandatory contribution to the merchandise fund contributed to the defection of some members, and a few prospective members, in still another way. Several of the early visitors to Fairhope came to inspect the site and to study the policies of the association before making application for membership. Just such a procedure was repeatedly urged by the *Courier.* What more natural than that some of these more cautious prospective colonists should resort to arithmetic to determine how much land they could obtain title to for $250? Several decided to employ this sum in the private purchase of land; hence, they failed to join the colony. Others withdrew from membership, winding up with real estate ventures of their own.[5]

From the outset many had opposed the mercantile department, holding that its existence was in violation of the principle of equal freedom. Several considerations contributed to the decision of the membership to abandon this aspect of colony life: the store consistently operated at a loss; there was no method of providing adequate capital; and some individuals desired to operate stores as private ventures. Even some of the

---

[5] A news item in the Fairhope *Courier,* April 15, 1895, notes that Dellgren, Smith, Michaels, and Tuveson have withdrawn from Fairhope and purchased a section of land which they will divide in ten and twenty acre tracts and sell outright. (There is no record that either Michaels or Tuveson ever applied for colony memberships.) Both Mr. and Mrs. Smith and Mr. and Mrs. Dellgren were elected officers in the first election on colony grounds. (Fairhope *Courier,* December 1, 1894.)

more persistent advocates of an association store were willing
to see it go. Mr. C. L. Coleman, the second and the last manager of the association store, wrote in the *Courier:* "I am not at
all as ready, as some are, to grant that the colony store was a
mistake. I think it was almost a necessity for the time being
and I stoutly championed its cause. I am reluctantly compelled
now to admit that it should be divorced entirely from the Fairhope Association, as such, and run independently of it, but by
members only. The store scrip has in large part been redeemed
and destroyed. It has served its purpose and served it well, but
sufficient funds to continue and maintain the store are, of
course, lacking and we MUST NOT GO INTO DEBT."
(Fairhope *Courier,* May 15, 1895.)

Convinced that $250 was an effective barrier against increas-
ing the number of families on colony grounds, and that the
colony store was a mistake, the executive council instructed the
secretary to prepare a petition for an election, and to put the
indicated constitutional amendments in proper form for submission to the membership. A special election was called for
June 2, 1895, and amendments achieving the following purposes
were approved.

1. The cost of membership was reduced by fifty per cent
(*i.e.,* the capital stock was reduced from $1,000,000 to $500,000,
and divided into five thousand shares of $100 each).

2. The constitution was divested of all provisions for co-
operative merchandising and production departments; the executive council was reduced from six to five by the elimination
of the office of superintendent of merchandising; and the issue
of scrip for the purchase and handling of merchandise stored
in the association warehouse was discontinued.

The elimination of the merchandising department provided
an occasion for Gaston, as editor of the *Courier,* to renew his
pleas for singletaxers to support the colony more liberally. As
he put it: ". . . while many singletaxers haven't helped Fairhope
because they believe it socialistic," the elimination of the
mercantile department should cause them ". . . to realize that
the tendency from the first has been away from socialism."

Henceforth, he prophesied, activities of the association would be confined to administration of land and to the performance of strictly public functions. Individuals, however, might be brought together in *voluntary* co-operation. Mr. Gaston recognized that it was unfortunate for Fairhope, that virtually all of the previous colonies had been predominantly socialistic. (Fairhope *Courier*, October 1, 1895.)

The possibility that the colony might incur a ruinous debt had worried many from the outset. An earlier attempt to amend the constitution by inserting in it a prohibition against indebtedness failed for lack of voting interest among the members. On a second try, July 13, 1895, an amendment carried providing ". . . no bonds or mortgages, or interest-bearing obligations of whatever character, shall ever be given or assumed by the association."

Also at the election of July 13, the capital stock of the association once again was reduced, this time from $500,000 to $50,000, the number of shares reduced from five thousand to five hundred. The principal place of business was shifted from Des Moines, Iowa, to Baldwin County, Alabama. The reduction in the capital stock reduced the cost of the annual corporation license tax, imposed by the State of Alabama, from $100 to $25, a saving not unimportant to the struggling corporation.

All of the foregoing amendments were approved within a period of less than eight months of colony life. The consensus was that the constitution was a workable instrument; that further changes in its provisions, if and when needed, would not be difficult to secure.

There is no evidence that the reduction in the total cost of membership from $250 to $100 added appreciably to the total membership fees received by the association. There was an immediate increase both in the number of fully paid up members and in the gross membership. The initial boost in the gross or total membership resulted from the private sale, usually at a discount, of the second certificate of certain members who had paid $200 for their shares. Sales of extra membership

certificates on private account followed an early precedent:
from the beginning those withdrawing from the association
were given a "certificate" showing the amount the member
had paid on his stock. The usual practice was for the retiring
member to sell this "certificate" to someone applying for
membership. Such sales were not necessarily final because,
under the constitution, stock was transferable only on the books
of the association and to persons acceptable to it as members.

Shortly after adoption of the amendments above referred to,
a few quite new but influential members took another look at
the constitution as a whole, and demanded a more complete
revision. The resulting bitterness and subsequent division
among the colonists were major adverse factors in the development of the colony—the cost was heavy in loss of material assistance from singletaxers generally.

Leaders in the demand for a more complete revision were:
Mr. J. H. Springer, formerly secretary of the Indiana Single
Tax League; Mr. W. E. Brokaw, formerly editor of the *Single
Tax Courier,* St. Louis, Missouri, and his wife, Mrs. Estelle
Backman Brokaw, formerly director of the Single Tax Propaganda Association of America. Mr. Springer was probably
better know to singletaxers generally than any other member
of the association. His application for membership was received and accepted on the same day, July 12, 1895, and the
colony officers openly rejoiced.

In accordance with local custom, Mr. Springer wrote a piece
for the *Courier* detailing his reasons for joining the colony
(July 15, 1895). He admitted that he came to Baldwin County
with the intention of settling outside the colony. He explained
that the cheapness of adjacent lands led him to think that
"access to land outside the colony would be easier" than within
it. With land selling at $1.25 an acre, and with ten acres suf-
ficient for his needs, Mr. Springer originally figured he could
obtain access to ten acres under deed and have $87.50 remain-
ing, the difference between the cost of the land and the $100
membership fee. After looking the situation over, he decided

to join the colony for the following reasons: all substantial improvements were on the bay front, on land then costing about $12 an acre. Bay front land was therefore easier of access through the colony than outside it. He found the country back of Fairhope too thinly settled for his taste, stating that it would be difficult to find three white families living in sufficiently close proximity to be counted as neighbors. Besides liking the Fairhope people and feeling at home there, he thought that with the completion of the Fairhope wharf, a project then under way, the community would become the trading center of the eastern shore.

With the arrival of the Springers and a few other new members, the colony for the first time was in a position to fill all offices with resident members. The paucity of resident members is illustrated by the election of officers in February. At that election four officers declined to serve and two offices were left vacant. Although Mr. Clements had been re-elected president, he had not found it convenient to move to the colony. Having an absentee president and an incomplete executive council was embarrassing to the colony in the conduct of its affairs.

At a special election held on August 30, 1895, just a few weeks after he became a member, Springer was elected the first resident president.

The Brokaws became colony members September 24, 1895. In meeting October 14, the executive council appointed them to serve as a committee to consider the revision of the constitution.

The October 15, 1895, issue of the *Courier* relates the background of the appointment of this committee: "Mr. and Mrs. Brokaw took advantage of a recent rainy day, which kept them indoors, to go over the Fairhope constitution, to see if they could suggest any amendments which would make its meaning clearer, or its details square more accurately with its fundamental law of equal freedom. It had been felt for some time that a revision of the constitution would be necessary, and we will be extremely fortunate to secure the assistance in this work of such recognized authorities on economics as Mr. and Mrs. Brokaw."

It seems probable that Mr. Gaston was exercising a degree of fortitude when he wrote in so charitable a vein, because he must have known that the newcomers were ambitious to unseat him and to reshape the colony to their own liking. For example, at the meeting of October 14, Mr. George Pollay, one of the original colonists, gave notice: "At our next meeting I shall move for the divorce of the Editorship and Management of the Fairhope *Courier* and the general secretary's duties, and also the election of a Superintendent of Industries by special election." One week later Mr. Gaston tendered his resignation as superintendent of industries to take effect as soon as his successor might be elected. He also asked to be relieved of the duty of editing the Fairhope *Courier*. The council accepted his resignation as a member of the executive council, and appointed Springer editor and manager of the *Courier* to serve at the pleasure of the council. (It was of course quite proper that Mr. Gaston resign from the council at the earliest opportunity, but there was no constitutional or other reason, except political, to separate the functions of editor and secretary.)

On October 17, 1895, a special meeting of members heard the report of the revision committee and December 3 was set for the vote on the revision.

The special revision committee proposed the following five major changes:

1. To reduce the membership fee from $100 to $25.

2. To increase the age for membership from eighteen to twenty-one and to abolish the privilege of a wife or husband of a member obtaining membership simply by signing the constitution.

3. To make it explicit that members only should reside on colony land.

4. To substitute a general assembly of members for the executive council.

5. To make the constitution amendable by majority vote.

For the next several issues the *Courier* (under the editorship of Springer) was filled with arguments urging adoption of the proposed revision. The principal arguments advanced were:

1. It is inconsistent with single tax principles to charge a membership fee to purchase land. Association activities should be financed out of ground rents only. Payment of the annual rental should be the only condition for leasing land. While the committee would like to abolish the membership fee altogether, it would be satisfied with reducing the fee to $25. This reduction would "place all adults on an equal footing" and would enable many to join who had thus far been unable to do so.

2. The suggested change in the age of membership from eighteen to twenty-one was based on the assumption that every adult on association lands would become a member. The committee argued that if the association continued to allow non-members to remain on the grounds, without payment of a membership fee, it would be discriminating against those who had paid the fee. It emphasized that until recently it was understood by all that a member could not rent land to a non-member.

3. The constitutional provision permitting husbands or wives of members to vote merely by signing the constitution discriminated against single members. The practice of two votes on one membership had no place in a single tax colony. "As long as we are a land owning association, we can do no more than to maintain equity between ourselves."

4. A general assembly would be more democratic than the existing executive council. All members not in arrears should be allowed to vote on changes in the constitution; but only those on the ground should vote for officers of the association. Five members would constitute a quorum. This would be "real democracy." "If the people, through the assembly, the initiative and referendum and an easy way of amending the constitution, cannot establish and maintain an equitable community, free from special privilege, they are incapable of self government."

Mr. Gaston led the opposition and directed most of the criticism to the proposals other than the substitution of a general assembly for the executive council. There was no organized resistance to this proposal. Those opposing the revision argued:

1. That the membership fee recently had been reduced from $200 to $100 and it had had an adverse effect on association funds. Members who had paid a $200 fee were given two stock certificates and were permitted to dispose of one of these. A further reduction in the face value of the stock would greatly reduce receipts from installment paying members and create many more certificates for private sale. Probably the market would be flooded with certificates for sale at a discount and association revenues from membership fees would be completely shut off. The colony's need for more land could be financed only from membership fees and donations. There was no reason to expect the proposed reduction to bring in more than four times as many members.

2. Mr. Bellangee, in a letter to Gaston, expressed the fear that a reduced membership fee could bring into the colony some members who had a "greatly reduced sentiment for the single tax."

3. Mr. C. L. Coleman, among others, feared a greatly reduced membership fee might result in an increase of colonists unable to finance themselves until they became established. "Even if memberships were reduced to $25 and we attracted 100 new members this winter is it to be supposed that such a class of people would be possessed of sufficient funds to build a house, clear and fence a farm, and live on their capital a year or more until they harvested and sold a crop?" Nor was Mr. Coleman in favor of permitting a bare majority to be "continually tinkering with the constitution." (Open letter to *Courier,* November 15, 1895.)

4. The most severe criticism was reserved for the proposal that all adult residents on colony lands must be members or leave the colony. The opponents argued that the word "reside" had no definite meaning, and that no court or government would dare interpret the meaning in such an arbitrary and narrow sense as was intended by those proposing the changes. The amendment, if adopted, would prohibit members from

making homes for matured children and aged parents. It would prohibit colonists from furnishing homes for help, and would mean the end to the colony's bright prospects of becoming an important resort. Many people had no interest in Fairhope policies but were anxious to reside there either in the winter or in the summer.

5. The opponents recollected that the colonists early discovered that it was important that prospective members should understand the constitution and the policies of the colony, and that they should be satisfied with its location and surroundings. The policy of the *Courier* had been to stress these points and it had frequently invited interested parties to visit the colony before making up their minds as to becoming members. This course would not be possible under the proposed amendment.

6. At least one member argued that there was a moral issue inherent in the proposal to prohibit non-members from residing on colony lands. An excellent statement of this view is contained in a letter from L. G. Bostedo, of Chicago, to Gaston, dated November 18, 1895. (Gaston files.)

. . . Single taxers rightly dwell forever upon the assertion that property in land cannot possibly be acquired by purchase or in any other imaginable way. But to exclude non-members from the lands of the association would be exercising the legal power of property in land; the very power that the founders of the Fairhope Association are seeking to abolish.

The committee overlooks the fact that at present the payment of a membership fee is voluntary, not compulsory. As all persons now have equal access to the colony lands and as all have the same opportunity to purchase stock in the company, why are their opportunities not equal so far as Fairhope memberships and Fairhope lands are concerned?

Any person remaining in Fairhope and failing to pay for membership when able to do so, would carry the taint of having been the recipient of charity. The people who go to Fairhope are not built that way.[6]

---

[6] Many visitors to Fairhope over the years have remarked on the superior nature of the people there. Mr. Bostedo, however, glorified them beyond all reason in his confident assumption that they would take out memberships as quickly as they could afford to. Some lessees of means not only failed to feel

7. The argument upholding the constitutional provision permitting spouses of members to be considered as members upon signing the constitution is interesting and of some validity. The framers of the plan felt that a married couple would need no more land than a single person and that to demand two memberships would be an undue financial burden. They also were sensitive to the fact that the success of the pioneer life would fall most heavily upon the shoulders of the women. They therefore argued that to permit wives to participate in the affairs of the colony would be only a small recognition of their services. Those seeking to retain this provision admitted that woman's suffrage had no part in the single tax movement, but asserted that "it was good of itself." (Fairhope *Courier*, December 1, 1895.)

8. The revision most feared was the one that would make the constitution amendable on a bare majority vote. This fear stemmed from the realization that all members were not single-taxers; at least agreement was far from universal among the colony members as to what policies constituted the single tax or how these policies could best be applied by a non-governmental association.

At the election the proposed revision of the constitution was badly defeated, both as a whole and in its separate provisions. Forty-five members were qualified to vote but only thirty-eight voted. Of these, fifteen voted against the revision as a whole and only three voted straight for revision. None of the individual proposals came close to having the requisite number of affirmative votes. (Fairhope *Courier*, December 15, 1895.)

The two factions created by the fight over the revision continued to quarrel. The executive council was presented with many petitions as each group sought to gain an advantage. Within a short period Mr. Gaston demonstrated his mastery of colony politics in the following sequence: at the meeting of

---

any taint of being recipients of charity but have been known to complain that the colony is not sufficiently generous with its substance. Also, Mr. Bostedo failed to recognize that not all lessees were acceptable as members even though they applied.

December 23, sixteen members petitioned the council, "That a pursuance of the present policy will be disastrous is, we think, shown by the almost total cessation of the receipts of the association and the fact that for the first time it is unable to meet the acknowledged claims of creditors who are growing impatient at delay in settlement of their accounts." The petitioners requested that Mr. Gaston be reinstated as editor of the *Courier.* The communication was placed on file. (Minutes, December 23, 1895.)

One week later the council adopted the following resolution offered by Mr. Gaston: "That in view of the fact that the association is already considerably in debt and the revenues for the last month have been insufficient to meet the expenses of the association that the Secretary's salary be reduced to $5 per month, and the *Courier* discontinued." (Minutes, January 6, 1896.)

At the annual election (February 10) Mr. Gaston was re-elected secretary and reinstated as editor of the Fairhope *Courier,* the publication of which was to be resumed as of April 1, 1896. As the *Courier* put it, the election "put the colony back in the hands of its friends."

At an election of March 26, 1896, five additional amendments to the constitution were approved. These amendments were designed solely to clarify the rights of members.

Two of these related to Article IV—Membership. The final clause of Section I of this article was changed to read: ". . . provided that on petition of ten per cent of the qualified membership filed with the secretary after ten days after action on any application by the executive council, such application shall be submitted to a vote of the membership." Under the original wording it was possible for ten per cent of the members to reject any applicant for membership simply by filing a written protest with the secretary within ten days of the time the executive council had accepted the application.

The following words "but only while such member remains in good standing" were suffixed (by amendment) to Section 2, Article IV, which read: "The husband or wife of a member shall, upon signing the constitution also be considered a member and entitled to a vote in the government of the association, while such relation exists in fact."

The third amendment approved changed, for the second time, Section 2, Article V—Supreme Authority, to read: "Each person not in arrears to the corporation shall be entitled to one vote and one only, at all elections involving changes in this constitution but on elections of officers and questions concerning local administration of affairs, only those shall be entitled to vote who are in person on the association grounds on the day of election and who are not in arrears."

A fourth amendment strengthened Article VII dealing with the initiative and referendum, by making it mandatory to hold a referendum election at the time specified in the petition, with two provisos: 1. that thirty days notice must be given where it is proposed to amend the constitution; and 2. that the members be given at least twenty-four hours notice on other matters.

Finally Section 2, Article VIII—Elections—was amended to read as follows (the italicized words constituting the amendment): "Special elections may be held at any time, at the discretion of the executive council, or on petition of ten per cent of the membership, after thirty days notice, *provided that the notice provided in Article VII as amended be given."*

On balance, it would seem that the colonists accomplished several constructive things during these early months. Certainly it was wholesome to amend the constitution and assure local self-government; to provide that the colony never could be wrecked because of any mortgage indebtedness; to reduce the cost of memberships; to abolish the association store; and to clarify the rights of members. In retrospect it seems fortunate that the first serious political and constitutional hassle within the colony ended as it did. Parenthetically, it may be noted that some of those who sided with the Springer-Brokaw group later acknowledged they were in error.[7] It may likewise

7 Mr. Henry Schakel, of Indianapolis, wrote as follows: "You will remember that I belonged to the Springer Party the time we set about to revise the Fairhope constitution. Our plan was a $25 membership and the leasing of land to members only. At that time I thought it the best plan, but now after eight

be noted that this bitter struggle over the constitution did not involve substantive questions of single tax doctrine. It was therefore primarily a struggle for control of the colony. It was, however, unfortunate in some of its after effects; some of the publicity and the subsequent vindictive behavior on the part of some of those who were defeated, combined to make it more difficult to enlist large-scale assistance from singletaxers generally.

years reflection, I frankly admit that your plan proved the best in the long run, because the non-member leaseholders help you to demonstrate your policy by their very presence." (Letter to Gaston printed in Fairhope *Courier,* February 3, 1905.)

$\mathcal{V}$

THE FIRST APPRAISEMENT

THE association leased its lands for over a year before it charged any rent. At first land was leased only to fully paid members, but in a short while special deals were entered into permitting members to reside on colony land before they had paid for their stock. There is no record of any general action taken by the executive council to repeal the offending by-law. It simply became ineffective in practice. The council, however, early adopted three resolutions controlling the leasing of its lands: 1. Each individual member was limited to a leasehold of five acres. The reason for this was the scarcity of cleared land. 2. Each member desiring possession of association land was required to give notice to that effect at a meeting of the executive council, describing the land desired, and securing the permission of the council before taking possession of the same. 3. The council provided for the appointment of a committee "to appraise the value of any clearing or other improvements on association land" and members wishing to lease such improved land would pay the association the appraised value of the "improvements." (Minutes, March 9, 1895.)

These rules caused some difficulties. The colony lost a member who withdrew in protest of the five acre rule when the

council refused an exception of permitting him to lease a certain fifteen acre tract. The member in question later was re-
admitted by the council but almost immediately a petition of
protest was filed by members and the council voted to refuse
him readmission and to reimburse him for the amount he had
paid in on his stock. (Minutes, July 29, 1895.) Another member asked for a reconsideration of the appraised value of the
"fruit trees and vines" on his land. A special committee was
appointed to review this appraisement and subsequently recommended a reduction in the valuation. (Minutes, September
17, 1895.)

The colony had been in existence almost a year before undertaking its first annual appraisal of the rental value of its lands.
The constitution charged the executive council with this responsibility. Earlier the council had appointed a special committee to study the broad problem of association rentals. This
committee made the following recommendations which were
adopted: 1. Appoint an appraisal committee to be composed
of three members of the executive council.   2. Assess rentals
semi-annually, in December and June and make rents payable
within six months thereafter;   3. Accord lessees the right to
complain of any injustice to the entire council within thirty
days after receiving notice of the assessment;   4. Give members
who are creditors of the association the right to pay their rents
by cancellation of an equal amount of the association's indebtedness to them. (Minutes, September 17, 1895.)

*The first rent assessment consisted simply of levying a charge
of five per cent against the appraised value of the land.* In dollars and cents this ranged from $1.25 for bay front lots (50' by
200') down to twelve and a half cents per acre for farm land.
Small as these sums may appear today they brought some complaints that valuations, and therefore rents, were too high. One
complainant stated that lots similar to colony lots which had
been assessed at the rate of $200 an acre could be bought out-
right for $50 an acre. (Minutes, December 23, 1895.)

In reply to these complaints the executive council admitted

that there had not been much data to serve as a guide for the first assessment, but the council had attempted to make a fair appraisal consistent with the available evidences of value, and that it had considered first the asking price of similarly situated land, privately owned. It further had taken into account the demand for certain lots, especially on the bay front. The council reported that in one instance three persons had applied for the same lot, and by common consent it had been let to the highest bidder. (Fairhope *Courier,* November 1, 1895.) In another case where there had been two applicants for the same acreage, a bonus of $6.50 was offered in addition to the rent.[1] (Fairhope *Courier,* May 15, 1896.) In the opinion of some, these two instances lent support to the view that the first rent assessment was too low rather than too high. Nonetheless, after much discussion the council decided that "assessments be reduced fifty per cent all around and stand as the assessment for one year, with such changes as may be shown to be necessary to a proper equalization of values." (Minutes, January 6, 1896.)

This experience with the first appraisal led to changes in the procedure for subsequent years. The following year, 1897, the council attempted to focus attention on relative rather than on absolute values; *i.e.,* it adopted a plan for appraisement of land values characterized as the "unit system." Under this plan the appraisal committee would select an "average" acre or lot, and instead of fixing its value in dollars and cents, would assign to it a value in units—perhaps twenty. All other lots or acres would be compared with this average land and if one was found to be worth one-half more, then it would have a unit value of thirty. All leaseholds would be rated in this manner and the units summed. *When the amount of money needed to be raised was determined* the absolute rental value per unit would be calculated by dividing the total amount to be raised by the total

---

1 This practice of letting a leasehold go to the person offering the highest bonus became standard procedure. Bonuses are payable only once and always to the colony.

units. (Fairhope *Courier,* December 1, 1896.) The initial result of this method was a rental value per unit of two and one-
half cents—one-half cent of which was to be earmarked for the
maintenance of a school.

Two things stand out from this first experience with the fixing of annual rentals. First, the executive council had not the
foggiest notion of how to calculate the full annual use value of
land, but it scarcely can be blamed for this failure. To this day
single tax literature offers very little assistance on this point of
important administrative procedure. In point of principle (as
opposed to procedure or technique) the first appraisement was
sounder than the second one, but there are definite shortcomings to the administration of a tax on economic rent by basing
it on market valuations. Second, the second appraisement based
as it was on an attempt to obtain mathematically sound relative
values was an improvement in technique, but when it came to
fixing the so-called unit values in terms of money, the association departed entirely from its basic principle by fixing the
rental on the amount of revenue needed, rather than by attempting to take the full economic rent and cutting the disbursements to fit the total receipts. As will be shown, within
only a few years the colony leaders were to reject both the
capital value method of appraisement and any rule limiting
the annual rent charges to a pre-determined expenditure
budget. Inadvertently the association in its first two appraisements afforded ammunition to those bent on giving it a hard
time in later years.

The relative unimportance of income from land rents in the
early years is evident from the appended table.

TABLE I.

SELECTED FINANCIAL DATA

FAIRHOPE INDUSTRIAL ASSOCIATION

1897-1904

SELECTED RECEIPTS

Year	Total Receipts	Rents	Membership Fees, Donations, Subscriptions	Net Wharf Receipts	Loans
1897	$ 564	$ 157	$ 122	$207	$ 18
1898	1,078	175	458	217	100
1899	1,359	251	118	222	450
1900	1,119	285	314	357	——
1901	1,313	480	215	246	——
1902	1,687	709	130	499	——
1903	4,027	928	1,767	328	285
1904	3,823	1,521	509	655	420

SELECTED DISBURSEMENTS

Year	Total	Property Taxes Colony	Property Taxes Lessees	Land Purchases	Roads & Bridges	School	Loans Repaid
1897	$ 469	$106*	$ 1	$——	$ 33	$ 33	$——
1898	899	67	16	——	49	105	18
1899	1,236	119	3	25	108	87	——
1900	1,053	140	6	232	52	82	——
1901	1,005	——	36	22	175	99	———
1902	1,506	167**	62	129	225	251	85
1903	4,274	409*	124	2,083	281	170	——
1904	4,000	393***	***	336	433	629	100

* For two years.   ** For 1901.   *** Not separated.

Other disbursements: Total for 1897-1904 for: Water $747

Telephone   457

Library   76

Cemetery   107

Source: Annual Reports of the Treasurer.

vi

SUGGESTIONS AND DEMANDS BY THE CHICAGO SINGLE TAX CLUB, 1897

A_N understanding of the Fairhope colony requires an appreciation of two facts. First, the colony was the product of the imagination and determination of a group of reform-minded individuals; it was not a planned offshoot of any organized or "official" group of recognized singletaxers. Second, the successful financing of the venture did depend, in part, on the willingness of single tax advocates and sympathizers to take out memberships, or to make donations of land, even though they had no intention of taking up residence on the colony site. The colony never actively sought either the endorsement or the financial assistance of *organized* singletaxers, although it would have been deeply appreciative of any material or morale building assistance which might have come its way.[1] However, partly because the colony did need outside assistance and partly because the activities and experiences of such an enclave would reflect in some manner on the greater

[1] Subsequently Mr. Gaston was tempted to seek the endorsement of the 1907 Single Tax Conference but was dissuaded from doing so because of the poor press the colony received during the 1904-1906 controversy. Among the few endorsements ever received by Fairhope was the following by the Women's National Single Tax League, meeting in New York City, June 26-28, 1902: "Resolved, that this conference sends its greetings to the Fairhope Colony, which is making the best attempt possible under present laws, to establish the Single Tax."

Single Tax Movement, editors of single tax organs and organized single tax clubs felt privileged to criticize, advise, assist, or otherwise interest themselves in the Fairhope venture. Many organizations and individuals, including Henry George, chose simply to ignore Fairhope.

Seeking outside assistance in a venture disapproved by many leaders in the movement, the Fairhope colonists simply could not isolate themselves from outside suggestions, notwithstanding that some of the suggestions seemed rooted in ignorance or bad faith. Some of the criticisms were both well-intentioned and constructive, and sooner or later were acted upon by the colony. Nonetheless, the relations between the organized single tax groups and the Fairhope colony were not altogether wholesome. Probably both the colony and the Single Tax Movement suffered by this failure to achieve a rapprochement.

The first intelligence received by the colonists from the Chicago Single Tax Club was that it was considering having a benefit picnic to raise money for the purchase of land for the Fairhope Industrial Association. No strings were to be attached other than the general conditions to be contained in the trust deed conveying the land. Such an opportunity did not surprise Mr. Gaston and other colony officers because Chicago was known as one of the principal strongholds of single tax sentiment. Naturally this possibility caused some excitement in Fairhope and Mr. Gaston was prepared to visit Chicago to help in the venture. (Fairhope *Courier,* August 1, 1897.)

It quickly became evident that the colony was not to receive any such windfall without conditions attached—conditions unacceptable to the colony. The rapid development of suspicion among the Chicago singletaxers with respect to Fairhope was attributable to the vindictiveness of some of those who were defeated in the 1895 controversy over the revision of the constitution. These embittered ex-Fairhopers charged the colony with fraud—a charge which was taken up in an editorial in the *National Single Taxer* in which the editor suggested the need of an investigation of Fairhope. (Ibid.)

These former members were persistent in their efforts to

discredit Fairhope. They charged: first, that some of the members of the Fairhope Industrial Association owned land adjacent to colony lands and refused to give the colony options on their holdings. Included among these members, they said, were Dr. Clara Atkinson, trustee and sister of the secretary; Mr. S. S. Mann, who served on the location committee; Mr. C. L. Coleman, the incumbent president of the association; and Mrs. C. P. Sykes. Second, they charged "fraud" because they felt the membership fee of $100 was inexcusably high in a colony located where land could be obtained so cheaply.

The important point related to the bringing of these charges is neither the degree of truth therein nor the inferences to be drawn from them, but the fact that the mere assertion of bad faith on the part of Fairhope gave ample reason for individual members of the Chicago club to attempt a critical re-appraisal of the colony. A considerable correspondence resulted and many suggestions and demands were made on Fairhope precedent to any donation of land. Some of these suggestions were constructive; some were either trivial or impossibly visionary.

One of the constructive suggestions arose out of a fear that the Fairhope constitution which provided that rent shall be collected for the benefit of the stockholders, whether resident or non-resident, meant that "a non-resident stockholder could certainly enforce his claim." Of course there had not been the slightest indication that any non-resident member of the association ever would request or enforce payment of dividends, but the legal possibility existed. Mr. L. G. Bostedo, a member of the Chicago club and an enduring friend of Fairhope, wrote: "Nobody but a few persons who are abnormally suspicious suspect that it was ever the intention of the promoters of Fairhope to use the corporation as a dividend earning speculation. We believe, however, that it will be wise to reorganize on a basis that will make such a thing impossible." (Letter to Gaston, August 30, 1897, Gaston files.) The colonists adopted this suggestion in the reorganization achieved with the incorporation of the Fairhope Single Tax Corporation in 1904.

A second criticism related to the fear of too much socialism within the colony. After the association store was abolished a voluntary co-operative called the "Fairhope Exchange" was organized. This had no legal connection with the Fairhope Industrial Association; it was sponsored by Mr. Coleman shortly before he was elected president of the association. Many single-taxers were fearful of such co-operatives. Among these was Clarence Moeller of the Chicago club who wrote Gaston on June 12, 1897, (Gaston files): "I understand some members are more socialist than Single Tax and I have feared that when your people figured out the details of the main principle of land franchises and money, there would be inserted additional institutions that jeopardize the principles so dear to us all and it would also be a violation of the law of equal freedom to divert rent paid by those engaged in individual enterprises to support cooperative ones or 'infant industries.' "

A third suggestion related to the omnipresent problem of how best to determine who shall remain in possession of the land. An apparently small minority in the Chicago club argued that all landholdings, *improved as well as unimproved,* should be offered to the highest bidder. These individuals, of course, contemplated that the highest bidder would pay for the improvements; he would take possession of a leasehold and its improvements upon outbidding the occupant and tendering to him the appraised value of the improvements. Most members of the Chicago club took a different view and supported the practice in Fairhope. Mr. Hiram B. Loomis wrote on July 18, 1897 (Gaston files): ". . . when land values rise, competition will show itself readily enough in the matter of subleasing, etc. The colony may then increase the annual rentals and the current possessor either pay more or relinquish his leasehold." This has been the policy of the colony and, as a subsequent discussion will disclose, has worked reasonably well over a period of time.

Mr. A. G. Pleydell of Philadelphia, editor of *Justice,* raised a technical question related to the policy of land tenure adopted in Fairhope. In a letter to Gaston dated August 16, 1897, (Gaston files) he expressed general agreement with the position of Fairhope in refusing to allow the highest bid to determine the value of land, but asked for a clarification of Article IX, Section 6, of the constitution which read: "If any lessee shall exact or attempt to exact from another a greater value for the use of land, exclusive of improvements, than the rent paid by him to the Corporation, the Executive Council shall immediately, upon proof of such fact, increase the rental charge against such land to the amount so charged or sought to be charged." Mr. Pleydell thought this, if interpreted literally, would work to prevent any increase in the value of land greater than that fixed by arbitrary assessment. He argued that a man would not offer land to another, for fear that if he overestimated and the other refused to accept, that the former would have an increased tax to pay when the land would not be worth it. "You have here the reversal of the highest bidder fixing the value of land, because you have the highest holder fixing it . . . It seems to me this would have a tendency to prevent the higgling of the market which is requisite as a guide to assessors or committees for the fixing of the rental of land." Once again a fundamental question of policy was raised during the formative period of the association—a question that became most acute during the period of the Florida boom—and one which has not been resolved in a wholly satisfactory manner to this day.

Fourth, a few members of the Chicago club suggested a complete reorganization of the association together with an entirely different name. To surmount certain legal problems these individuals suggested that the Fairhope Industrial Association be incorporated as a municipal corporation. The new city would reimburse the members of the private corporation in scrip or bonds and in return the association would deed its land in trust to the municipality. Mr. Charles G. Foord in a letter dated June 21, 1897, wrote Mr. Gaston: "Our latest and best plan for Fairhope, one which seems to have many points to commend it, is to incorporate as a town or city with a municipal organization. This plan as it seems to me will array all the State, local and national powers on our side and give added dignity. Another suggestion is to change the name to Alabama

City. This will give us all the powers of the Southern sentiment and tradition." The colonists quite sensibly dismissed this suggestion as impossibly visionary or unrealistic in terms of Alabama law and sentiment.

Finally, members of the Chicago club were most indignant and critical of the colony for permitting individuals who owned land adjacent to it to retain their memberships and even to hold office in the association. The fact that Mr. S. S. Mann had given the colony an oral option to buy the land held by him did not satisfy the Chicago brethren who wanted a written option. Strongest criticism was directed at Dr. Atkinson and Mr. Coleman who persistently refused to give the colony any sort of an option to purchase lands held by them except (in the case of Mr. Coleman) at the prevailing market price. (Minutes, November 16, 1903.) Mr. Hiram B. Loomis felt so strongly over what he considered a major defection of character among colony members that he wondered whether ". . . it would not pay the colony to move elsewhere rather than try to carry such a burden?" (Letter to Gaston, July 10, 1897, Gaston files.)

This last criticism cut deeply. It was true but circumstances were such that little could be done about it. The individuals whose professions with respect to the single tax were most in variance with their practices were among the most useful and most sympathetic resident members. In so far as can be determined each understood the single tax doctrine and each believed in it as an abstraction. Undoubtedly they did lack a measure of faith in Fairhope succeeding as a single tax venture. They wanted some measure of security for themselves in the event of failure. The extent to which either Dr. Atkinson or Mr. Coleman actively sought an unearned increment cannot be determined, although it is incontrovertible that they automatically would receive such a windfall with the growth of the community.[2]

---

[2] In response to an inquiry from the present writers, C. L. Coleman's son, Mr. Henry George Coleman, wrote, June 25, 1953: "Although my father believed in the principle of the Single Tax as laid down by Henry George, he did speculate in land, not only up North where he came from but in Baldwin

A few years later the colony announced it would not consider anyone for membership who owned land adjacent to it and who refused to option such land to the association. This decision was part of an effort to screen those applying for membership. Another precaution taken in 1901 to insure a loyal membership was the inauguration of committees to examine applicants for membership on their knowledge of and belief in the single tax. Also in 1901, the executive council instructed the secretary to insert in all original stock certificates after the words "transferred only upon the books of the association in person or by attorney upon surrender of this certificate," the following: "and to persons acceptable to the association as members." All members were asked to send in their certificates to have these words appended thereto. (Minutes, October 7, 1901.)

Although it may come as a surprise to the uninitiated, speculation in land was actively indulged in by many if not most professed singletaxers. In part this was a deliberate propaganda technique. A lecturer or worker for the single tax also known to be a land speculator, or land owner, could profit from publicizing his real estate deals as "horrible examples." To questioners the singletaxer would reply in effect: "Yes, I do own land and I do profit undeservedly from a land and tax system permitting me so to gain. Until the system is changed someone must get the socially created values. You people are permitting me and others who own land to receive privately an income which we have not earned and which should go to the public. Although I am one of the beneficiaries I think the system should be changed to prevent any individual from receiving any community created values."

It is one thing for a singletaxer to own land at a distance from an enclave, which is designed as an organized protest against the prevailing system. It is quite another matter to own land adjacent to such a colony. Perhaps the ethical distinction is not well taken, but from a practical point of view, the refusal

---

County after he joined the Colony. However, if laws were passed prohibiting the sale of land for private gain, he would have willingly and without bitterness abided thereby."

of members to option land adjacent to the Fairhope colony effectively limited the extent of the positive demonstration. The colony was not well endowed materially, and if the local members were not disposed to help the colony acquire land at no sacrifice to themselves, it is not difficult to understand that non-resident singletaxers should be suspicious and non-member residents should be unimpressed.

As a general proposition a member of any radical reform movement, or any organized aspect of the movement, must keep his or its behavior beyond reproach from the point of view of fundamental doctrine. The mores of so-called radical groups typically permit their members to be tolerant, even sympathetic, toward any program to reform the existing system, but discourage them from deviating to any degree from the strict orthodoxy of the creed adopted by the group to which they belong. Many of the brushes the Fairhope colony had with other singletaxers and single tax organizations were rooted in its unorthodoxy. The means for ushering in the single tax generally accepted among singletaxers was that of political action. Many of the faithful simply could not condone the Fairhope method and felt compelled to fight it with all available means. Although singletaxers are among the strongest of individualists and are determined to uphold individual liberty, when organized they fail to escape this deep rooted psychological compulsion of all organized reformers who are dedicated to a particular cause having a definitive creed or official program.

The dilemma faced by the colony was that of how to reconcile the substantive principles of the movement with the continuing necessity to compromise in the conduct of a social experiment. A functioning social group such as the Fairhope colony necessarily finds it most difficult to purge its membership for any cause other than the grossest defection of character or behavior. Obviously it would not have accomplished anything to move away from the offending members; wherever the colony might go it would have to deal with essentially the same human problems.

The Chicago Single Tax Club did not hold its picnic for the benefit of the Fairhope land fund. In the long run this was unimportant since not much money would have been raised. At the time, however, the controversy hurt, following as it did the recent division among colony members over the revision of the constitution. The colony was put on the defensive. The next ten years were to be characterized by many activities and policies designed to improve the colony's relations with non-resident singletaxers and to consolidate its position with its own lessees, members and non-members alike.

vii

INITIAL PROVISIONS OF
PUBLIC SERVICES AND FACILITIES

*F*AIRHOPE was unique among colonies of this period. The colony as such accepted no responsibility for the material needs of its members who were expected to build their own homes, clear and fence their lands, and find their own employment. The colony promised only to make land available to members on an equitable basis; to collect the full economic rent; and to use the rents collected for the benefit of the lessees. But no community can exist without some public facilities and services; hence, arrangements had to be made for the organization and financing of essential common requirements.

Some of the first community improvements resulted solely from voluntary co-operation among the colonists. An example of this was the building of the first roadway from the beach to the building sites on the bluff. This improvement was indispensable in order to haul lumber from lighters to the locations of the first homes and store buildings.[1] With few exceptions, however, major facilities and services were not provided wholly

---

[1] See Fairhope *Courier*, January 1, 1897: "Much of the early work on streets and roads, parks and beaches, was done by volunteer workers. Members agreed to devote certain hours or to give two Saturday mornings a month to such work without compensation. Such work was often rewarded by a beach picnic prepared by the colony women."

from voluntary labor and contributions of supplies or equipment. The executive council therefore formulated certain rules relating to work on colony improvements.

At first the council provided that paid-up members would be entitled to preference in employment on colony projects. Early conditions governing this employment included an eight hour day with a scale of $1.50 per day for skilled labor.[2] These conditions were considerably better than those prevailing in the rural South of 1895. They were, in fact, too liberal for the colony to maintain.

The financing of the early improvements presented a serious problem. The colony treasury had been seriously depleted by the initial expenses and land purchases.[3] Further, new memberships and payments on stock purchased on installments were coming in slowly. The colony collected no rents until after a full year of existence. Special donations for land were kept separate in a land fund and unavailable for current expenses or for public facilities.

The scrip provided for in the constitution proved indispensable to the financing of the colony during the early years. These certificates were prepared in Des Moines in denominations of five, ten, twenty-five, and fifty cents, and of $1.00, $2.00, $5.00, and $10.00. The scrip was used with a high degree of success because its issue was limited to estimates of certain colony expenditures for the period of one year, and because no individual was under any obligation to accept it, although the

[2] The first Saturday of each month was set aside for a general meeting of resident members at which time the financial reports of the colony would be given and at these meetings the pay sheets of work done in various departments would be presented, reconciled and audited. (Minutes, December 31, 1894.)

[3] The financial experience of the Fairhope Industrial Association for eleven months from February, 1894, to January, 1895: *Receipts,* $2,255.59, of which $2,207 was paid in on stock or penalties for arrearages and $43.59 was received from subscriptions to the *Courier. Disbursements,* Secretary's salary ($40 per month), $440; Expenses of locating committee, $195.50; Paid on land, $771; For typewriter, $67; For publishing *Courier,* $76.68; For *Liberty Bell* and printing the constitution, $65; and Miscellaneous, $212.03; total $1,827.21. To which, add $428.38, making $2,255.59. Of this $428.38, the Secretary held cash of $241.95; Cash held by Treasurer, $30.50; Bills received and since paid, $100; and personal accounts in process of settlement, $55.93.

colony was contractually obligated to receive it on any indebtedness of the bearer to the colony. At no time did the issue seriously get out of hand. There is, however, some evidence that it did occasionally circulate at a discount with lawful money, but there is no evidence that the discount ever became more than nominal. The colony did remarkably well with its "shinplasters," for the officials were highly responsible and intelligent, and there was a sufficient flow of "money" from non-resident benefactors and from wharfage and other local receipts.

While it was still meeting in Battles Wharf, the executive council instructed the superintendent of public services to procure a well and pump for a public water supply. (Minutes, December 31, 1894.) This instruction was not acted upon; several months later the colonists petitioned the executive council for action, pleading an urgent need for such a facility. (Minutes, July 23, 1895.) The petitioners were told that a well was under consideration and the council subsequently announced that water had been secured, that the well was a splendid one, but that the colony could not finance a pump.

Within a few weeks one of the members, C. L. Coleman, offered to install the pump at his own expense on condition that he be reimbursed out of the first new membership or if a new membership proved not to be forthcoming he would accept payment in wharf certificates. This offer was accepted by the council. It was the first of many similar offers accepted during the early years of the colony.[4]

4 Mr. Coleman was one among several Fairhope personalities who deserve a more extended treatment than can be accorded herein. In the early years he did many things to help the colony, its active members, and many retiring members; e.g., on April 29, 1895, he moved that the council give Mr. E. Smith (who arrived in the covered wagon on round-up date) a certificate for the amount paid on association stock, urging Mr. Smith's great need, that Mrs. Smith was a very deserving woman and that such action might stop Mr. Smith from talking against the colony. Coleman offered to buy the certificate from Smith for cash. On March 11, 1896, Mr. Coleman purchased the house and improvements of the Brokaws in an effort to appease this couple. He took the lead in organizing the Fairhope Exchange—which had no connection with the Fairhope Industrial Association—the purpose of which was to facilitate exchange of the products of

The colony, as such, was destined never to be wholly successful in furnishing a public water supply. This problem occupied the colonists for many years and was the basis for a considerable amount of bitterness among two groups of members. One group wanted to borrow for physical facilities, through water trustees so that no indebtedness would be created for the colony, and charge for the services. The other group wanted to make do with whatever funds were available but furnish the services free out of rents.

The division among members over the water works issue in 1906 will be remembered by some of Fairhope's older residents as the "Bulletin-Board-Controversy."[5]

The weekly publication of the Fairhope *Courier* was not frequent enough to keep its readers abreast of the latest ideas, arguments, and pronouncements in regard to the water works. Consequently, one of the interested parties inaugurated the use of a bulletin board. In true Fairhope spirit the opponents were urged to make full use of the bulletin board—and they did!

Arguments and refutations developed to such a volume and with such rapidity, that interest in "daily mail check," so important in any small town, gave way in Fairhope to the daily, in some cases hourly, bulletin-board check.

A wharf was a basic necessity to Fairhope since the only means of transportation to Mobile was by water and the nearest wharf was several miles distant. Within seven months after arrival at the colony site steps were taken to remove this deficiency.

---

the colonists and to accumulate capital and conduct enterprises to provide profitable employment for its members.

Mr. Coleman undoubtedly possessed great faith in the single tax (he named his son "Henry George" Coleman) but he was not convinced that anything should or could be done except by government. At any rate he purchased forty acres adjoining the colony and refused to sell it to the association except for more than he paid, and he homesteaded another adjoining forty acres. This caused much criticism both in Fairhope and nationally. In 1905, he moved off colony grounds and never again served the association in an official capacity. Although he was somewhat active in his association with the "protesting tenants" in 1904-1906, his intent was neither vicious nor malicious, but was designed to clarify certain issues.

[5] This bit of Fairhope history was related by the late Mrs. Anne B. Call.

Mr. Bellangee and several others of the original membership consistently insisted that all public improvements should be financed out of ground rents. With respect to the wharf, however, the consensus was almost unanimous that the need was so great that it could not wait the accumulation of land rent, but must be financed from other sources. The colony as such could not borrow because of the constitutional restriction against contracting any interest-bearing indebtedness. Further, the young colony could not appeal to any wealthy benefactor for material assistance, for none had appeared up to that time. Mr. Bellangee is credited with the suggestion that the wharf be financed in the manner employed in the construction of the Guernsey Market House. (Clipping, New York *Herald,* August 30, 1903.)

Under the Guernsey Market House plan (as applied to the Fairhope wharf) all contributors of money, materials, and labor were issued wharf certificates in the amount of $1.25 for every $1.00 invested. These certificates were redeemable at face value for wharfage for both passengers and freight. They were also acceptable on subscription to the stock of the association, but only to the equivalent of the actual cash value represented. (Minutes, May 6, 1895.) Later these wharf certificates were made receivable for payment of any indebtedness to the association. (Fairhope *Courier,* July 20, 1896.)

The colony management estimated that not more than twenty-five per cent of the certificates issued would be presented for cash redemption. To meet such a contingent liability the council provided that ". . . the entire proceeds from the operation of said wharf over and above the cost of operation and maintenance be applied to taking up the certificates outstanding in the order of their issuance." (Minutes, May 6, 1895.)

The young colony was yet too poor to finance the wharf entirely from local barter and the issue of wharf certificates. Sensing this, the *Courier* advised distant friends of the great need for the wharf and solicited their financial support. The response to this plea was favorable; outside purchases of wharf certificates probably provided the bulk of the cash used in financing the wharf.

The first wharf cost about $1,300 and proved to be one of the colony's most successful ventures—at least financially. (Fairhope *Courier,* July 1, 1896.) Apparently this surprised neighbors of the colonists. Writing in the *Courier* (January 15, 1899), Mr. Gaston reflected: "Time was when our neighbors looked askance upon us, when they thought us a few impractical enthusiasts and our organization one that would go to pieces, laughed behind our backs at our wharf scheme and our 'shinplasters' and prophesied that our improvements could be bought for 'six-bits' in a year or two."

The first wharf was a colony-owned and colony-operated enterprise. Its management was directly under the executive council which determined wharfage charges, selected and supervised the wharfinger and administered the details of maintenance and improvement. The wharfinger worked on a percentage basis and his relative share declined as the total receipts increased. Taxes assessed against the wharf were considered operational costs and were subtracted from wharfage receipts before net earnings were calculated and before payments were made on outstanding certificates.

The association did not receive any *cash* from wharf receipts until September 19, 1898. (Fairhope *Courier,* October 14, 1898.) By the end of 1898, $765.40 of the $1,172.40 in wharf certificates had been retired. During many of the early years of the colony the net wharf receipts exceeded the net rentals from land as a source of revenue to finance colony expenditures.

Provision for free schooling for members was mandatory under the constitution, but this service was not provided until April 17, 1896. The delay is understandable not alone because of the relative poverty of the colony, but also because the number of children in residence was comparatively small. The first school provided both day and evening sessions, the latter for the convenience of older children. The colony paid the teacher $10.00 per month in scrip, but the teacher was permitted to supplement this by subscriptions from students. Students living on association lands were charged only half as much as non-colony children. The school at first received nothing from Alabama public school funds and later obtained an insignificant amount for several years. In financing the school during the early years the colony charged, or refrained from charging, an incidental fee as the state of its treasury permitted. At best the amounts received from the State of Alabama were sufficient to finance only four months of schooling. The colony, on its own, supplemented by occasional incidental fees, extended the school year to about eight months. The goal, kept always in mind, was a school free of any charge to students.

The first school building was the colony store moved to a lot located on the first colony leasehold, which was held by the secretary. To obtain this site the colony council exercised the constitutional right of eminent domain, and thus Mr. Gaston lost his sweet potato patch. Most of the labor on the school building was voluntary but at one time work almost ceased when voluntary help was not forthcoming. This crisis was met by the executive council which instructed the schoolhouse committee to procure the necessary labor which the association would pay for in scrip.

The schoolhouse increased in size as the colony grew. In a short time a second room was added to the building. Shortly before the incorporation of the town (1908) the colony completed a three room school building. The Town of Fairhope immediately assumed its responsibility for the operation of public schools.

Fairhope secured its public library years before it had any reason to expect one. Mrs. Marie Howland, a former member and editor of the news organ of the "Credit Foncier Company" located in Mexico, joined the Fairhope colony in 1898. With her she brought her late husband's library, the Howland and Lowell Collection comprising about twelve hundred volumes. (Mrs. Howland served as librarian until her death in 1921. She also served as associate editor of the Fairhope *Courier*.)

The library started in a modest fashion when Mrs. Howland

allotted one room in her home for this purpose. It gave a tremendous boost to the morale of the colonists who enjoyed boasting that not even Mobile had a public library.

It was in connection with the library that the colony received its first offer of help from Mr. Joseph Fels, a wealthy soap manufacturer, social reformer, convinced singletaxer, and philanthropist of Philadelphia and London. For the next ten years Mr. Fels was to be the colony's greatest benefactor. Fels became interested in the colony upon reading an article on Fairhope published in *Justice*. He outlined his initial plans to aid the colony in a letter to Gaston dated April 25, 1899:

If it can be arranged, get the use of a room in some private house or elsewhere for the books; I will cheerfully pay for the cost of shelving, etc., but bring these books into immediate use in the community . . . A good many of them are considerably more ambitious than is usual for a colony library . . . As you suggest I shall be glad to entertain the proposition from your executive council looking to an advance by me of from $200 to $500 for the purpose of establishing a telephone line.

The Fairhope Public Library became one of the more successful local institutions. Ultimately it acquired a separate building which has been improved and enlarged more than once. Other than free utility services it receives nothing from governmental sources; it is financed entirely by the colony, supplemented by very modest individual contributions in the form of dues from members of the "Library Association."

As indicated in the exerpt from Fels' letter to Gaston, the executive council early had outlined its idea of establishing a telephone system in Fairhope. This was to be the first public service paid for out of land rents. This proved to be one of the colony's greatest mistakes. It was costly and it engendered dissension, even bitterness, among members and lessees.

Criticism of the telephone involved two points. First, many thought the service was provided too far in advance of a general public demand. Second, many made the point that the resources of the colony would be strained to provide an adequate water system—a public service much more in public demand at that time. The initial expense of installing the telephone service was $457.42. In the same year it was necessary to make relatively heavy outlays for a new schoolhouse, a wharf warehouse and wharf repairs. As a result of these unusual disbursements the colony operated at a small deficit in 1904.

To a degree, the differences among members over when and how to make capital outlays for public services were doctrinaire. Mr. Bellangee, spokesman for one faction, held that all public services (he excepted the wharf because of its absolute necessity) should be financed from land rentals. From the information now available it is impossible to determine precisely what Mr. Bellangee had in mind. He might have meant that land rents should provide the capital outlays only or that they were to be used to pay operating expenses as well. The group for which he spoke contained individuals endowed with common sense; hence, it would appear reasonable to assume that they would have permitted some charges to consumers of publicly owned utility services in the interest of economy in consumption and to achieve equity among consumers. It is clear that Bellangee wanted to finance all capital outlays from annual rentals. Such a policy would mean that a new community must forego for an indefinite period all public services requiring large capital outlays. Gaston and most members of the executive council were unwilling to accept such a strict "pay-as-you-go" program. They held that most Fairhopers had been accustomed to conveniences, such as the telephone, and that they should not be denied these advantages simply because Fairhope had not grown fast enough to furnish them from land rents. They argued that such public services would serve to accelerate the growth of the colony; that they could be maintained and expanded out of future rentals.

The first telephone system was financed without any additional issue of certificates or the contracting of any formal indebtedness. Colony revenues and "loans" by Fels and others supplied the financing. The system was placed in operation in the fall of 1904, with only twelve subscribers. Each user furnished his own telephone and paid for his dial and switch, but the service was free to the individual user. In practice the upkeep of the system proved costly. It is easy to understand the growing unhappiness among the lessees, an increasing proportion of whom were not members, and had no official voice either in the determination of the annual rent charges or in the disposition of the colony revenues. To these disaffected elements it looked much as though a small group of telephone users were benefitting at the expense both of unnecessarily high rentals and of inadequacies in the water system, public school, and other facilities of wider usefulness.

Several of the boats serving the eastern shore also served Fairhope upon the completion of the wharf. Many Fairhopers, however, were not satisfied with such services. If any appreciable number of Mobile families were to be attracted to spend summers in Fairhope, it was imperative to provide a boat leaving Fairhope early in the morning and leaving Mobile after working hours. Certainly it seemed necessary to ensure a reliable *daily* service of some sort. Experience demonstrated that private owners of existing boats could not always accommodate their interests to those of Fairhope. (Even the establishment of a post office in Fairhope did not ensure daily service of a mail boat until pressure was brought through the Post Office Department.) Finally, some residents of Fairhope believed some competition was required to combat the automatic increase in boat fares put in effect during the winter season.

On October 8, 1900, colony leaders called an open meeting of all citizens interested in securing a boat for Fairhope. A plan was offered designed to furnish Fairhope with a boat to be operated for its sole interest, but offering investors "security and a reasonable profit." The Fairhope Industrial Association as such could not undertake the venture because the constitution forbade any direct interest-bearing indebtedness. The plan approved at the meeting was to use the device of a "trusteeship" instead of a corporation in order to avoid the costs of incorporation and annual license taxes.

Subsequently Mr. Gaston was appointed trustee to carry out the terms of the contract, which provided that the first charge against the earnings of the boat would be the payment of six per cent interest on the stock. Under the plan adopted, all earnings from the boat, after operating expenses, were pledged to retire the trustee's certificates. Upon the retirement of these certificates or stock the boat would be turned over to the association to be operated as a public service of the colony.

Following formulation of the boat plan the colony established a boat yard near the wharf and appointed a building committee as provided in the trust agreement. The committee was composed of E. B. Gaston, J. Bellangee, and P. A. Parker. Actual building of the boat provided benefits for Fairhope; *e.g.,* much needed work was supplied to members and lessees, many of whom were willing to take their pay in trustee certificates. The boat advertised to the outside world that the colony was determined to do everything possible "to make good theories work."

Early in 1901, Gaston travelled to Philadelphia, New York, and Boston to interest singletaxers in the colony but especially to secure subscriptions to the boat fund. (Fairhope *Courier,* January 15, 1901.) His efforts were successful and the steamer *Fairhope* was financed, as the wharf had been, largely from outside sources. Mr. Fels was the largest contributor ($2,200), and after the launching on June 27, 1901, the *Courier* asked, ". . . was it not appropriate that the boat would slide down the ways on Fels Naptha soap, with a Fels Naptha wrapper on her bow?" (Fairhope *Courier,* July 1, 1901.)

The *Fairhope* was not a financial success although optimistic statements were issued from time to time. She burned in the fall of 1905 shortly after a complete overhaul of boiler and machinery. This overhaul followed a general rebuilding during the summer at a cost of $6,000. At the time of the fire most of the original cost and the cost for the repairs remained unamortized. The boat was not insured despite the provision in the trust agreement which stipulated that insurance be carried. In the judgment of the trustee, marine insurance was too expensive.

Mr. Fels visited the colony shortly after the steamer burned and exonerated the trustee and the colony from any responsibility or liability in the loss of the boat. He declared that "... for the money invested and the effort made, Fairhope was doing the most practical and effective reform work being done in the world today." (Fairhope *Courier*, December 29, 1905.)

Creditors for the repair and overhaul of the boat brought suits against the stockholders, principally against Joseph Fels, as they felt his backing of the boat had lent considerable influence in their decision to offer credit. Settlements were made out of court and the colony and her individual members, as well as the holders of trustee's certificates, were relieved from further responsibility. Later the Fairhope Improvement Company, which had no legal connection with the Fairhope Single Tax Corporation, rebuilt the boat and operated it for a period of years. (Mr. Fels was also the largest stockholder in the Fairhope Improvement Company which was managed by Mr. R. F. Powell.)

Although the financing and management of the steamer *Fairhope* was technically divorced from the Fairhope Industrial Association (and its successor the Fairhope Single Tax Corporation), the umbilical connection was so strong that the financial failure of the boat was used rather effectively by many in attacking colony management. Friends of the colony should be willing to admit that, with the exception of the wharf, public ownership of public services by the colony left much to be desired. With respect to the steamer, however, it should be made clear that the colony as such was not burdened financially because of its failure. Colony ineptness in managing public utilities in no wise reflected on the single tax aspects of colony experience.

Article XII of the constitution was interpreted to require the colony to furnish free burial spaces for its members. A beautiful site was set aside for the cemetery and by 1900 the trustees had proposed rules to govern its upkeep and use. The regulations adopted provided that members and other persons residing on colony land were entitled to free burial space. Lessees were permitted to secure lots for future use on the payment of a small annual rent until the space was used. Non-residents of colony land were allowed to purchase burial space. (Fairhope *Courier,* October 15, 1900.)

The rules adopted in 1900 are largely in effect today. The committees who have supervised the cemetery have been interested and capable. The colony has contributed liberally to cemetery upkeep as the treasury permitted and the needs demanded. Very early, the colony started setting aside funds received from the sale of cemetery lots to finance its maintenance.

One of the early actions of the executive committee was the setting aside of some of the most beautiful bay front lands to be used as parks and to assure access to the beach for members and lessees. The free access of the public to the beach long has served as a marked contrast to the situation in the neighboring communities which failed to provide public beach facilities. As additional public services, the executive council early provided free bathhouse facilities and pavilions for the use of the lessees. Before long, however, the council found it necessary to impose charges for the use of such facilities by the general public.

While the colony management was busy developing public services, the colonists concerned themselves with the art of living. Indications were numerous that the early colonists were more adept at living than at making a living. In one of his caustic moods, Fels wrote Gaston from London, February 10, 1909: "Your community is further behind in agriculture than in economic discussion, and I suppose the cultivators themselves differ in their ideas quite as much."

Societies, organizations, clubs, and forums mushroomed in Fairhope. Some of the organizations were designed to further the work of the colony. Others existed only to serve the colonists' cultural interests and talents. Early Fairhopers were individualists and intellectually curious. Almost any cause or idea could get a hearing and a following. The broad range of interests among the colonists may be indicated by listing a few of the organizations which sprang up within the first few years of the colony's existence: Henry George Club; Socialist Club; Library Review Club; Fairhope School of Philosophy; Progressive League; Dancing Assembly; Village Improvement Association; Woman's Suffrage Association; Fairhope Winter Assembly or Chautauqua; Fairhope Society of Arts and Crafts; Fairhope Dramatic Club; Academy of Science and Art; Henry George Athletic Club; Fairhope Library Association; Arbitration Society and the Fairhope Band.[6]

Although Fairhope was both young and very small, apparently its citizens needed these varied and numerous outlets. One explanation is the unusually high level of intelligence of its people. From its inception Fairhope was referred to in neighboring communities as "intellectual" and "arty." It was accordingly suspect by some, but not by many. For example, Judge J. H. H. Smith, of Bay Minette, in speaking at the fourteenth anniversary celebration remarked that he found the extraordinary intellectual activity of the people a great attraction. He thought Fairhope must have a greater proportion of intellectual and independent thinking people relative to the population than could be found "anywhere else in the world." The *Courier,* January 8, 1909, quoted him as saying that he would "like nothing better for his children than to live in such an environment to develop their reasoning faculties and stimulate thought and action."

Possibly the most important and typical organization in the colony was the Progressive League, sometimes referred to as "the forum." Meetings of the league were held on Sunday afternoons, either in the park or in the colony hall, according to weather conditions. Members took turns in speaking on subjects of their own choice. It was customary for the talks to close with a question and answer period. It mattered little the subject of the address—the single tax was certain to come up in

6 "Fairhope as a place to bury oneself seems to me like a joke. Why, it is the bother of my life to have time to stay home and enjoy home life. The whole time seems to be given to societies, clubs, leagues, sociables, concerts, dances, endeavor meetings, commemoration services, anniversaries, surprise and other parties, and I don't think this is a complete list." Extract from "Mrs. Howland's Letters." (Fairhope *Courier,* January 1, 1903.)

the discussion period. Occasionally a member would suggest that as these meetings were held on Sunday it might be well to limit addresses to sacred subjects. The general practice, however, was for each member to choose his own subject; problems of the day, the money question, socialism, and the single tax were thoroughly discussed.[7]

Colony residents used the beach and parks intensively. The Village Improvement Association built a platform around a huge magnolia tree in the beach park and it became a focal point for many festivities. Of some interest to antiquarians is the fact that the colony revived the Fourth of July celebration in Baldwin County. It early observed Memorial Day, decorating the graves of all war veterans, Northern as well as Southern.

The following summary of the accomplishments of the Fairhope colony to the time of incorporation of the municipality is taken from Mr. Ernest B. Gaston's remarks on the occasion of the thirteenth anniversary. (Fairhope *Courier,* November 15, 1907.)

Fairhope was founded on cutover pine lands in a practically uninhabitable area. By 1907 it owned 4,000 acres of land with a bay frontage of about three-fifths of a mile. Nearly 500 people were living on colony leaseholds in approximately 125 dwellings. The following commercial and community facilities were provided by 1907: four general stores, one doing a $50,000 annual business; one millinery and ladies furnishing store; one drug store; one notions store; two bakeries, one with a restaurant; three hotels; one meat market; a blacksmith shop; one saw and planing mill with a corn grinding and rice hulling mill in connection; a brick yard; a power printing plant; central stations for Baldwin County of the Home Telephone Company and the Southern Bell Company; the only central water works

---

7 Mrs. Howland, Fairhope *Courier,* December 22, 1905, defended the usual practice: "Formerly there used to be much complaint in the League because our teachings there were too secular, especially because we rung in the single tax on every occasion. We have now learned that the fundamental principles of the Single Tax are consonant with, not ecclesiastical dogma, but with the very essence of the highest religious faith."

system in Baldwin County comprising two miles of mains and supplying forty premises directly connected and many others using water from the tank; a two room schoolhouse with a third room in progress; a colony operated telephone system; a wharf (recently destroyed by storm but in process of rebuilding at a cost of $4,000); bathhouses; a free public library of over three thousand volumes; and generous reservations of lands for parks along the bay. Also the colony had spent much money on roads and gulleys.

viii

INCORPORATION OF THE FAIRHOPE SINGLE TAX CORPORATION

OFFICERS and members of the Fairhope Industrial Association long had desired to incorporate the Fairhope colony under the laws of Alabama. The most important reason for this desire was to find some way to obtain perpetual legal existence. They also wanted to perfect their charter in order to make it clearer that theirs was a non-profit organization, to be judged and taxed as such. The Alabama General Assembly paved the way for this step when, on October 1, 1903, it passed a statute which enabled the incorporation of organizations not for pecuniary profit in the sense of paying interest or dividends on stock, but for the benefit of organization members through their mutual co-operation and association. The statute of 1903 grants a perpetual charter to such an organization subject to revocation by the legislature.

Some of the arguments urged by the colony's attorney, Mr. James H. Webb, in support of such a law, are of interest to the Fairhope story. Mr. Webb wrote members of the Alabama General Assembly in part: ". . . but a few years ago, where now flourishes the village of Fairhope, there was merely an indifferent cow pasture, assessed at probably fifty or twenty-five cents an acre. But a little band, that we considered harmless cranks, came down from the Northwest and cast their fortunes there to put in practice a theory that to them seemed wise and which they held dear. As I have said, they succeeded, and the Colony of Fairhope is the most thriving village on the eastern shore, a credit to the county and to its promoters and a benefit to the state and county in more ways than the largely increased tax returns occasioned thereby." (Fairhope *Courier,* October 15, 1903.)

The procedure for obtaining an Alabama charter and the manner of making the required adjustments deserve detailed portrayal. Hence, certain official actions and documents are fully reproduced herein. These include: (A) A resolution adopted by the resident members of the Fairhope Industrial Association, in a special meeting held May 26, 1904; (B) the Declaration of Incorporation of the Fairhope Single Tax Corporation; (C) the Charter of the Fairhope Single Tax Corporation; and (D) A summary of the Minutes of the Meeting of Charter Members of the Fairhope Single Tax Corporation.

A

RESOLUTION ADOPTED BY RESIDENT MEMBERS
OF FAIRHOPE INDUSTRIAL ASSOCIATION
MAY 26, 1904

At a meeting of the resident members of the Fairhope Industrial Association, held at Fairhope, Alabama, on May 26, 1904, the following resolution was adopted: WHEREAS it was contemplated at the organization of this association as provided in article ten of our charter, that when a site for our colony had been selected it might be desirable to become a corporation under the laws of that state, and

WHEREAS through the kindness of the legislature of Alabama very favorable laws have been passed for the benefit of this association, and to get the full benefit of same it will be necessary to incorporate under the laws of this state.

NOW THEREFORE in consideration of the premises, and to accomplish such result, BE IT RESOLVED that the following proposition be submitted to a vote of the members of the association for their ratification, viz: That the President and Secretary of the Fairhope Industrial Association are hereby Authorized, empowered and directed to convey to the Fairhope Single Tax Corporation—a corporation organized under the laws of Alabama, (which has adopted the constitution of the Fairhope Industrial Association, with such changes in phraseology as were obviously necessary, reaffirmed all general rules and procedure of said association and assumed all obligations thereof), all of the property of the Fairhope Industrial Association, and to execute in behalf of and in the name of said association suitable conveyances, that the Fairhope Industrial Association shall thereupon be dissolved and cease to exist; that in consideration of said transfer, the Single Tax Corporation shall obligate itself to issue to the recorded holders of the certificates of membership and stock of the Fairhope Industrial Association certificates of membership in the said new corporation which shall have the same value as the certificates surrendered, and which shall be delivered on the surrender of such certificates.

(This election was completed July 15, 1904. The vote was unanimous in the affirmative.)

B
DECLARATION OF INCORPORATION OF
FAIRHOPE SINGLE TAX CORPORATION

We, the undersigned, desiring to form a corporation under the provisions of an act for the organization of corporations not for pecuniary profit in the sense of paying interest or dividends on stock, but for the benefit of its members through their mutual cooperation and association, approved October 1st., 1903, do hereby declare:

1

The name of said corporation shall be The Fairhope Single Tax Corporation.

2

The names of its chartered members are Ernest B. Gaston, C. K. Brown, H. Creswell, J. Bellangee, George Knowles, Clara

M. Gaston, Mary Hunnell, Mary E. Mead, Marie Howland, Wm. Call, G. M. Bancroft, N. Mershon, D. K. Bancroft, Anna B. Hail, Wm. Stimpson, Frank L. Brown, Geo. W. Wood, Clara E. Atkinson, M. V. Watros, J. A. Patterson, Wm. Brown, Mrs. F. L. Brown, A. H. Mershon, C. L. Coleman, Sarah L. Coleman, Edith R. Wilson, C. H. Wilson, Anne B. Call, C. E. Littlefield.

3

The purpose of said corporation is to demonstrate the beneficence, utility and practicability of the Single Tax theory with the hope of its general adoption by the governments in the future. In the meantime securing for ourselves and our children and associates the benefits to be enjoyed from its application as fully as existing laws will permit, and to that end to conduct a model community free from all forms of special privilege, securing to its members therein equality of opportunity, the full reward of individual efforts and the benefits of cooperation in matters of general concern, holding all land in the name of the corporation and paying all taxes on the same and improvements and other personal property of lessees thereon (monies and credits excepted), charging the lessees the fair rental value, and in the prosecution of its plans for the general welfare of its members to do and perform all the acts and exercise all the powers permitted under Section 5 of said act.

C

CHARTER OF THE
FAIRHOPE SINGLE TAX CORPORATION

I do hereby declare the parties aforesaid, their successors and associates, duly incorporated under the name of the Fairhope Single Tax Corporation; that the existence of said corporation shall be perpetual subject to the right of revocation by the legislature. Said corporation has the power to elect such officers as it may deem necessary in such manner and for such terms as it may provide and remove the same at any time and adopt such constitution and by-laws as it may see fit not in conflict with the constitution and laws of this state. Such corporation shall have the power to buy, sell and lease real estate, to build and operate wharfs, boats and other means of transportation and communication; build, erect and operate water works, electric lighting and power companies, libraries, schools, parks, and do any other lawful thing incident to its purpose for the mutual benefit of its members, and may admit such other persons to participate in its benefits as it may see fit and upon such conditions as it may impose.

(The above declaration and charter went to Judge of Probate, Baldwin County, Alabama, and were returned "Given under my hand this 10th day of August, 1904.")

D

SUMMARY OF MINUTES OF MEETING OF
CHARTER MEMBERS OF THE
FAIRHOPE SINGLE TAX CORPORATION,
OCTOBER 26, 1904

Officers *pro tem:* F. L. Brown, Chairman; E. B. Gaston, Sec. Actions taken:

1. All members of Fairhope Industrial Association whose names did not appear on the application for the charter were elected members of the Single Tax Corporation.

2. The officers of the Fairhope Industrial Association were elected officers of the Fairhope Single Tax Corporation for the terms to which they were elected by the Fairhope Industrial Association.

3. The constitution of the Fairhope Industrial Association was adopted as the constitution of the Fairhope Single Tax Corporation except for some obviously necessary changes. These changes were adopted separately; then the constitution as a whole was adopted.

4. The president and secretary were authorized to accept and sign the conveyance turning the property of the Fairhope Industrial Association over to the Fairhope Single Tax Corporation, as drawn by Attorney James H. Webb.

ix

"DO YOU SEE THE CAT?"[1]

$\mathcal{T}ROUBLE$ came to Fairhope in the winter of 1904. Not that the colony ever was free of problems before or since, but the trouble which arrived late in 1904 was so different in degree and in results as to deserve intensive analysis. In retrospect this crisis, known nationally among single taxers as "The Fairhope Controversy," was climactic. By comparison most of the earlier and later differences and divisions appear either anti-climactic, vestigial, or of narrower import, despite some evidence that many of the other differences evoked more personal bitterness among the protagonists. The struggle from about 1902 to 1907 but climaxing during late 1904 and 1905, literally was one over the basic integrity of the Fairhope plan as a tactic for furthering the Single Tax Movement, and was accepted as such by singletaxers.

The most basic principle at issue was whether single tax doctrine necessarily demanded that an attempt be made to collect the full annual use value of the land irrespective of the

1 Meaning: "Do you see things from the single tax viewpoint," According to Arthur Nichols Young, *Single Tax Movement in the United States* (Princeton University Press, 1916), p. 270, "The expression was contributed to single tax phraseology by Judge Maguire, Henry George's San Francisco friend. Judge Maguire told the story of a landscape picture which bore the sign, 'Do you See the Cat?' A first glance at the picture failed to reveal the hidden feline, but after closer study the figure of the whole animal burst suddenly into view. Thereafter one might see in the picture nothing but cat."

desires of the community for public services. The next most proximate basic principle in dispute concerned the propriety of characterizing as "single tax" a plan which had to operate within a framework of state and local taxation which actually levied taxes on improvements and personal property. Such a plan could not comply literally with single tax conditions, but would have to simulate them by refunding to lessees (certain) taxes paid by them. The third basic principle in dispute involved the degree of democracy in the government or management of the colony which would be necessary to square the experiment with Henry George's emphasis on the importance of freedom. A fourth disputed principle, to some extent a corollary to the others, concerned the desirability of the Fairhope scheme in managing the land through leases rather than through issuance of deeds.

It would not be proper to infer that the problems and conflicts of this period were resolved by logical analyses alone. On the contrary, and despite the fact that the protagonists often invited one another to consider basic principles, much of the controversy involved questions of procedure and judgment (*e.g.,* fixing of rents and disbursements), impugning of motives, and inevitable clashes of personality. Of discussion there was a full plenty—Fairhopers loved to discuss, dispute, argue, and contend—but the outcome was not decided by reason or argument alone. Political tactics of organization and propaganda were resorted to by all parties and the tide of battle both ebbed and flowed.

Whether logical analyses or simply political and material considerations determined how members voted on a particular issue, the soundness of the decision itself must be judged in terms of principle. The purpose of this chapter is to analyze the operations of the Fairhope plan, its policies and procedures in terms of fundamental single tax principles.

To some extent it is unrealistic and perhaps unfair to apply strict single tax tests to the behavior of the colony in 1904, because not all of the members and lessees were exclusively single tax in philosophy. Only recently, in 1901, a number of socialists had joined the Fairhope community, coming mostly from Ruskin Colony. The Fairhope colony, however, was rapidly divesting itself of its more socialistic features, thus bringing the single tax aspects into greater prominence. Appeals for members and for contributions to the land fund were being directed almost exclusively to singletaxers. In 1903 and in 1904, Mr. Bellangee made two extended and quite successful lecture tours in behalf of the single tax program of the colony. By 1904, therefore, the colony as such could reasonably be judged primarily a single tax venture.

RELATION OF ANNUAL RENT TO TOTAL USE VALUE

The first and most fundamental problem encountered by the colony in establishing itself as a single tax demonstration was that of obtaining a consensus that colony rents should absorb the total use value of colony lands, without regard to the desires of the lessees as to public services. The issue of rents did not involve an interpretation of the constitution of the corporation; this document clearly contemplated that holders of colony land should pay into the common treasury the full use value of their leaseholds. The issue became a political one when the executive council attempted to comply with the constitutional mandate and its decision to do so was upheld by the membership. The following tabulation of rents collected by the colony clearly shows why this issue became serious after 1903.

TABLE II.

RECEIPTS FROM RENT
OF COLONY LAND: 1900-1906

Year	Receipts
1900	$ 285.40
1901	479.63
1902	817.20
1903	928.46
1904	1,520.67
1905	2,293.93
1906	2,140.16

During this period the usual procedure for determining the annual rent list involved four stages. First, the executive council made tentative appraisals usually at its first regular meeting in November. Second, the secretary furnished each lessee with a copy of the complete rental list showing not only the appraisement for the land held by the individual lessee, but that of every other lessee. Third, the executive council sat during December as a board of equalization to hear complaints and to explain the appraisals. Finally, the annual rentals were ratified by the resident membership of the corporation at the annual meeting held in February.

VIEWS OF COMPLAINING TENANTS

As might be anticipated every new rent appraisement brought some complaints, and necessitated explanations to justify it. Probably no annual appraisal ever was completely satisfactory to all lessees. The appraisals made in 1903 for the year 1904 resulted in the council holding an unusually active equalization session. This meeting was held on December 16, 1903. The chairman took note of the large number in attendance and announced that the council would first hear all objections before attempting any reply. The principal questions and objections raised included:

Why any raise at all this year, and if any raise, why so large?

Did the council claim that land values in Fairhope had increased by two-thirds in the last year?

Was it desirable to make the increase if rental income was to be used to refund taxes paid by lessees on their improvements, stocks of goods, etc.?

One non-member lessee did not object to his own rent but stated he wanted the money to be wisely expended—that he thought it had been squandered.

Perhaps the most fundamental issue was raised by a member and sometime officer. This individual discussed the single tax as he understood it. He asserted it was no part of the single tax to "rack rent." On the contrary, he understood that Henry George had proposed the land owner or holder would be left a

small portion of the rental value in order to cover the services
rendered by him and to help prevent loss in the sale of his
improvements in the event increasing taxes made it necessary
for him to move.

In their turn the colony officials made a general defense of
colony rent policy and took special note of certain questions
and criticisms. For example:

1. Rental value of Fairhope lands had not increased by two-
thirds in 1903. Rents previously charged, however, were much
too low, and there was need for a sharp raise to catch up.

2. Objections that the land was assessed too high because of
low productivity for agriculture were irrelevant. The lands in
question were not assessed as farm lands but for other purposes
for which they were in demand.

3. The council took issue with certain judgments that certain
locations were not superior to others. Officers were able to
show a great demand and a long waiting list for bay front lots.
They argued that the large increases were justified because
much land was held out of use and many who desired certain
sites for use could not get them unless bonuses were paid.

4. In answering one assertion that the rentals charged in
Fairhope had caused county tax officials to raise assessed valuations in Fairhope, the council stated that Fairhope rents
afforded no proper basis for assessing of taxes. Lessees were
urged to understand that the rentals covered advantages accruing from colony policies and not exclusively inherent in the
land. For example, one complainant was shown that the tuition
paid by the colony for his children exceeded his rent. Further-
more, the council proposed to see to it that the county tax
officials did not discriminate against the colony, "even if it
were necessary to spend some of the people's money to do so."

Apparently the officers did a good selling job. At the close
of the meeting the chairman asked, "All who think the rents
are, generally speaking, too high, rise." One stood up. He then
asked, "All who think they are not, generally speaking, too
high, rise." Nearly all arose.

It would be erroneous to read too much into the apparent

consensus that the rent appraisals for 1904 were not unreasonable. Subsequent events disclose that there was a persistent undercurrent of dissatisfaction among colony residents including some of the members. It is safer to conclude that at this time the issue was not truly joined—that the meeting of December 16, 1903, was merely a preliminary skirmish to the major battles of the next two years.

In an attempt to reduce frictions within the colony, the executive council adopted the following resolution as presented by Mr. Bellangee:

WHEREAS, it was the intention of the founders of Fairhope to secure to all residents within her borders perfect justice and equality of opportunity through the application of the Single Tax principle, to the use of her lands, making no distinction between lessees, whether members of the Association or non-members, so far as the benefits of her policy may affect them, therefore,

BE IT RESOLVED, by the Executive Council of the Association that it will recognize the equal interest of all in all public matters, by giving the same consideration to petitions and suggestions from non-members as from members and, in case of a referendum being desired by non-members the same per cent required of members to make such reference mandatory will be recognized as of equal force when coming from residents of the Association irrespective of membership.

The Council considers such action permissible under the constitution but does not find itself authorized to refer such matters for final action to any but members of the Association.

BE IT RESOLVED FURTHER, that public notice is hereby given that the regular meetings of the council are open to the public, and at such meetings all reasonable suggestions and requests from any one interested in the public administration of Fairhope will be welcomed and considered by the Council. (Minutes, January 18, 1904.)

In November 1904, the executive council made its customary annual rent appraisals and recommended another substantial increase. The lessees immediately organized and requested a special meeting of the membership for the purpose of hearing complaints against the proposed rentals. At this called membership meeting a statement by tenants was read to the membership stressing the following complaints:

1. Rentals on leasehold lands have increased to such an extent that they have become a burden. A reasonable capitalization of the proposed rentals would put the value of Fairhope lands equal to that of city and improved suburban properties in the North. Moreover, the appraisement was unreasonable because " . . . the fact remains that all this property is of very little more value than good farm lands, as is evidenced by the valuations placed on the same by your body on county and state taxation."

2. Exact detailed financial statements should be made of all monies received and expended, from all sources and for whatever purposes, by the corporation.

3. The complaining tenants were entitled to ". . . know the exact status of all transactions relating to or with individuals that affect this corporation or association and which may have caused the expenditures of monies or money for, or is liable to create an obligation in the future."

In summary those signing this statement protested against paying the assessment as made for 1905, stating ". . . that before taking further steps to protect our interest against what we believe to be the unjust and unwarranted rents you have made, we respectfully ask that these rentals be reduced to a more equitable basis that would represent the actual value of these lands without any subjective value attached thereto." They further requested ". . . a more full understanding as to the financial conditions and obligations of this corporation in order that we might determine and judge as to whether or not we have made good theories work." (Minutes, December 29, 1904.)

Apparently the complaining tenants made a favorable impression on the membership. At this meeting three propositions were voted upon:

1. A proposition to admit non-member lessees to participation in the expenditures of the revenue for 1905. The vote was: Yes, 25; No, 4.

2. A proposition to accept the council's appraisement of 1905 rents. The vote was: Yes, 14; No, 15.

3. So few votes were cast on the proposition as to what the percentage of increase on rents should be that no decision was reached.

Following the inconclusiveness of the third proposition, a motion carried to the effect that a committee of lessees, which it was understood had been appointed at a meeting of complaining tenants to make an appraisement of rentals, should be requested to go ahead with its appraisement, and when completed, should meet and consider the matter further with the council, after which the matter again should be referred to the members. (Minutes, December 29, 1904.)

At the council meeting of January 7, 1905, the secretary was instructed to advise the committee of complaining tenants that " . . . we will take up with them the matter of more detailed reports of receipts and disbursements when they are ready to take up the rent matter." (Minutes.)

On January 14, 1905, the objecting tenants met and unanimously adopted certain resolutions and memorials addressed to the president, the executive officers, and the members of the Fairhope Single Tax Corporation. These memorials and petitions, and the reply made by the executive council, are of sufficient significance as to warrant their reproduction in full as an appendix. (Text of documents taken from Fairhope *Courier,* January 27, 1905.)

The resolution adopted by the lessees having the greatest interest from the standpoint of principle was one requesting the executive council: " . . . to fix a legal limit beyond which the rating board cannot annually raise the rents to double and triple, quadruple and even quintuple the rents of the year previous . . . there will be no peace until there is a limit fixed to this non-ending and excessive taxation." The tenants suggested fixing the limit on a percentage of the actual cash value of the land leased. They implied that rents occasionally might exceed a modest legal limit by vote of the leaseholders on a proposition to increase rents to finance a particular public improvement.

The objecting lessees directed their arguments and suggestions almost exclusively to that aspect of the Fairhope plan which advocates using the rental value of its lands in lieu of monies raised by taxation. The lessees' chain of reasoning may be summarized as follows: under the Fairhope plan rent should be used in lieu of customary taxes; taxes ought not to exceed the sums necessary to provide for the necessities, welfare and prosperity of a community; when such needs are determined the actual assessment of taxes becomes " . . . a matter of simple arithmetic; the needs and desires of a community can be best determined by the whole people . . . no satisfactory method of separating the wise and virtuous from the unwise and unscrupulous has ever been discovered." Also, " . . . any system of taxation that cannot be safely trusted with the whole people is not worthy of consideration."

The extent to which the resolutions and memorials of the protesting tenants were contrived to accomplish certain ulterior motives of leaders among the lessees, or actually reflected lessees' understanding of the Fairhope plan, cannot now be determined. A categorical judgment can be rendered that the reasoning was faulty.

REPLY OF EXECUTIVE COUNCIL

In the very first paragraph of its reply, the executive council attempted to correct the misunderstanding of the lessees, stating: "The Fairhope plan as originally promulgated and steadily adhered to, contemplates that every holder of Fairhope land shall pay its full rental value from year to year into a common fund to be expended for the common benefit, in lieu of taxes levied in the usual way, *the first purpose being to prevent land speculation and to preserve for all who might ever desire to locate in Fairhope equal opportunity to enjoy its advantages.*" (Emphasis supplied.) If this "first purpose" be accomplished: "in the very nature of the case no minimum rate of increase can be guaranteed nor is it at all likely that a uniform rate of increase over a preceding year will ever be practicable because of the changing relative values which will arise from various causes. And there is nothing more certain in the light of all past experience not only at Fairhope, but everywhere else, than that land values tend constantly to rise and that where population increases rapidly land values, also, will rise rapidly."

Thus was joined the first issue of principle—that of the full collection of economic rent. If the Fairhope plan contemplated this, then the issue regarding the role non-member lessees might play in the determination of annual rentals becomes significant. It seems reasonable that the determination of rents could not safely be entrusted to those who either failed to understand or were antagonistic to the "first purpose" of Fairhope.

The basic situation is quite different with respect to making decisions as to the disbursing of rental income. The executive council made this explicit, stating: "Your attention is directed in this connection to the fact that before the Council knew of your criticism in this regard, it recommended to the members the admission of lessees—both members and non-members—to equal participation in determining the use to be made of the common funds, which proposition carried by a vote of five to one."

The specific issue of rentals for 1905 was settled at a special membership meeting on January 30, which debated at length the revised rent appraisements. Speakers on the motion to adopt the appraisement were limited to five minutes and no one was allowed to speak a second time until all desiring to speak had been heard. After discussion the vote was taken; eighteen voted for the appraisement, eleven against.

The adoption of the 1905 rent appraisement by the membership was not accepted by the tenants without a protest. The tenants' league met the next day (January 31, 1905) and resolved " . . . that we protest against the action of the Executive Council, whereby at a meeting of said body held on Monday evening, January 30, 1905, they did irregularly adopt a schedule of rentals for the year 1905 on the ground that the action of said Council was taken without sufficient notice to all concerned and interested in rentals and that said proceedings were irregular throughout." The council took no action on this protest.

The adoption of the 1905 rent appraisement did not restore harmony within the colony. Disaffected parties merely shifted their attacks. First, there was a struggle among the members for political control of the offices and over the policies of the corporation. Second, disagreements among the colonists and tenants spread to outside forums such as the Baldwin *Times,* the Daphne *Standard,* the Mobile *Item,* and the *Single Tax Review.*

POLITICAL MANEUVERINGS

As will be demonstrated in recounting the election of 1905, the membership of the corporation was so evenly split over some of the judgments and policies of the executive council as to create a political problem. In the 1905 election every vote was important. With this in mind a requisite number of members addressed a petition to the council urging that no new members be admitted within thirty days prior to the regular annual election. This petition was presented and the resolution adopted at a special meeting on January 30. The petitioners argued that the spirit of that clause of the constitution providing for a referendum vote on new memberships would be violated unless the membership were given ample time for such a vote. They further argued that it is neither ". . . good policy nor good taste, to risk the imputation of ulterior purposes in the appointment of a new member just before an election." As a result of this resolution the council tabled an application for membership from Mr. W. A. Baldwin. This resolution notwithstanding, an attempt was made as a first order of business at the annual meeting of February 2, 1905, to accept Mr. Baldwin's application. This attempt failed, but Mr. Baldwin was accepted for membership to take effect one week afterward.[2]

Before voting on officers for 1905 the membership adopted a resolution submitted by Secretary Gaston to the effect that all who had been placed in nomination as candidates for office be

2 Mr. W. A. Baldwin was one of the three who signed the memorials and resolutions of the protesting tenants dated January 14.

requested to pledge themselves as follows: "That they fully and heartily approve not only the single tax policy in general but the Fairhope plan of applying the single tax principle as far as possible under existing conditions, *by collecting the full annual rental value of its land,* and in consideration thereof *paying the taxes of the county and state on the improvements and personal property of the lessees held upon its land,* and that if elected, they will to the best of their ability, apply the principles of the corporation as expressed in its constitution and its lease contracts." (Emphasis supplied.)

Presumably all candidates so pledged themselves but the official minutes are silent on this point.

Precisely what transpired in the election of February 2, 1905, cannot be determined. The first report on the vote was as follows:

President: F. L. Brown, 25; C. K. Brown, 16.

Vice-President: William Stimpson, 22; H. Cresswell, 21.

Secretary: E. B. Gaston, 22; G. W. Wood, 21.

Treasurer: J. Bellangee, 16; C. L. Coleman, 20.

Because there were from one to three additional nominees for some of these offices, only the presidency was determined; Frank L. Brown defeated his father, C. K. Brown, for this office.

The tellers (trustees) failed to agree on the votes cast and a recount of votes was called for the next day. This difficulty over the vote tally arose because a delegation (or delegations) had gone to at least three members, who were absent because of illness, and collected their votes.

The result of the recount of the ballots on the first election was:

President: F. L. Brown, 24; C. K. Brown, 16.

Vice-President: H. Cresswell, 20; William Stimpson, 20.

Secretary: E. B. Gaston, 21; G. W. Wood, 21.

Treasurer: C. L. Coleman, 19; J. Bellangee, 15; C. K. Brown, 2; C. Wilson, 1; G. W. Wood, 2.

The run-off election was held on February 16, 1905. E. B. Gaston and J. Bellangee declined to run, perhaps as a gesture toward harmony. Mr. Wood was elected secretary, and the very new member, W. A. Baldwin, was chosen treasurer. Elected to the council as superintendent of public health was C. K. Brown, and Mrs. Anna B. Hail was elected trustee.

RECALL OF CERTAIN OFFICERS

This did not end either the campaigning or the elections for 1905. On September 26 a recall election was held in response to the following petition signed by thirty-three members:

WHEREAS, certain officers of this Corporation have openly declared themselves in hostility to fundamental features of its policy; have circulated through the public press, and otherwise, statements regarding the colony misleading, to characterize them mildly, detrimental to the reputation of our community and harmful to the interests of all its people; have joined with those not members of the Corporation, some notoriously hostile to its policy, and some even having personal interests in this vicinity contrary to the interests of Fairhope as a single tax colony, in an agitation against its Constitution and lease contracts:

And WHEREAS, such officers cannot be expected to work sincerely and with enthusiasm for the success of Fairhope along the line which its members are pledged by the Constitution, and both members and non-members are bound by their lease contracts; and whereas such officers do not represent the sentiment or choice of a majority of the resident members:

Therefore BE IT RESOLVED, that we hereby petition for the submission to a vote of the resident members at a special election called for Thursday evening, September 26, of the following questions:

Shall W. A. Baldwin be removed from the position of Treasurer?

Shall C. K. Brown be removed as Superintendent of Public Health?

Shall Anna B. Hail be removed as Trustee of the Fairhope Single Tax Corporation?

This petition was countered by the following remonstrance signed by sixty-two tenants:

We the undersigned, members and tenants of the Fairhope Single Tax Corporation, realizing that the signers of the call for a referendum to remove . . . from their respective offices, represent a majority of the resident membership, and that their decision will be final under the present Constitution of this Corporation:

Therefore we respectfully call your attention to the fact that these officers have been faithful in the performance of their duties;

and that the indebtedness of the Corporation has been greatly decreased during the time they have held office; and we feel that the best interests of the people of Fairhope will be conserved by their retention in office.

The prophecy of the signers of the remonstrance was accurate. The officers were removed by affirmative vote on each question. In the issue of September 29, 1905, the Fairhope *Courier* taking note of this recall election, commented: "Fairhope is now in the hands of its friends."

The inference to be drawn from the recall election and the comment of the editor of the *Courier* is that between February 16 and September 26 a majority of the resident membership became convinced that the basic integrity of the Fairhope plan was in mortal danger. The decision of these members was one of principle. It is not to be interpreted as a blanket endorsement of all previous official programs, judgments and procedures.

RESIDUAL PROBLEMS AND ISSUES

Before proceeding to analyze the questions of basic principles, the following important problems and issues should be noted as not having been resolved by the removal of certain officers.

1. The annual rent appraisement remained too much a matter of personal judgment, a condition which continued until 1914, when the Somers System was introduced.

2. Many of the lessees, member and non-member alike, were relatively poor and, moreover, had not learned how to live and manage investments within the framework of the single tax. Mr. Bellangee recognized this as basic when he wrote:

One of the worst obstacles in the way of the experiment of Fairhope, is the fact that none of us has been able to see far enough into the future to know what is wise for us personally and almost without exception have made unprofitable improvements which we cannot dispose of to an advantage. Of course the single tax should not be held responsible for that but most of us do not like to accept the blame ourselves, but we find it more convenient to charge it up to Fairhope than to providence. (Fairhope *Courier*, March 3, 1905.)

Some, however, found it difficult to agree fully with Mr. Bellangee that the single tax should not share the responsibility for this condition, if only because it introduces another uncertainty into the calculations of the investor of improvements on land. At any rate the question proved a perennial one and we have the testimony of Mr. Bellangee that many colonists did make unprofitable improvements. The issue was presented clearly, in question and answer form, in the columns of the Fairhope *Courier,* January 15, 1901:

Suppose a tenant leases land and suddenly finds because of growth of population that his land values have grown too high, and he has a difficult time disposing of his improvements, *e.g.,* a small house?

The answer given by the editor was: "If the community is entitled to the value accruing to land because of its presence and demand for land—all being equally entitled to the use of land—that value must be taken by the community if justice be done, and the community must not be held responsible for the mistakes in judgment of individuals." The editor went on to express his conviction that under the single tax, land would increase in value so gradually that individuals would readily adjust themselves to changing conditions. The editor further remarked, however, that land values probably would increase more rapidly in Fairhope than they would if the single tax were generally applied. Clearly this creates a contingency to be considered in any decision with respect to improvements on leaseholds. If to the uncertainty over the rate of increase of the economic rent of Fairhope land is added the difficulty of making an accurate annual rent appraisement, the prospect of making profitable improvements becomes ever more problematical. These observations do not weaken the doctrinaire view of the nature of strict justice under the single tax philosophy. They may, however, throw some light on the effects of the operation of the single tax in Fairhope from the point of view of the investor. If so, they may help explain the disappointments and the negative, sometimes bitter, attitudes of tenants.

3. Problems related to spending public funds are neither

unique to Fairhope, as opposed to other communities, nor, within Fairhope, are they confined to this period. Disbursement issues were particularly acute during this period; the judgment of colony officials was questioned by many members who were otherwise loyal to these officers.

The principal cause for complaint was the inauguration of a telephone service, largely at the expense of the corporation, a service which many characterized as premature. The consensus was that only a few business and professional men had an immediate need or desire for this service. Apparently a large majority (there is no way to measure this consensus because the issue was never posed at a referendum) would have preferred an improved water system, a liquidation of colony indebtedness, additional repairs and improvements on the wharf, or lower rents. The fact remains, however, the members did not exercise their constitutional privilege of petition and referendum with respect to the telephone service.

4. The recall of certain officers, with all attendant implications, could not resolve basic conflicts of philosophy, material interests, social status, and other reasons for differences among individuals and cliques; the action merely implemented a membership decision to support the constitution and lease contract.

Causes of continuing contention among individuals, of a non-doctrinaire nature, are difficult to evaluate under the best of conditions. Five decades of perspective are of little assistance in determining the extent to which certain hands are unclean, or certain feet besmirched with clay. How, for example, determine the extent to which Mr. Prescott A. Parker, of Volanta, and the editor of the Baldwin *Times,* were motivated in their antagonistic stand against the Fairhope colony by the fact that they were "promoting a private railroad and town-site speculation" within one and one-half miles of Fairhope.[3] Did Mr.

---

[3] Such an explanation was implied by Mr. Gaston on several occasions, *e.g.,* in an editorial in the Fairhope *Courier,* "Fairhope in the Public Eye," January 27, 1905; "Reply to Prescott A. Parker," *Single Tax Review,* IV, Winter (January 15, 1905), 20-22. In this communication Mr. Gaston refers to Mr. Parker as ". . . so good a singletaxer" and as a long time member of the corporation.

E. Q. Norton, editor of the Daphne *Standard,* write and behave toward the colony as he did because he felt the management of the colony never listened to him as it should have in view of his great prestige as the Alabama Committeeman of the National Single Tax League? How determine the extent of any truth in allegations that Mr. Gaston was prone to identify the best interests of Fairhope with his own views and therefore, upon occasion, appeared dictatorial, excessively stubborn, even conspiratorial in getting his own way?

Such questions largely are rhetorical because motives cannot be measured. Nor, in the absence of an objective rating scale, can they be ranked in any ethical sense. It is herein assumed that the motives of all those involved in the Fairhope controversy were mixed. What is now sought is not an explanation of events and actions in terms of personalities, but an analysis of the issues and contentions in terms of demonstrable effects with reference to single tax principles.

Moralists may not be satisfied with such a decision; they may prefer to examine not only the rightness of actions but also the rightness or wrongness of the reasons for taking them. Likewise cynics and self-styled "realists" may be unhappy because of their belief that the essence of "truth" in the explanation of a social phenomenon lies in the motivations of the contending parties, with the almost universal implication that these motivations are basically material in terms of personal wealth, power or social prestige. The decision to emphasize principles rather than personalities in no wise denies all merit to the positions of the moralists and the realists. The single tax doctrine and program is rooted in ethical idealism or justice; it is not exclusively a fiscal reform. Its proponents always have been a minority and usually a very small minority, however articulate and influential upon occasion. Its first objective—the elimination of speculation in land or of private receipt of net income from land—would remove one of the important avenues toward rapid accumulation of personal wealth, and initially would destroy or greatly reduce some individual accumulations. When the society adopting and protecting private property rights long has been a predominantly democratic one, it should not be surprising to find widespread resistance to such proposals based in part upon individual material interests. But it is one thing to recognize the roles of both idealism and individual self-interest; it is quite another thing to attempt a judgment of a social experiment in terms of the motivations of the individuals involved.

REAFFIRMATION OF COLONY'S INTENTION

In their action to recall certain officers, the members of the Fairhope corporation reaffirmed the clear cut and original intention of the colony—to take in rent the full use value of the land for the first purpose of preventing land speculation. This reaffirmation disappointed many lessees who had hoped to convince the membership that it would be sufficiently Georgian to take in rent only that part of the annual use value needed to meet the common expenses as determined by the wishes of the whole community. In some respects the dispute was one of orthodoxy, each side looking to a single prophet, Henry George, and to one authoritative source, *Progress and Poverty*.

The views of the two groups may be simply stated. Those desiring a change in Fairhope rental policy attempted to show that George ". . . believed that for all practical purposes we should have the single tax when we had abolished all taxation save that upon land values." On the other hand, the official Fairhope policy and the considered views of most of the membership was that in addition to abolishing all other taxes, the tax on land values should equal the full economic rent of land.

The issue over the proportion of economic rent to be taken in taxes did not originate in Fairhope, nor has it yet been settled to the complete satisfaction of all who have some claim to be considered as singletaxers. The reason for this doctrinal uncertainty lies partly in some of the things George said and wrote, but even more in some reinterpretations of George's position by Thomas G. Shearman, and C. B. Fillebrown, who became the most influential advocates of what George called "the single tax limited."

The anti-Fairhope forces frequently quoted from, and to a large extent based their case for "low rents" upon, an editorial signed by Henry George in the August 17, 1889, issue of his weekly, *The Standard*. The editorial cited is one commenting on a resolution passed by the Cleveland Single Tax Club in favor of taking all economic rent for public uses. Mr. George wrote:

I, too, would like to take the entire economic rent. But I wish the Cleveland club had added another resolution explaining how they propose that it shall be done, for it is here that the difficulty comes . . . But first as to Mr. Shearman: Whatever percentage of economic rent he may think will suffice for the necessary expenses of government, he is as good a single tax man as those who wish to take it all. For he is for one single tax, or to speak more precisely for levying all taxes on one single source of revenue—land values. If that does not constitute a single tax, what does? And while he declares that he would "demand only so much of the ground rent as is needed by the State for public purposes," he sets no limit to the increase of the needs of the State, but on the contrary, shows his appreciation of how these needs will increase with the opportunities for supplying them, by declaring that "the natural increase of taxation is always far more rapid than the increase of either population or wealth."

Yes, George wrote those words, just as he wrote many others both in the same issue of *The Standard* and upon other occasions. A few months earlier (*The Standard*, December 29, 1888, p. 3) he wrote:

There are some who see the injustice of present taxation. There are some who would go so far as to substitute for our present modes of raising revenue this equal, simple, cheap method that does not ·hamper production, and then stop. Them we may call single tax men, limited. *We who want to go all the way—we are single tax men unlimited.* But there is no reason why we should not go together until we get to the point where our limited friends want to stop. They can then stop, if they choose, while we keep on. (Emphasis supplied.)[4]

In the August 17, 1889, issue of *The Standard*, the issue from which the complaining Fairhopers were fond of quoting with

4 Young, *Single Tax Movement in the United States*, pp. 262-263.

approval, the burden of Mr. George's total remarks was that
although he believed taxation should take the entire economic
rent of land he was not sure how this might be done in practice.
He wrote: ". . . This is a point as to which I am not and never
have been clear . . . About the best . . . anyone . . . could do in
this regard would be to formulate some plan that would take
about the whole of economic rent."[5] It is true that George did
think that the best plan for administering the single tax would
be to leave a margin of economic rent with the land owners.
This could be rationalized as a commission for the collection
and payment of the taxes but its practical advantage would be
to leave land with a selling value which would make it easier
to assess. George, however, recognized as a disadvantage of this
plan that ". . . in this way we could not collect the full amount
of economic rent."[6]

THE PROBLEM OF ADMINISTRATION

Only a minute fraction of single taxers have been confused
over the intention of Henry George. The great majority understand that neither the prophet nor the word, taken in context,
could be cited in support of taxation of less than the full economic rent, except as it might be administratively impractical.
What is the nature of this difficulty?

Singletaxers typically have been reluctant to discuss the question of how the single tax should be collected. Their position
is that the first task is that of securing popular approval for the
single tax; they fear that discussion of the details of the program
might provoke such differences as to weaken the effort to secure
its approval. They rightly state that no one possibly could
anticipate the form of any statutes passed to implement the
reform.

In the taxation of property the practice among the American
states has been to levy against the value of property as opposed
to directly taxing income from property. Statutory definitions
of assessed value vary considerably but they rather clearly contemplate that the base shall be *market,* or cash or selling value.

5 Loc. cit.
6 Loc. cit.

It is not difficult to demonstrate that retention of market valuation as the base for taxing land means that it would be mathematically impossible to take all of the economic rent in taxation. This follows because, first, a tax resting either on the net return from land or on the value of land cannot be shifted but must be borne by the present owner. Second, buyers presumably are reasonably well informed and are rational people who take into account the effect of unshiftable taxes. If these assumptions are correct, every increase in land value taxes reduces the market value of land. If the taxes equaled the net income from land (before taxes), the market value of land would disappear altogether. Obviously if this happened there would be no base remaining for the assessment of annual taxes. If, therefore, the single tax should be administered by levying against the market value of land, the rate must be something less than one hundred per cent. The principal factors setting the maximum proportion of economic rent that could be collected would be: the fidelity with which market (and assessed) values of land are determined by the capitalization process, and the rate of capitalization. Assuming land is desired for income yield alone, and the average net income can be fairly determined, then the significant variable is the rate of interest or yield expected by marginal purchasers of land; the lower the rate of return demanded the greater the proportion of economic rent could be taken before the capital value of the net rent (*i.e.* rent after taxes) fell below the total economic rent.

There could be, quite clearly, alternative methods of administering the single tax. For example, the base might be net income rather than market value; or the concept of taxable value might be changed to permit the capitalization of economic rent, or the capitalization of the sum of taxes taken and (net) rent remaining after taxes. An analysis of the several alternatives would lead far beyond the relevancy of this question in the story of Fairhope. Let it suffice that the Fairhope method simulates a system which would take land income directly, rather than indirectly, by basing taxes on some concept or measure of "value." George's dilemma does not apply to Fairhope except for the ever present problem of exercising sound judgment in the annual estimation of economic rent. There is not now, and there probably never will be, any completely satisfactory objective method for determining the *total* economic rent of land within a given community; there do exist, however, reasonably satisfactory methods for determining the *relative* values of the different parcels of land.

With respect to the basic question of principle it seems fair to conclude that those who proposed that the colony collect in rent something less than the full annual use value of the leaseholds were in serious error both in their understanding of Henry George's intention and of the relevancy of his dilemma with respect to its administration as applied in Fairhope.

THE ISSUE OF A SIMULATED SINGLE TAX

The Fairhope colonists never claimed that their demonstration could be a literal experiment in the operation of the single tax. A private corporation obviously cannot have taxing powers, and thus cannot "abolish all taxes except those levied on the value of land." It must operate within the framework of federal and Alabama state and local taxes which grant to the residents of Fairhope no special exemptions or other tax privileges. Literally all that the colony can do is to prevent speculation or individual profit in colony lands and to use the rent collected for the (public) purposes of the community. Rents in Fairhope were intended to absorb the total economic rent to fulfill the *primary* purpose of the single tax—to destroy land speculation by the simple process of leaving as little economic rent as possible in the hands of the owners or occupiers of land. Those with even a cursory familiarity with the single tax will understand the reasoning, both ethical and economic, for such a policy. To singletaxers, the Georgian program is one of basic institutional reform; it is not a mere tax reform.

Similar ethical and economic reasoning is employed by single taxers to support their proposal to abolish all other taxes. That is, public morality cannot justify *compelling* individuals to contribute to the support of the government out of income or wealth which they earn. Aside from this ethical consideration, singletaxers (of that period) argued that the full economic rent easily would equal the justifiable expenditures of government. Indeed some of them (including George) believed economic rent would be sufficient to permit the financing of greatly extended public services. They further believed that the two-fold effects of a more complete utilization of land, and the lifting of taxes which tend to repress thrift, investment, and work, would tend to a great expansion of production and to achievement of many other desirable results. The soundness or reasonableness of these expectations is not here at issue. What needs to be understood is that it is almost as important to singletaxers to abolish all taxes other than those on land as it is to take all economic rent from landholders. It is "almost as important" because singletaxers tend to take the position that the private receipt of economic rent is even more immoral than the taxation of "earned" values. They believe the adverse economic effects from land speculation are greater than the repressive effects of taxes on sources other than land rent. More recently, singletaxers recognize the likelihood that justifiable government activities will require revenue in excess of total economic rent.

It seems to follow that even an approximate demonstration of the single tax could not be convincing or valid unless (the effects of) taxes other than those upon land were minimized. The only conceivable manner in which a private corporation, such as the Fairhope Single Tax Corporation, could accomplish this result would be to refund taxes paid by the lessees on their personal property and improvements. Ideally, other taxes paid by lessees also should be refunded, but this was manifestly impracticable (even in 1905) both because of the difficulty of determining the incidence of indirect excises and customs, but also because in a new community, located on lands of very low value, the total economic rent would not be sufficient to refund all federal and state taxes. The instant issue is that of the desirability in principle and in practice of refunding taxes levied on property other than land.

Defenses of Tax Refunding

This policy of the Fairhope colony is one of the most difficult to defend. It proved too esoteric even for many who unquestionably were fully in sympathy with the colony and who accounted themselves knowledgeable singletaxers. It is therefore
easy to understand how the policy, presented in certain lights,
would tend to magnify misunderstanding and promote dissatisfaction. At any rate, the management of the colony discovered
that it was necessary to make repeated explanations and defenses
of this practice. A recounting of one of the earlier and generally
characteristic series of questions and answers relating to this
issue may suffice to explain the position of the colony. As
reported in the *Courier* of January 15, 1901, the following
questions were addressed to the editor and the following
answers were given:

The *Courier* was asked to define the policies of the association as to the payment of taxes on movable property, in particular ". . . do provisions of the constitution mean that the
association agrees to pay taxes on pianos, jewelry, diamonds,
and all such articles of luxury?" The editor answered, "Yes."

The inquirer then asked whether ". . . this would be the
policy of the corporation even if the tax on them should exceed
the amount of land rents paid by the possessor?" The editor
answered, "Yes," and continued with an explanation which
may be paraphrased as follows: the organizers of the colony not
only believed in the single tax but believed that it was possible
to apply it in practice, by the option of its members, without
waiting the aid or consent of anybody else. County and state
(and in municipalities, local taxes) are now raised according to
the estimated needs by a levy on all forms of property. Assuming that in an average community the taxable value of land is
equal to the value of improvements and personal property
thereon, it is evident that to raise in taxes a given sum from
land values alone would require twice as high a rate of taxation
as if levied on improvements and personal property also. We in
effect say to the tax assessor, "You may levy the taxes of this
community on any basis you see fit, but we will accept the

burden as a community and distribute it over our individual residents on the only just basis of the value of the land they individually hold—the value being due not solely to their individual enterprise and industry but to the presence and collective activity of the community."

"Isn't this taking from the poor to pay for the rich?"

The editor answered, "No." The colony merely takes the value of land from anyone, rich or poor. It could not get anyone to locate here on the proposition of taking the full value of the land and then subjecting the lessee to unjust taxes on his improvements or personal property. "Our lands are open to all the world under definite written leases . . . but membership in the association is limited to those who heartily approve its principles and no others need apply."

"Unless all own an equal amount of personal property, would not the payment of personal property taxes by the association be unfair?" (This is one of the seemingly endless variations of the preceding question.)

The editor replied in effect: the policy which helps the holders of large amounts of personal property (the rich) also helps the small owner as well as the would-be owner (the poor). If the fund from which the association pays the taxes were drawn from necessarily increasing taxes on the small holder, the injustice would be clear. Exemption of personal property increases the demand for land and therefore its value—the increased value providing for the increased taxes. In an average community the total taxable value may be equally divided into land values and other values. The only way anyone can make a plausible showing of danger in our plan is to imagine someone coming into the community with the deliberate intent to injure it and making improvements or bringing in personal property in excess of our ability to pay taxes upon them in excess of our land value. Our rents are between two to three times our taxes. It is safe to depend on the law of averages. (Fairhope *Courier*, April 15, 1901.)

"Will not refunding of personal property taxes before long change the single tax into a single personal property tax?" and:

"When Fairhope personal and improvement taxes get to be as large as your annual rental, it will take all your land rental to refund the personal property taxes, will it not?"

The position of the colony as articulated by the editor of the *Courier* may be stated as follows: even if state and county taxes were wholly levied upon personal property and were sufficient to absorb all the land values, there would still be a single land tax to the people who paid them if they paid according to the value of the land they occupied, and paid no other tax. The colony holds the belief that the tendency is for land values to increase faster than the values of improvements and personal property. In practically every settlement the state and county taxes are the smaller amount of the total tax, the local (municipal) taxes being greater. Fairhope will have none of these local taxes to contend with. It therefore can apply part of its land rent in payment of state and county taxes and have the greater part left to spend at home. (Fairhope *Courier*, January 1, 1902.)

One of those fond of raising the issue of policy involved in refunding of taxes was Edward Quincy Norton, editor of the Daphne, Alabama, *Standard*. For whatever reason, Mr. Norton was a persistent and generally unfriendly critic of the Fairhope plan, notwithstanding his great assistance in locating the colony and his intention to join as evidenced by his having signed an application for membership and having made the then customary down payment of $5.00. It must be noted that whatever caused his disaffection happened within the first few months of the colony's existence because Mr. Norton left the colony in June of 1895. (Minutes, June 3, 1895.) Whatever else may be said with respect to Mr. Norton's views it is clear that he never was overly enthusiastic about the enclave idea preferring the strategy of general propaganda and political action in the advancement of the common cause. This preference was an honest one and may explain his tendency simply to reiterate that Fairhope was not a single tax colony because in fact it had not succeeded in abolishing any taxes. If upon occasion he went beyond a literal doctrinaire or technical critique of Fairhope, it may be because he entertained a very real fear that the colony would do damage to the greater movement in which he fancied himself an important leader. Regardless of whether this characterization is substantially accurate (or charitable), Mr. Norton did reach rather far in his attack on this aspect of Fairhope policy. Writing in the *Single Tax Review* (V, Summer Number, July 15, 1905, 18), Mr. Norton said: "The Fairhope plan does not 'equalize the varying advantages of location and natural qualities of all tracts of land' because it undertakes to repay to renters the taxes they pay to the state and county on their personal property and improvements, and an inspection of the Rent List for 1905 *will show that the amount of such personal property and improvements may enable one to occupy some of the most desirable lots and be paid for doing so, instead of having to pay for such occupancy.*" (Emphasis supplied.)

It would be difficult to state the issue in more prejudicial terms. The implication clearly is that some lessees (the rich—who can afford expensive improvements?) are bribed to reside in Fairhope. Lessees receiving refunds for taxes are therefore pictured as parasites. There is in this manner of presenting the issue (and Mr. Norton was not atypical of his group) nothing that would assist the public to understand the theory back of the policy of refunding taxes. Likewise there is nothing to aid in an analysis of the soundness of the policy.

In presenting his illustrations from the rent list, Mr. Norton likewise makes little constructive contribution to the issue from the point of view of principle. To demonstrate this it is sufficient merely to reproduce two or three of Mr. Norton's illustrations and Mr. William Call's comments upon them.[7]

Illustration by Norton: Mrs. M. E. Mead. Rent $25.00. State and county taxes, $5.60, repaid by the colony, leaving $19.40 as the price she pays for occupying the lots.

Comment by Call: Here are the facts: Mrs. Mead rents two valuable lots on the bay front, appraised by the colony at $25.00. She pays this to the treasurer and also $5.60 to the county tax collec-

---

7 *Single Tax Review,* V, Autumn (October 15, 1905), 44-45.

tor, making her total payment $30.60. The colony then pays to Mrs. Mead on presentation of her tax receipt, $5.60, as refunded taxes, leaving her *net* payment $25.00; her land rental.

Illustration by Norton: Mershon Brothers. Rent $214.15. Last year, 1904, their rent was $130.83 of which $87.49 was refunded in taxes; this year's refunding I have not yet been able to ascertain. I am assured that for a number of years their taxes refunded to them was greater than their rents, so that they were paid for occupying colony land.

Comment by Call: Another case for net rent. As even under his manipulation of figures it appears that Mershon Brothers paid to the colony $43.34 more than their state and county taxes came to, he is compelled to state that he is assured, etc. . . . From my own knowledge as treasurer and deputy, and Mershon Brothers' own statement to me, their taxes have never been in excess of their land rent.

Illustration by Norton: W. A. Baldwin. Rent $15.00 on 90 x 112 feet *adjoining* lot on which is store owned by C. K. Brown. Rent of second lot from store . . . $7.50, total on two lots, $22.50. Taxes refunded, $33.18, leaving him $10.68 ahead. If to the above is added the rent of the lot *on which* is the store of C. K. Brown, rented by him, it would bring his rents up to $45.50.

Comment by Call: A sudden qualm of conscience causes Mr. Norton to add " . . . if to the above, etc. . . ." Certainly it would and it should be added, for the $33.18 taxes refunded is mainly the taxes on this stock of goods on C. K. Brown's lot and as he rents the store he (Mr. Baldwin) naturally pays the ground rent. But whether added or deducted, it proves nothing, as the point he tries to make, that the net rent is what it isn't, has become very badly blunted.

POSSIBLE DANGERS FROM REFUNDING POLICY

It is herein submitted that the substance of Mr. Norton's attacks against the policy of refunding taxes is representative of the argument offered by those who agreed with him. Occasionally, however, the point was made that the colony could not afford to persist in such a policy, but no facts or extended argument were offered in support of this point. It can only be surmised that these critics did not believe that in a growing community land values would increase even more rapidly than other wealth. For example, Joseph Dana Miller, editor of the *Single Tax Review* (V, Autumn Number, September 15, 1905, 50), wrote: "It will be clear, owing to its plan of refunding all State and county taxes on land, improvements thereon, and personal property, moneys and credits excepted (as set forth in the third clause of the lease) that, as Fairhope increases in population and wealth, its real difficulties will begin."

Mr. Gaston could not let this prophecy pass without a reply. In a column headed "Strange Statement for a Single Taxer," he wrote:

This seems to us a most remarkable statement for the editor of a single tax journal to make. We can imagine no ground for it save the belief that with increase of population the state and county taxes will increase more rapidly than the ground values. This is a common enough fear on the part of non-single taxers, but it is quite astonishing to us to find it entertained by the editor of the *Single Tax Review.* Fairhopers are not such weak faithed single taxers. We not only believe land values to be the only just source of public revenue, but that they will furnish a more adequate revenue than is derived from the present system. If we are right, there will be no increasing difficulty to meet the state and county taxes from our land rentals, as our population and wealth increase, but the contrary. If we are wrong, the single tax is not a practical proposition.

It is the mission of Fairhope to put just such problems to the test of practice. (Emphasis supplied.) (Fairhope *Courier,* November 3, 1905.)

In making his reply to Mr. Miller, Mr. Gaston chose not to reiterate a previous judgment of his that "real difficulties" conceivably could result from deliberate malice on the part of corporation tenants. Such untoward behavior might take two forms: 1. Malicious individuals might bring into the colony considerable sums of personal property of such a nature that little if anything would be added to the economic development of the community. 2. Such evilly intentioned persons might deliberately over-assess their improvements and personal property. Such an action is quite possible under Alabama property tax assessment procedures. There is no evidence that any came to reside in Fairhope bringing with them any great concentration of wealth let alone doing so for malicious purposes. There is evidence, however, that some tenants, demonstrably antagonistic to the Fairhope plan, did tend to over-assess their personal property and improvements. In the judgment of colony officials, this practice was sufficiently widespread and costly as to cause them to change the procedure of the listing and assessment of such property located on corporation lands. This defensive action will be detailed later as will the action taken years later to limit the refunding of taxes paid by lessees to the amount of rent paid by them.

The colony's case on this issue of refunding taxes is much superior, in terms of adduced arguments and facts, to the contentions of the critics of the policy. The argument of greatest validity against refunding of taxes was that the Fairhope colony did not, indeed legally could not, abolish any taxes. Such an argument is of course purely rhetorical; the colony could, and largely did, abolish the *effects* of property taxes based on wealth other than land. It could, and did, alter the incidence or distribution of the burden of Alabama property taxation, relieving personal property and improvements of the effects of taxes so based.

THE ISSUE OF DEMOCRACY

Must a single tax demonstration, to be valid in a Georgian sense, be conducted within a framework of democratic organization and procedure at least roughly comparable to the traditional town meeting? If so, can Fairhope qualify in view of its inherent organization which lodges final decisions as to both rents and disbursements in the membership of the corporation?

The issues posed by these questions clearly are neither fiscal nor economic. They are, nonetheless, highly relevant to an estimation of Fairhope as a single tax community. Although it should be made explicit that many who criticized Fairhope on grounds of its somewhat oligarchical organization were basely motivated, this in no wise weakens the philosophical bases for such criticism. There were some sincere singletaxers or single tax sympathizers who criticized the imperfect democratic organization and procedures of the colony on purely objective or idealistic grounds. There were others whose motives would be difficult to impugn except, perhaps, to make definite their vested intellectual interest in an entirely different strategy for advancing the single tax movement.

Among those whose motives were reasonably above suspicion was Mr. Joseph Dana Miller, editor of the *Single Tax Review*. Although Mr. Miller offered additional criticisms of Fairhope, and a careful reading of the *Review* for this period leaves the impression of considerable bias (to a degree conscious and deliberate) against Fairhope, there is little doubt but that his feelings on the importance of democratic organization and procedures were deeply and sincerely held.

Mr. Miller firmly believed that under the plan adopted for the government of Fairhope, any success achieved by the colony could not be cited as furnishing a complete demonstration of the soundness of the single tax, nor could any failures reflect on the single tax as such. He expressed his conviction as follows:

The Single Tax contemplates a system "broadly based upon the people's will," arising out of an intelligent apprehension of much if not all that it includes. A belief in the single tax without an accompanying fundamental faith in democracy is likely to lead its believers far astray . . . the Single Tax is important because it makes for fuller freedom. Outside of the domain of freedom its application is unthinkable. So, too, would be its practice without its spirit. If the plan of Fairhope contravenes essential democracy, then such application of the Single Tax as rules in that colony is not the Single Tax as Mr. George taught it. *And that is just as true whether or not the adoption of an undemocratic system is made necessary in the effort to retain this partial application of the Single Tax, or whether or not a more democratic system would entail its utter abandonment.* (Emphasis supplied.)[8]

Mr. Miller did not make the mistake of charging autocracy by conviction or by desire of the members, but rather by its inherent organization. He strongly urged that ". . . the govern-

8 Editorial, "A Reply to Our Critics," *Single Tax Review*, V, Summer (July 15, 1905), 45.

ment of Fairhope is the business of all the people of Fairhope. . . . Democracy is the only principle we know of. A demonstration of the Single Tax under any other form of government, we fear, must be too faulty and incomplete to be of any great value."[9]

Mr. Miller was essentially correct in his estimation of Henry George's general position. The spirit of the single tax *is* the spirit of freedom, and many of George's utterances may be interpreted fairly as believing not only in freedom of access to land, in freedom from monopoly, especially in land, and in freedom from taxation of the fruits of individual effort, but also in other manifestations of freedom. Mr. George clearly implied upon many occasions that he believed in freedom of individual choice which might be made operative in the area of political and social, as well as economic institutions, organizations and procedures. This particular indictment by Mr. Miller therefore must be given serious consideration.

Spokesmen for the official Fairhope colony did not fully agree that the organization of Fairhope was inherently autocratic. They made four points:

First, they submitted that within the membership of the colony there existed the purest kind of democracy. The executive council was not a self-perpetuating oligarchy but merely "a standing committee which attends to business details." They further pointed out that upon petition of five per cent of the resident members any act of the council, or any measure proposed by the petitioners, must be submitted to a vote of the membership upon twenty-four hours notice. They further pointed to the fact that the membership must decide upon the retention or dismissal of any officer upon petition of ten per cent of the membership. In all instances a simple majority governs.

Second, they argued that membership in the corporation is not closed but is open to all who desire a voice in the control of the colony. The conditions for membership are two-fold: payment of the fee of $100 and an understanding and an acceptance

9 Loc. cit.

of the principles of the colony, the latter to be determined by the council, which may be overruled by the membership in a referendum.

Third, those who spoke for the management and members of Fairhope pointed out that the council and the membership had extended many of the privileges of membership to tenants. Lessees could petition for mandatory referenda, and they could participate in decisions as to how the net rentals would be disbursed. They also were consulted in fixing of the annual rentals; lessees were given the privilege of the floor in meetings and could attend all business meetings of the executive council. However, they could not vote for officers and the final decisions on disputed matters were left to the membership.

Fourth, they made the valid point that the corporation possesses no governmental powers, and that non-member lessees have precisely the same citizenship rights, privileges and responsibilities as the members. Closely related to this point were statements and arguments that the corporation is a private one; therefore, it was natural that control be restricted to members. No tenant was coerced into signing a lease.

Critics of Fairhope countered on some of these points. They characterized the $100 membership fee as "an unheard of price to qualify for voting," and they argued that the test of belief in the single tax as a condition to membership was both arbitrary and indefinite. Their position was that under such a test the "corporation may and does admit or exclude members at its pleasure. . . . Anyone may claim to be a single taxer without being so. Anyone may be excluded because he does not hold the right kind of single tax theory, or he may be excluded on other grounds."[10]

These critics countered the contention that the Fairhope Single Tax Corporation, being a private corporation, should be privileged to operate through majority decision of its members. They argued that the organization and operations of the Fairhope colony was the business of the wider single tax public

[10] *Single Tax Review,* V, Summer (July 15, 1905), "Communication" from N. O. Nelson of LaClaire, Illinois.

because singletaxers generally were urged to contribute to its land funds, and because the colony was being presented to the public as a bona fide single tax experiment.

Colony officials, members, and friends argued that the integrity of the Fairhope experiment could not be maintained if all lessees were permitted a vote on colony policies and decisions. They reasoned that "not one in a hundred" of the general public either understood or agreed with the single tax reform, and that the great majority of the tenants would vote lower rents than would be necessitated by single tax doctrine.

One member who spoke out in an unequivocal manner certainly had every right to be heard. That member was Mr. Alfred Q. Wooster, one of the framers of the original constitution. He was a colleague of Mr. E. B. Gaston's on a leading reform paper of Iowa, the *Farmer's Tribune,* and a founder of the *Liberty Bell,* the official organ of the colony until the *Courier* was established.

In a letter published in the September 1, 1905, issue of the Fairhope *Courier,* Mr. Wooster wrote:

. . . Especially have I "kept tab" on the efforts made to make of Fairhope a failure by so changing its constitution that its very foundation principle would be overturned and the structure fall into the chaos of prevailing commercialism.
. . . Most emphatically do I now assert that the proposition to give to lessees of the corporation's property the right to vote for corporation officials and determine its policies, is wrong, absolutely wrong, unjust, irrational and illogical, and if done will sound the death knell of Fairhope as a single tax experiment. As well might an orthodox church invite atheists to determine its creed . . . Its constitution is strictly democratic, but aliens, although they may abide within its borders, have no moral right and should never be given a legal right to either control or influence in any way the corporation's affairs.

Not all Fairhope critics were willing to concede that giving control to non-member tenants would "sound the death knell of Fairhope as a single tax experiment." For example, Mr. Nelson argued: "When the people of Fairhope should be thrown upon their own resources, vote their own assessments, vote a disposal of the revenue, I think a majority would vote wisely." In support of this optimistic view he argued that a large minority will be those living on or near marginal land; many others are naturally public-spirited and want liberal public utilities; still others are convinced singletaxers. Mr. Nelson thought the total influence of these three groups would add to make "the single tax idea and self-government safe in Fairhope."[11] Most of those opposing the Fairhope organization stopped short of attesting to such a degree of faith in the understanding and sweet reasonableness of the majority of tenants. Many acknowledged singletaxers took the position that the colony could not survive and adhere to single tax principles under majority rule. But this did not concern them to nearly the same extent as did the lack of what they conceived to be an inadequate degree of democratic organization. They simply did not like the enclave strategy, a view which would have been perfectly acceptable to enclave singletaxers if only the critics had not insisted on professing a sympathetic interest in, and friendship for, Fairhope. Orthodox Fairhopers found it difficult to understand such a friendship.[12]

LEASES VS. DEEDS

Can the Fairhope plan to implement its particular single tax experiment through leases be considered valid, in a Georgian sense, in view of Henry George's characterization of his proposal as one of leaving land in the private possession of individuals with full liberty on their part to give, sell, or bequeath it?

The frame of reference of this issue of principle centers about the activities in the late summer of 1905 of the Leaseholders' Protective Union. This organization was composed of some colony members, but mostly non-member lessees, who desired fundamental changes in the Fairhope plan. In referring

11 Loc. cit.
12 "Letter" from J. Bellangee, *Single Tax Review*, V, Autumn Number (October 15, 1905), 48: Mr. Norton has every right to his opinion except ". . . he has no right to claim friendship for what he is striving to destroy, or for those whose interests and property he is trying to injure."

to themselves, they preferred the term "patriots" and they were fond of characterizing the opposition as "royalists." The "royalists" in their turn preferred to denominate the complaining tenants as "kickers" or "low-renters." Among the leading spirits of the Protective Union were W. A. Baldwin, C. K. Brown, Anna B. Hail, and C. L. Coleman, all colony members. Among the more prominent non-member lessees active in this group were Dr. Greeno, A. Swift, and E. T. Molyneux who served as secretary. Dr. Greeno had applied for membership twice during 1905 but without success. He subsequently became the first mayor of the town of Fairhope and, in answer to a congratulatory letter from Mr. Joseph Fels, dated July 14, 1908, replied: "I have not been and am not now in sympathy with what is known here as the 'Fairhope Plan.' . . . The whole scheme to my mind and to the mind of any business man is unattainable and can prove of no benefit to the settlers on their lands."

During 1905 the Leaseholders' Protective Union engaged in the task of rewriting the constitution of the Fairhope Single Tax Corporation. One of the articles as proposed by this group read:

Each lessee may receive a deed from the corporation in lieu of a lease, which shall provide that the annual rental value of the land shall be taken for such public municipal purposes as can be better maintained by the municipality for the people than by the individuals themselves. Those who hold memberships for which money has actually been paid into this corporation may apply these membership certificates in paying their rent.

The self-styled "patriots" found doctrinal support for this radical proposal in an open letter Henry George had written to Pope Leo XIII which stated in part: "We do not propose to assert equal right to land by keeping land common, letting anyone use any part of it at any time. We do not propose the task, impossible in the present state of society, of dividing land in equal shares; still less the yet more impossible task of keeping it so divided. We propose leaving land in the private possession of individuals, with full liberty on their part to give, sell, or bequeath it, simply to levy on it for public uses a tax that shall equal the annual value of the land itself, irrespective of the use made of it or the improvements on it."

The implication that Fairhope could not be judged a bona fide single tax experiment because the colony used leases rather than deeds is manifestly unsound. Henry George did not approve of private property in land. In another context he wrote: ". . . private property in land is a bold, bare, enormous wrong, like that of chattel slavery."[13] Although he did not propose to abolish private property in land, he did intend to take away the most important incident of ownership—the right of any individual to receive an income from land. Assuming that a tax levied either on the value of land, or on economic rent, is unshiftable—the single tax would destroy the market value of land. George maintained that land nationalization and periodic divisions of land among individuals would be both unnecessary and impractical. In comparison with his plan for making land generally accessible, nationalization would have serious propaganda weaknesses, and it would not provide the security of physical possession so necessary to induce individuals to invest in expensive, specialized and durable improvements.

The Fairhope "royalists" were perfectly clear in their own minds that the giving of ninety-nine year leases, with the continuing privilege of renewal, would afford all the security of tenure necessary for anyone contemplating an investment in improvements. They further felt certain that their liberality in permitting transfer of leaseholds was a sufficient equivalent of "full liberty" on the part of lessees "to give, sell or bequeath" their improvements. In this last sub-point, however, those who urged using deeds rather than leases may have had a point. Much later in Fairhope history the colony found it desirable to place certain restrictions on the right of lessees to transfer leaseholds. The nature of these restrictions, and the reasons and resultant effects are discussed in Chapter XVII.

Under the conditions governing the privilege of transferring

---

[13] George, *Progress and Poverty*, p. 356.

leaseholds existing in 1905, this particular proposal to change the constitution of the corporation clearly rested on tenuous grounds, and it is easy to understand that the majority of the membership viewed it as a distinctly unfriendly proposition. It is more than coincidental that officers W. A. Baldwin, C. K. Brown, and Anna B. Hail were recalled within twenty-four hours of the formulation and acceptance by the protesting tenants of this proposal to amend the constitution.

APPEALS TO COURTS TO COLLECT RENTS

One immediate effect of this 1904-1906 controversy was an increase in delinquent rents, which compelled the colony to take legal action.

Typically the Fairhope Single Tax Corporation has been considerate of tenants delinquent in their rents but the number and extent of such delinquency must have been unusually large in 1905. This may be inferred from the action of the executive council on May 21, 1905, when the treasurer was instructed to send *printed* notices to tenants who had not paid their rent for the first half of the year. The notice also was to include a statement that the treasurer did not wish to put the tenants to any trouble and expense (presumably legal) which could be avoided, and therefore asked them to pay at once, or at least to let him know within ten days what they would do.

At the meeting of September 18, 1905, the council adopted a rule designed to reduce future delinquency of new tenants. Henceforth an applicant for corporation land must tender rent at least equal to one-half the rent for the year; any excess above the rent for the remainder of the year would be credited on the rent for the next year.

On November 27, 1905, the secretary reported that he had been informed by the corporation's attorney that "to collect rent from delinquent tenants with improvements, the legal method is an action of assumpsit; before a Justice of the Peace if the amount is less than $100; before a Circuit Court if it is more." The council voted to proceed at once to collect delinquent rents.

On March 5, 1906, the treasurer again was directed to proceed against delinquent tenants placing the accounts in the hands of Attorney James H. Webb for collection. This was done and Fairhope had its first experience with the courts in September and October of 1906.

The first of these cases was before a Justice of the Peace at Point Clear. The defendant argued: 1. that the annual appraisement of rentals was not based on the theories of Henry George; 2. that such rentals were made and raised in an arbitrary and illegal manner; 3. that such rentals were inequitable and excessive. The court found that the leases contained no reference or requirement that the leases should be based on the theories of Henry George, and that defendants had not shown the rentals were made in an arbitrary and illegal manner. There was, therefore, one issue: whether or not the rentals of the defendants were inequitable and excessive. The court found they were not excessive, largely because the evidence showed that the plaintiff had fully complied with the terms and conditions of the leases; that the rentals were made openly and publicly; that the executive council consulted the lessees, considered objections made, and only after revision, with approval of the majority of the lessees, were the rentals finally promulgated; and that the constitution and by-laws of the corporation, relating to the fixing of rentals, had not been changed since the execution of the leases. (Fairhope *Courier,* September 14, 1906.)

The second case, against George Fredericks, was heard before the district court. The corporation successfully defended against the demurrer that the lease contract was void because of its indefiniteness and uncertainty and the absence of any adequate provision for making the rent definite and certain. The defense was based on the argument that in *the very nature of the case* a definite rent could not be fixed in advance for future years, the lease, however, *providing a definite method* for the determining of the rent from year to year. The corporation also successfully defended against the alleged illegality of refunding state and county taxes paid by lessees. The corporation's lawyer, Mr. R. T. Ervin, gave a single tax argument in defense of this policy, but he also insisted that it was not the business of the court to inquire into the justice or injustice of contracts; such an inquiry should have been made by the defendant before entering into the contract.

The court sustained an objection on behalf of the corporation against the use of Mr. C. K. Brown as an individual "expert" on valuations in Fairhope. In substance the court found his testimony not competent and his opinion not pertinent because the lease contract provided that the judgment of the council (subject to a referendum of the membership) should be the standard by which rents should be fixed. (Fairhope *Courier,* November 2, 1906.)

Clearly the outcome of these first court tests was most gratifying to the corporation and more than disappointing to some who had been freely predicting that the Fairhope Single Tax Corporation could not withstand a legal test.

Upon analysis of the issues of single tax principle in contention during 1904-1906, it seems reasonable to assume that most singletaxers, after studying the Fairhope landscape, would, indeed, "see the cat."

X

INCORPORATION OF THE TOWN OF FAIRHOPE; ADJUSTMENTS OF THE COLONY THERETO

O*N* April 9, 1908, the qualified voters residing within an area of approximately one and one-half square miles voted eighteen to one in favor of incorporating the village of Fairhope. Soon thereafter the Probate Judge of Baldwin County declared the town "endowed with the rights and powers of a municipality." Of the land within this area about one-fourth was owned by the Fairhope Single Tax Corporation and the remaining three-fourths was privately owned. An unofficial census taken by a citizens' committee determined that within this area there were four hundred sixty-six white and one hundred three Negro residents. (Fairhope *Courier,* April 10, 1908.) The governing body of the new municipality was to be a mayor and five aldermen; these six officials were to be chosen from a list of qualified voters numbering, at the date of incorporation, only twenty-four. During the remainder of April and May, however, several additional voters were qualified and there were actually forty votes cast for the office of mayor at the election held early in June. (Fairhope *Courier,* June 5, 1908.)

Sentiment for incorporating the Town of Fairhope crystalized during the late summer and fall of 1907. A series of citizens' meetings were held to plan incorporation. At that time the Alabama law required at least twenty-five signatures of qualified voters and freeholders on any petition for incorporation. This law had to be changed because most of those living on colony land were not freeholders. The legislature accommodated to this condition and dropped the freeholder qualification for petitioners. That Fairhope needed this legislation is obvious. Only nine qualified voters attended the citizens' meeting called for the purpose of organizing the movement toward municipal incorporation, and not one of these nine was a freeholder. (Fairhope *Courier,* September 13, 1907.)

The scarcity of qualified voters residing in the area to be incorporated was not the most significant political peculiarity of this community. There is little doubt but that the members of the Single Tax Corporation, in common with the total community, had become extremely sensitive to the ideals embodied in the concept "the will of the people." For example, the colony trustees made a unique suggestion to the members just before the annual colony election of February 14, 1908. They recommended ". . . that those candidates to be elected tonight as well as those officers now holding over to pledge themselves to serve the popular will of our people as done under what is known as the Winnetka plan, subject of course to such limitations and guaranteeing such privileges as are set forth in our constitution."

At this meeting the members also discussed the importance of the poll tax as a qualification for voting. As a result the trustees subsequently recommended that lessees' poll tax receipts be accepted in partial payment of rents for all years subsequent to 1907.[1]

During April and May, 1908, there were several citizens' meetings. These culminated in the adoption of the two following resolutions, the first of which amounts to a recommendation of the Winnetka Plan for the town of Fairhope, and the

[1] Years later the executive council ruled that application of poll tax receipts of lessees on rents shall include both those of husband and wife where either is a lessee. (Minutes, October 22, 1924.)

second an attempt to obtain political harmony within the community. (Fairhope *Courier,* May 22, 1908.)

RESOLUTION I: . . . that this meeting of resident citizens of the town of Fairhope, hereby pledges itself to the principle of complete democracy, and asks the qualified electors to support no candidate for mayor or alderman, who will not pledge himself in writing, if elected, to obey the will of the people at any time they may express the same, even to the extent of resigning his office in case a majority shall request him so to do, and that any adult person, regardless of sex, who shall have maintained a bona fide residence in Fairhope for six months, shall be entitled to participate in such expression of the public will.

RESOLUTION II: . . . that this meeting approve the proportional representation plan, to be applied in this way: that immediately after the registration of voters on next Friday and Saturday, a committee to be appointed by this meeting shall go over the census of residents as taken recently, and ascertain the number respectively of members of the Fairhope Single Tax Corporation, including adult members of their families, the number of residents on single tax corporation lands not members of the corporation and the number of those residing outside the lands of the single tax corporation the total to be divided by five, the number of aldermen to be elected, to ascertain the "quota" necessary to elect a candidate.

That on this basis the said committee shall apportion to each such division of the citizenship the number of candidates to which it is entitled, the same to be nominated by such division and reported to said committee which shall prepare a ballot accordingly for which all agree to vote.

Provided, that if the colored residents within the limits of the municipal corporation, are not allowed to participate in the selection of the candidates of the division in which they reside, their number shall not be credited to such division.

Neither of these resolutions carried without much discussion and many expressions of doubt as to their wisdom. Some citizens questioned the legality of officers pledging themselves to abide by the will of the people when the law provided that only "qualified electors" shall have effective voice in public affairs. The rejoinder made by the proponents of the resolution was that the device proposed was merely an attempt to secure something within the law but not provided by it, that it was just a question of whether a candidate wanted to trust his own judgment or preferred to rely on the judgment of the majority of the citizens. (Fairhope *Courier,* May 29, 1908.)

The committee appointed by the citizens' meeting to implement the second resolution failed to do so. The consensus of this committee was that the divisions proposed by the resolution were simply an outgrowth of the Fairhope colony conflicts and should not now be considered. Rather ". . . all divisions should be wiped out and the people join in nominating a ticket from and for the whole people." (Ibid)

The fact that only a small minority of adult residents were qualified voters did not dampen general interest in the first election or in the process of "nominating" candidates. The same citizens' meeting which adopted the above resolutions attempted to nominate the candidate for mayor. The vote taken was: Gaston, 29; Greeno, 2; Wood, 3; Bellangee, 3; Staples, 1; Beckner, 1; Clifton, 1; and W. E. Sweet, 1. Gaston expressed appreciation for this vote but would not agree to the "nomination" until a further effort was made to secure "an expression of the wish of the people." Gaston moved that an effort be made to put a ballot in the hands of every adult person who had resided in the town for six months. He further moved that another delegation of citizens, who were meeting at the same time in another place to secure "nominations," be invited to join in submitting their nominees to the people at the same time. Both motions were adopted.

In the meantime both the membership of the colony and the Henry George Club had urged Gaston to offer himself for the Office of Mayor, and in the event he was unable to do so, these groups urged that Bellangee be the candidate. The Henry George Club went on record as considering ". . . it fitting that the first mayor of the town shall be a recognized singletaxer." (Fairhope *Courier,* May 29, 1908.)

Mr. Bellangee stated that this action by the membership of the colony was ill-advised, and that in no event would he consider himself a candidate. In letters addressed to Gaston, he urged his (Gaston's) withdrawal from the race. Bellangee made this request after the citizens' committee had prepared and distributed ballots containing names of all candidates to all adults in the area to be incorporated. This committee announced as "The People's Choice," Gaston, with sixty-nine votes and Greeno with thirteen. The conclusiveness of this straw vote was marred by the fact that the other faction had declined to join in such a test of popularity with the general citizenry, and had remained content with its previous nomination of Mr. Greeno, an avowed opponent of the single tax corporation and a two-time loser in previous applications for colony membership. At any rate the formal election resulted in a victory for Greeno with twenty-one votes to nineteen for Gaston. However, three members of the single tax corporation won places among the five aldermen selected. (Fairhope *Courier,* June 5, 1908.)

Shortly after the incorporation of the town, the *Eastern Shore* (July, 1908) predicted that "Fairhope will be known hereafter as a town, and the name 'colony' will go out of use, except to describe certain local usages, such as 'colony rents' and 'colony lands.' " In the course of time this prediction was fulfilled in so far as the general public was concerned, and the high probability that the colony would lose status may have been one important reason why such non-resident members and friends of the Fairhope colony as Joseph Fels, Bolton Hall, and Daniel Kiefer, were considerably saddened by the act of municipal incorporation—particularly when the charter of the newly incorporated town failed to contain any provisions for "home rule" in matters of taxation, let alone requirements for the single tax.

On April 21, 1909, Bolton Hall wrote Gaston that he was dismayed at the prospects of the Town of Fairhope issuing bonds or levying special taxes of such a nature as to "practically nullify" the single tax features of the colony. He stated that in the future ". . . we must look for the main results of Fairhope in the attention, and spirit that it has inspired in Arden and in other similar places as well as in its general propaganda." (Gaston files.)

In a letter to H. S. Greeno (undated copy in Gaston files)[2] Mr. Fels wrote: "As for myself, I have never believed in the necessity for a municipality such as has been formed there, but I never raised any objection because the people down there should run their affairs. My interest in Fairhope is purely that of wanting to help carry out the plan by which all public revenues shall be raised out of land values."

Fels wrote Gaston from London, June 24, 1908, to the effect that he thought Gaston's candidacy for mayor a "little immodest," and continued: "Fairhope has long since been too much in the hands of a few men, and that is unhealthy to last a long time. I am glad you feel yourself that some new blood ought to come in. Whatever is worth perpetuating at Fairhope will be perpetuated, and the change in local matters will teach a lot of people lessons." Somewhat later, August 3, 1908, he wrote Gaston that he was concerned about the relationships between the town and the colony. He asked: "Do you not think it a good idea to correspond with Bolton Hall, Kiefer and perhaps Pleydell about the best to do and not to do in the dealing with the town authorities of Fairhope? In the multitude of counselers there may be safety."

Fels continued to live with this worry.[3] On October 5, 1908,

---

[2] The present writers are grateful to Joseph Fels for one of his habits. In writing to E. B. Gaston, he customarily enclosed letters he had received from other respondents if they bore upon the matter he wanted to discuss with the colony. Frequently he enclosed copies of letters he had written to others. In this way it has been possible to write with more assurance of the nature or significance of early events in Fairhope than would be possible solely from official documents, published accounts and bi-lateral correspondence.

[3] Whether the incorporation of the town was a deciding factor in Fels' decision to cease aiding the colony financially, is purely conjectural. In 1909 he incorporated the Joseph Fels Fund of America at which time he wrote: "After many years of pretty close devotion and the spending of a good many thousand dollars to help the colony on its firm feet, I became of the opinion that I could spend the money for the Single Tax more effectively in other directions." (Fairhope *Courier,* March 13, 1914.)

For ten years Fels gave generously to the colony, not only of his money but of his time. He made many trips to Fairhope sometimes to render specific aid and sometimes "to straighten them out." He invested heavily in private business and lent or made outright gifts to individuals to enable them to stay in the colony. He invested heavily in the Steamer *Fairhope* and gave $10,000 to the Organic he wrote Gaston: "What occurs to me now is on the subject of the corporation transferring any of the franchises to the town organization without the greatest possible protection, and always with a string tied to it, so that these functions can be withdrawn if *every* condition is not carried out to the benefit of the *entire* community. You have got too far along now to make mistakes, and even a small one might be fatal as it would establish a precedent."

There can be no question but that incorporation of the Town of Fairhope was an important turning point in the history of the community and the single tax colony. The single tax corporation necessarily assumed a position subordinate to the municipality, however influential its philosophy and policies may or may not have been in shaping subsequent city policies and programs. Nor is there any question but that municipal incorporation was inevitable in view of the rapid growth of the village and the widening schisms among the residents. Creating the Town of Fairhope helped to settle some problems and to cause still others.

To a considerable extent municipal incorporation resolved the problem of how to inject a satisfactory degree of democracy within the community, a result which could not have been accomplished by any action of the colony. Municipalization was not unacceptable to the great majority of members of the single tax corporation. Years later Bellangee stated his position as follows:

However necessary it may be to retain in the hands of the faithful the title to the land; and to guarantee absolutely that all values created by the public be reserved to the public, I am thoroughly convinced by our experiences, that beyond thus safe-guarding our experiment, the Fairhope public, without distinction of economic beliefs or relation to the Fairhope Single Tax Corporation, should be permitted in the most democratic manner possible to decide absolutely for what those values should be devoted; and that no service should be undertaken or promoted by the arbitrary authori-

School, $1,000 to the Library, and twenty-two hundred acres of land to the colony—all with the hope that the colony might better demonstrate the single tax.

ty of the Executive Council until it has been authorized by the public, in some unmistakable manner. *Single Tax Review*, XIII, No. 3, May-June, 1913, 20.)

In addition to making the local government more representative, incorporation of the town improved the position of the colony in another direction. Prior to 1908 all "municipal" services and facilities were financed by the single tax corporation. Many of these facilities, such as streets, the school building and parks, benefited those living off colony lands and enhanced the value of privately-owned lands. Henceforth the single tax corporation would pay a portion of its rental income into the town treasury and would be relieved of that portion of the burden of financing public services which would be paid by those living on and the owners of privately-owned lands. The executive council lost little time in approving a method of relieving corporation lessees of some municipal taxes. In December, 1908, the council *ruled* that the Fairhope Single Tax Corporation would accept receipts for municipal and road taxes in payment of rents. In the event the road taxes were worked out, in accordance with the custom of the period, a receipt for the time worked would be receivable on rents to the amount necessary to discharge the tax in cash. (Fairhope *Courier*, December 11, 1908.)

To a degree, therefore, it would seem that the single tax corporation remained in substantially the same position with respect to fundamental principles. The corporation retained the right to collect annual rentals equal to the economic rent of its lands and it continued the responsibility of using this income for the benefit of the lessees. It further retained the policy of refunding taxes paid by lessees, even enlarging its commitments in this respect by refunding poll taxes, municipal and road taxes. The budget of the single tax corporation would be relieved of the direct financing of public services and those not on colony lands would contribute to the overhead and other costs of the new government on whatever tax or other revenue source adopted by it. Such a view is somewhat too sanguine. Some of the conditions that made the Town of Fairhope inevitable necessarily weakened the colony as a single tax demonstration. First, three-fourths of the area of the new town was privately owned. Second, the municipality did not obtain a home rule charter permitting it to choose land value taxation to the exclusion of all other taxes. In the Town of Fairhope, therefore, there was neither legal authority nor universal sentiment for following the principle that "all values created by the public be reserved to the public." Nor was there any method (other than on colony lands) to achieve the *first* purpose of the single tax reform—the destruction of land speculation and the making of land more readily accessible for the use of all. These shortcomings were not created by the act of municipal incorporation; initially the fault was in the failure to secure a solid block of urban or urbanizable land, preferably at least three or four square miles in area. In addition, the combination of "natural limitations," managerial errors and the deep-rooted desire to obtain material gain from enhancement of land values, resulted in a failure to generate sufficient sentiment in favor of one hundred per cent land value taxation to assure that the municipality would rely solely on the land value tax as the source of revenue. The effects of these weaknesses and failures were magnified by superimposing the larger and legally stronger unit of municipal government on the structure of the single tax corporation. Henceforth it would be even more difficult for the uninitiated to perceive any effects, beneficial or otherwise, resulting from the unique land management policy of the private corporation. The single tax corporation was destined to lose much of its personality, and to the extent its presence was felt *and understood* by the citizens of Fairhope, too often the reaction was to be one of frustration and resentment. In short, the single tax corporation would become less important to an increasing number of local residents as the municipality grew in significance.

This progressive undermining of the *popular* influence of the single tax corporation was not immediately apparent. Two conditions limited the initial importance of the municipal government. These were: the single tax corporation owned all

public facilities; and the municipal government was weak
financially for a considerable time. The immediate problem
was whether, how, and on what terms to transfer public facilities owned by the colony to the jurisdiction of the new city.

Some of those most opposed to the colony seriously proposed
that the single tax corporation turn over all public facilities,
franchises and net rentals to the new municipality, without
compensation or strings of any kind. This view was rationalized by recalling the promise of the corporation membership to
turn over net revenues to an acceptable corporation controlled
by all the lessees. This promise, which never was realized, of
course did not contemplate that the revenues of the colony
would be spent for the benefit of those living on non-colony
lands; hence, this rationalization did not impress many Fairhope residents. The feeling in Fairhope was widespread that
the municipal organization should be one to represent all views
and interests and that all should contribute to its support.

The executive council of the colony formalized and presented
to the town government a plan for the conveyance of certain
streets then open and in use. The plan forbade the town's
granting private franchises for public services upon the streets
conveyed. The grant stipulated that ". . . the policy of municipal ownership and operation shall be pursued as fast as law and
custom will permit." The single tax corporation reserved the
right to enter upon the streets conveyed by it, to perform necessary services for its lessees until such time as the town was able
to take over such public services. The plan contemplated that
whenever the town was able to take over any public service performed by the Fairhope Single Tax Corporation, it could do
so ". . . on the payment of its then valuation, to be determined
by a board of nine appraisers, three from the councils of each
corporation and the remaining three chosen jointly." There
was an expressed hope ". . . that the town should endeavor to
secure from individual owners of land within its limits a similar
and contemporaneous conveyance." (Fairhope *Courier*, October 30, 1908.)

Within a year Mr. Bancroft, superintendent of lands and

highways, reported that the colony had conveyed thirty-nine acres of streets to the town. (Minutes, November 3, 1909.)

One of the first efforts of the Fairhope colony had been to establish a school. Both land and buildings had been furnished by the colony and the operating expenses largely had been financed by the single tax corporation and supplemented by monies raised by various women's organizations. With the incorporation of the town, however, community opinion was that the school should become the financial responsibility of the town government.

Because the school building belonged to the colony, several of the members felt the single tax corporation was entitled to the receipt of rent from this facility in the event it should be used by the town. These members reasoned that now that there existed an organization capable of distributing the cost of public services over a wider area, there was no reason why the colony should continue its contribution beyond its fair share. The executive council accepted this point of view and decided that rent should be charged the school district for the use of the school building. (Fairhope *Courier*, September 25, 1908.)

This decision prompted a general "school meeting." The County Superintendent of Schools stated that he was opposed to paying rent for the building. He stressed that he and several persons not living on colony land previously had expressed themselves as preferring that the school be more centrally located in the school district and that it belong to the district, and he asserted that the group referred to had been willing to contribute to such a school. He further stated that the colony, in order to have the school located on its land, and in order to secure a share of the public school fund, had furnished the building. (Fairhope *Courier*, November 25, 1908.)

On the other hand, members of the colony argued that when the colony built the schoolhouse, there had been no agreement that the school either would belong to or would be under the supervision of the public school district. Later on the colonists stated that there was nothing obligatory about the colony furnishing the building; on the other hand, there was no obligation on the part of the school district to continue the school in its present location, but, they argued, at least four-fifths of the children in attendance lived on colony land. (Fairhope *Courier,* April 23, 1909.)

In an endeavor to co-operate, the colony, while maintaining its "moral and legal" right to charge rent for its building, took the position that if the people in the school district voted against paying rent, the council ". . . is not disposed to hamper the school by pressing the matter at this time." (Minutes, November 30, 1908.) The people in the school district voted against paying rent for the school building.

The executive council then offered the town a two-acre site for a school and made an additional offer to contribute its share in the cost of a new building either by donation or taxation. Although this offer seemed generous the town requested a better proposition.

The school building in use had recently been enlarged by the colony. The expansion had been financed by borrowing, with Fels' consent, the $1,000 which he had contributed to the Library Fund. Some of the colonists were willing to turn the school building over to the town but wanted the town to assume this $1,000 debt. A majority of members objected on the ground that this would force the colony, as a part of the town, to pay a large share of the library debt while those living off colony land would escape the burden of paying the colony any equity in the school building beyond a small share on this library debt. (Fairhope *Courier,* April 23, 1909.)

The colony council subsequently made many generous offers to the town on the school matter. One of the final offers was a gift of the two acres already mentioned together with a colony donation to a proposed new schoolhouse of an amount proportional to the number of children living on colony lands to those living off colony lands, or alternatively, if the town wanted to buy the present school building, the gift of two acres of land would go with the building. (Fairhope *Courier,* April 23, 1909.)

When this offer was turned down at a town meeting, it was

evident to many that there was a small though highly articulate element in the community which was willing for the colony to contribute much more than its equitable share. The justification for this point of view seemed to be ". . . had there been no municipal incorporation the colony would have continued to carry this unremunerative school burden indefinitely." (Fairhope *Courier,* May 14, 1909.)

In the meantime the colony received and accepted an offer of $2,000 for their school building from the Organic School.

During these months of meetings and referenda the attitude of the town aldermen had been somewhat neutral. This body preferred to let the various factions—colony and non-colony— argue it out. They were unwilling either to take away colony property by condemnation proceedings or to compel the so-called outsiders to contribute toward the previously incurred cost of the school building. (Fairhope *Courier,* May 14, 1909.)

One practical consideration coloring the attitude of the town officials was that the town had little or no credit. One of the aldermen hinted, perhaps facetiously, that if the colony sold its building to the Organic School it might like to invest the money in town bonds "without interest," or perhaps even make the town a present of one-half the bonds. This alderman remarked: "That of course could remain an open question for discussion as Fairhopers love to argue, and it would be cruel to remove all cause for argument." (Reported in Fairhope *Courier,* May 14, 1909.) The town council thought poorly of suggestions that the colony be enjoined from going through with the sale of the school building to the Organic School, stating that it thought ". . . the Fairhope Single Tax Corporation had manifested a liberal spirit in the matter." (Fairhope *Courier,* June 18, 1909.)

The final outcome was that the school building was sold to the Organic School and the colony agreed to contribute $1,000 to a new public school building provided those outside the colony would pay $250. (Ibid.) In addition, in a special meeting of August 3, 1909, the executive council conveyed land for the public school to the town on condition that it would be used for school or other municipal purposes, and "in no event to be sold, but if not directly used for such purposes to be leased and the rental collected and used for public school purposes." The conveyance also contained a provision whereby the land would revert to the colony if the terms were not complied with. Obviously, the executive council had accepted Fels' advice against conveying land except ". . . with the greatest possible protection and always with a string attached." In this instance, however, the time came when the strings were removed. In 1924 the land given by the colony was deeded to the town for school purposes. It was necessary to waive the reservations in the original conveyance to permit the town to secure state funds for a new school building. (Minutes, July 1, 1924.)

The conveyance of land to the town enabled the *Courier* to point out a single tax moral:

By taking the rental value of the land from year to year, no selling value attaches to the land and when a site is wanted for a public purpose, no purchase price need be paid for the land, the lessee only having to be compensated for improvements (if leased). Were it not for this policy the cost of a site would be the first and no doubt a heavy charge, against the proposed new public school and hall. We will have a hard time enough to get our building as it is but thanks to the "Fairhope Plan" and to the Fairhope Single Tax Corporation we have our choice of sites. (Fairhope *Courier,* June 25, 1909.)

In 1908 the single tax corporation boasted the only water works system in Baldwin County. The system comprised about two miles of mains directly supplying forty premises. Many other residents obtained their domestic water supply directly from the colony well. The system had been a continual worry and drain on the colony. It was anything but successful. Those who had paid connection fees had some justification for the feeling that they had an equity in the system. These two situations impelled many members of the colony to want to hold on to the system unless they could obtain some compensation for the previous outlays made in its development. A further factor which complicated the water problem was the existence of a considerable sentiment among colony members that "the town should pursue the policy of furnishing water substantially at cost." (Fairhope *Courier,* July 17, 1908.)

Partly because the colony-owned water system was not a financially successful facility, and partly because there was no general conviction among colony members as to the proper agency for owning and managing this utility, the issue was not resolved for almost seven years. During August, 1915, the water system was transferred to the town, without compensation and without imposing any condition other than that the town should put it in order and operate it in its best judgment for the benefit of the people. (Fairhope *Courier,* August 20, 1915.)

Incorporation of the Town of Fairhope did not immediately result in confining the colony to a program of administering its lands. Even after the water system issue was disposed of the colony retained for a while its telephone system, and it did not turn its parks and wharf over to the town until 1932. In the meantime the colony encouraged and assisted other ventures of a public character—especially the People's Railroad and the School of Organic Education.

xi

TWO FAIRHOPE INSTITUTIONS: THE PEOPLE'S RAILROAD AND THE SCHOOL OF ORGANIC EDUCATION

*T*HE People's Railroad and the School of Organic Education are juxtaposed largely because their contrasting natures reflect so faithfully the struggle within the still young community to define its destiny. The People's Railroad was largely the product of the strong conviction held by Ernest B. Gaston that all such public facilities either should be publicly owned or co-operatively managed. The railroad was destined to be the last fling at semi-socialism sponsored by the colony or its leaders. It was not to be the last venture in public ownership within the Fairhope community, because the municipality of Fairhope has remained faithful to the condition included in the deed of streets by the colony to the town, that no private exclusive franchises were to be granted thereon. Subsequently the municipality was to own and operate the water, electric and gas systems. The colony, however, was fated to confine itself to administering its lands in accordance with single tax principles after it disposed of its water, wharf and telephone facilities.

The School of Organic Education was largely the result of the advanced thinking and dedicated service of Mrs. Marietta Johnson. It was destined to achieve considerable success. This school found a natural habitat in Fairhope, partly because the nature of the people was such that they enjoyed innovation and therefore tended to support any proposal which appealed to them as making sense and as being in the public interest. What more natural than that a school built around the *whole needs* of children *as individuals* should be founded in a community populated largely by individualists strongly imbued with the spirit of freedom?

The People's Railroad Company was not formally a part of the Fairhope Single Tax Corporation although the colony did enter into an agreement with the railroad granting material privileges so valuable as to constitute virtual sponsorship. Also it was more than coincidental that the secretary of the colony, E. B. Gaston, served as president of the railroad.

The People's Railroad was started in 1912 but it long had been in the thinking of some of the colonists. As early as 1897, Mr. Gaston had outlined a plan for securing a railroad for Fairhope. The details of the plan as contemplated in 1897 are not available but it is known that it received some opposition. For example, Mr. T. E. Mann, of Gladbrook, Iowa, wrote to Mr. Gaston on June 19, 1897: "I do not like father's outline of your R. R. scheme. It is Shylockish with hardly a suggestion of co-operative reform about it. Though possibly the end would justify the means." (Gaston files.)

Early in 1912, Mr. Gaston outlined the advantages of a railroad to the community and submitted a plan for its accomplishment before the colony council. The main benefit stressed by him would be the increased accessibility of colony land. His plan called for the construction of fourteen miles of track from the bay at Fairhope east to the Louisville and Nashville Railroad at Robertsdale, via Silver Hill. He was able to show that several individuals along the proposed route were interested (subsequently they became members of the railroad company); therefore the venture was not solely one of the Fairhope community.

The wharf, Gaston argued, was a vital connecting link between Mobile and points along the proposed railroad route. He expressed the belief that the railroad and the wharf could be most economically managed by the same group. Therefore: ". . . it is believed by the officers of the said Railroad Company that it would greatly facilitate the securing of funds for the building of its proposed road, if it were given the right for a limited and definite time to administer the said Wharf as a part of its line and have the earnings of the wharf, to make up possible deficiencies in the earnings of the road proper until its business can be built up to a profitable point."[1]

After hearing Gaston's proposals for the railroad and the manner in which he hoped the corporation would co-operate, the executive council endorsed the general plan of the People's Railroad and expressed its willingness to co-operate on "any reasonable basis for the administration of the Fairhope Wharf in connection with such a railroad." (Minutes, April 1, 1912.) Shortly thereafter the executive council took definite steps to co-operate with the railroad, subject, of course, to a referendum of the membership and an agreement on the part of the railroad company to assume certain responsibilities.

Key provisions in the agreement between the Fairhope Single Tax Corporation and the People's Railroad were:

1. The corporation agreed to grant a right of way for tracks and to provide land for depot and terminal tracks. In return the railroad would accept the responsibility of making a settlement with any lessee of the corporation whose improvements might be damaged by the railroad exercising the colony grants.

2. The colony agreed to turn over the management and income of the wharf to the management of the railroad for a period of five years from January 1, 1913, on condition that the railroad reimburse the holders of wharf certificates either by giving them obligations of the railroad company or by paying cash. The railroad was further charged with meeting all expenses of repair or betterments to the wharf during the term of its use. The agreement further stipulated that the wharf be

1 See "Memorandum of Agreement" between the Colony and the People's Railroad. Mr. Gaston formed a paper organization of the proposed railroad before the colony council was asked to take formal co-operative action. This "Memorandum of Agreement" is in the Gaston files.

insured against tornadoes and fires at least to the amount of insurance then carried by the corporation; any insurance benefits collected were to be applied to the wharf.

3. The agreement prohibited the railroad company from charging higher wharfage than that imposed by other wharfs along the coast and it prohibited any increase in the rates currently charged.

4. The railroad agreed to pay all taxes assessed against the wharf and to keep the wharf free from all liens during the time it was in possession: "it being the intent and purpose of this agreement that the said Railroad Company shall not have power to create any liability of indebtedness for which said property would be liable, and should it fail to strictly comply with this condition, the Fairhope Single Tax Corporation may, at its option, declare this contract forfeited and resume possession and control of said wharf."

5. The People's Railroad agreed to provide ample space for foot wharfage.

Conditional to making this agreement effective, the People's Railroad must have completed its first mile of track connecting with the wharf and have furnished "suitable means of transportation thereon," as well as having made satisfactory arrangements with all wharf certificate holders.

In subsequent referenda the membership of the colony voted approval of the action of the executive council in granting land and right of way to the railroad, and endorsed the execution by the council of any instrument necessary to give legal force to these actions. With respect to turning over the management and receipts of the wharf to the railroad company, the members were anything but enthusiastic; only by the narrow vote of twenty-two to twenty was this action approved.

One of the reasons many members wanted to retain the wharf and its receipts under colony management was that since the storm of 1906, which had destroyed the wharf, the colony had been without any wharf receipts. The company organized to rebuild the wharf had issued certificates for its financing, and had retained managerial responsibilities until all charges against the wharf had been paid. Now that the wharf indebtedness was nearly eliminated many within the colony looked forward once again to the wharf as a source of income for colony purposes.

There were, of course, some who objected on principle—not all singletaxers agreed on the principle of public ownership and operation of railroads and public utilities. Mr. Fiske Warren, wealthy singletaxer, founder of two single tax enclaves inspired by Fairhope and a large investor in the railroad, wrote on this point in a letter to Mrs. Anne B. Call, February 12, 1923: "I agreed with him [Gaston] then on the plan, but we differed profoundly upon an important point, as we do still. He was and is a believer in the public ownership and operation of railroads and their equipment, and I was not and am not, and thus, on its theoretical side, the plan appealed to him and me from different angles. He liked it as being the nearest to the public ownership practicable in view of the inhibition, in the constitution of Fairhope, of interest-bearing indebtedness, while I liked it because it was legally a private venture, whose success (partly because of its co-operative features) I hoped would put to sleep beyond resuscitation the very idea of public ownership." (Letter in Bellangee-Call files.)

Mr. Gaston estimated that Fairhope's share of the cost of the railroad would be about $95,000. (Fairhope *Courier,* January 10, 1913.) He proposed to raise the necessary funds in two ways: first, individuals would buy memberships in the People's Railroad Company for $5.00. These memberships carried no investment rights but merely denoted an interest of individuals in the venture and gave them the privilege of helping to plan and to work for the success of the railroad. Second, six per cent interest-bearing bonds would be sold to investors. Mr. Gaston wrote that the People's Railroad Company considered these bonds as ". . . a better and safer investment than those of any railroad company now operated in this country." (Fairhope *Courier,* October 10, 1913.)

The railroad company did not postpone construction until it had completed its financing; in fact it was in such a hurry to build the first mile necessary for the agreement to become operative so it could take over the wharf, that it started immediately following the affirmative referendum by the colony membership. Such hasty action, however, proved unnecessary because it was not until the fall of 1914 that the Wharf Company was able to liquidate the debt against the wharf and return it to the colony. Further, the railroad company had encountered delays in finishing the first mile of track. It therefore asked that the contract for the use of the wharf be extended for five years from the date of termination of control by the Wharf Company. The council acted favorably on this request and the membership agreed at a referendum election. (Minutes, June 13, 1916.)

The first mile, in fact the *only* mile, consisted of a narrow gauge track and was equipped with small cars which carried both freight and passengers. Capital funds proved not forthcoming in an amount sufficient to finance construction beyond the first mile. The railroad also was handicapped by keen competition from other wharves and from truck lines.

A severe tropical storm swept away the wharf in July, 1916. This catastrophe disclosed that the railroad company had not carried the tornado insurance specified in its contract with the colony. Trustees Anne B. Call and A. M. Troyer reported this lack of insurance to the members of the colony and also charged that the wharf was not being kept in proper repair. The trustees recommended that the entire contract with the railroad company be rewritten, that the railroad be required to create a fund to be available in case of future damage to the wharf. (Minutes, September 18, 1916.) The executive council laid over to a future meeting both the report and the recommendations therein.

At a meeting on November 6, 1916, the council resolved: "that the council is satisfied that the officers of The People's Railroad Company are making a laudable effort, under difficult circumstances to further the mutual interests of the colony and the investors in the railroad and should be dealt with in a generous spirit." The council disapproved imposing any requirement to keep a sinking fund for the amortization of the wharf stating that it would embarrass the railroad in its efforts to pay off its other indebtedness and its attempt to establish its credit ". . . by the payment of interest on its bonds, thus keeping the faith really of the community, which approved the proposition for the building of the railroad which is the real beneficiary." (Minutes, November 6, 1916.) The council reasoned that the people had subscribed as generously to the repair of the wharf after the last storm as they had after previous ones. Inferentially this eliminated any reason (from the point of view of the council) for making any attempt to build up a fund to meet future catastrophies. Although it seems inexplicable, the council seemed almost indifferent to the fact that the wharf and its earnings represented the major asset of the railroad.

The executive council was presented with several petitions seeking the cancellation of the agreement and contract with the railroad. All referenda, however, supported continuation of the contract.

In addition to the unhappiness of some over the failure of the railroad company to carry insurance, and over its unwillingness to build up a fund for the rebuilding of the wharf if destroyed in the future, many lessees objected to the railroad charging foot wharfage. The colony had charged foot wharfage only when its treasury was badly depleted and most of the time the lessees had received free foot wharfage. Resentment over these charges grew to the point that the council discontinued permission of the railroad to make this charge. (Minutes, May 7, 1917.)

Rather quickly it became evident that the railroad would not be a financial success. However, as late as January, 1917, Gaston, in his capacity as president of the railroad, thought it might have a chance if the "people were patient and had a proper attitude . . . but unless it be looked upon as it really is, solely an unselfish agency in behalf of the people and treated accordingly, the effort might as well be abandoned." (Minutes, January 15, 1917.)

Early in 1921, and prior to the termination of the contract between the colony and the railroad, Mr. Gaston made one of his last pleas on behalf of the railroad. He admitted that it had not been possible to carry out the original plan but he thought the railroad should not be abandoned in view of the contractual obligations to investors, especially non-resident investors. He asked that a study be made of the municipalization of the wharf *and* of the People's Railroad, considered as a single entity. In his judgment a small additional investment would complete the line to the town limits. (Fairhope *Courier,* February 4, 1921.)

Apparently there was little sentiment for the colony to assume complete responsibility for the railroad. On March 5, 1923, the council "approved the sense of a petition" signed by a large number of lessees and members requesting that the corporation not take over or operate the People's Railroad Company.

The decision to allow the railroad to go into receivership was not unanimous. Mr. Fiske Warren, in a letter to Mrs. Call dated March 5, 1923, wrote: "With a fund from the pier to draw from . . . is it good enclavian policy to let The People's Railroad Company go into bankruptcy?" Many residents felt that the colony had a greater responsibility to the investors of the railroad than was included in the letter of the legal agreement, and that the railroad should continue as an entity to receive wharf receipts in order to liquidate its debts. Those so contending, however, were in the minority. Most members insisted that the Fairhope Single Tax Corporation had a greater obligation to its lessees than to the investors in the People's Railroad Company. Consequently, with the expiration of the agreement a receiver was sought for the railroad, and the wharf was once again returned to colony management.

The "organic school," as it is popularly called, became one of the more unusual Fairhope institutions—and one of the most widely known. In the years of its greater success it attracted to the small community a great many people—many of whom were of national and international prominence. Those attracted to Fairhope because of the organic school were not necessarily singletaxers although some became intrigued with the economic philosophy and activities of the founders of the community.

Mrs. Marietta Johnson, founder of the organic school, previously had taught in the Fairhope public school. She had received her training in the public and normal schools of Minnesota and had taught in the public schools of that state. She accounted as her most enjoyable work in Minnesota her service as "training teacher" for the State Teachers' College of Minnesota.[2]

At the time Mrs. Johnson was receiving her training one of the criteria of a successful teacher was the ability to teach six-year-old children to "read through four first readers in three months!" Mrs. Johnson supervised the training of teachers who, in their turn, entered the teaching field to accomplish this and similar goals.

Mrs. Johnson's keen interest in children and her wide reading in the fields of education and psychology caused her to question the then current methods of teaching and to reappraise prevailing educational standards and objectives. Her primary inspiration, she wrote, came from Nathan Oppenheim's *Development of the Child.*

"I began to see the child in an entirely different light—began to realize that he is unformed, unripe, immature; that he is in no condition even to be trained. 'Training' and 'growing' are quite different. In training we often dominate or force in order to accomplish certain definite external results. In growing we provide the right conditions—included in the process—and the moving power is within! If the child is wholesomely, happily, intelligently employed, he is being educated! . . . *The Develop-*

2 This account is neither a biography of Mrs. Johnson nor an evaluation of the "organic school." Much of the material and the quotations used are from Mrs. Johnson's "Thirty Years with an Idea." This little monograph was not completely finished at her death and the version available for use here is a posthumous publication carried as supplements to the Fairhope *Courier.* For this reason it is not practicable to give precise bibliographical data on the citations contained in this section.

ment of the Child became my educational Bible, and its frequent perusal has been a marvelous stimulation and support through many years of experimental work."

This view of the responsibility of the school as one to serve the needs and interests of the child rather than to have the child pressured into fulfilling certain standards set by adults, led Mrs. Johnson to visualize a new type of school, a school where the six and seven-year-olds would not be confronted with books but would be given "occupational" or "activity" work. Reading, writing and numbers would best be postponed for nine and ten-year-olds. Each age group would have activities suitable to its interests and needs. In her ideal school there would be no examinations or report cards; an activity or a piece of work well done was all the reward needed. Under this system no child would ever need to feel the "stigma of failure." When a child had done his best he would have succeeded. The new school would view education as life rather than as a preparation for life. It would be as much concerned over the physical and spiritual well-being of the children as with their purely mental development. The new school would be concerned with training "the entire organism" of the child.

While Mrs. Johnson was turning over in her mind these ideas of a new type of school, she was in communication with friends in Fairhope. In the summer of 1907, Mr. and Mrs. S. H. Comings, resident members of the Fairhope Single Tax Corporation, offered Mrs. Johnson $25 a month if she would return to Fairhope and establish a free school based on her new ideas. Mrs. Johnson wrote: "I had been in Fairhope some years before and was longing to return . . . I was fully committed to the idea of starting a school and gladly embraced this opportunity. I was so anxious to try out the idea that I should have been willing to pay children to come and let me experiment."

Mrs. Johnson rented a cottage for $15 a month; this left only $10.00 for supplies and salary. With this tiny material assistance she sought to answer the question, ". . . would knowledge and skill be an inevitable accompaniment of a normal process of growth?" If rapid growth and nation-wide favorable acceptance of the school is any criterion, the question was answered in the affirmative.

The Fairhope *Courier* at once began publicizing the organic school as one of the prime attractions of Fairhope and the colony. The executive council quickly expressed its great appreciation of the school and announced its "disposition to give as liberal appropriations to it as its revenues would allow." (Fairhope *Courier*, June 5, 1908.)

Joseph Fels was one of the early benefactors of the school but his interest was not so much in pedagogy as in attracting people to Fairhope. He gave $5,000 for building and equipment and $1,000 a year for five years for maintenance. (Fairhope *Courier*, June 1, 1909.) Doubtless this was one of the school's most important gifts if only because it came during the early years before the school had obtained widespread support from friends in the North and East.

Mr. Fels' gift may be used to illustrate a type of consideration that led to differences among friends and members of the colony. He tendered the gift with the expectation that it would serve to illustrate the benefits to those living on colony land; Mrs. Johnson's chief interest was in free education for all children. Fels expressed his point of view in a letter to Mrs. Johnson written from London, March 4, 1909:

"The more I think of the matter, the more certain do I become that the benefits of the Organic School should go to the people living on Colony land. Indeed, so certain am I now about this that, had I considered it well, I should have made my contribution from the beginning conditional on this being done. It is against my usual style to have a string tied to a gift!

"If the School is to treat people in or out of the Colony alike, and so be no inducement to people to come and live at Fairhope on Fairhope land (if they can get the same benefits on private land) then one of my reasons for helping the school has been defeated.

"I know your great goodwill to all people, and I know you lean towards what you believe to be the right kind of Socialism.

For myself, I believe in most of the things you do, though I do not stamp myself anything, but Socialism will not come by nationalizing the land or by purchase but by taxing land values. The school itself gets the benefits of being on Fairhope land, it gets exemption from outside taxes which are put on privately owned land. If our work is to be of any constructive use, it will have to more and more draw the line between public and private ownership." (Letter in Gaston files.)

Almost immediately the enrollment of the organic school equaled that of the Fairhope public school. Within a short period several organizations and individuals were contributing financial assistance. The school was endorsed at "The Single Tax Conference" held in Chicago in 1911, and the conference contributed $175 to it. (Fairhope *Courier,* December 15, 1911.) Mrs. Woodrow Wilson invited Mrs. Johnson to call upon her and discuss "Organic Education." (Fairhope *Courier,* January 17, 1913.) Several years later Mrs. Henry Ford contributed $12,000 and sponsored a series of twelve lectures to be given by Mrs. Johnson in Detroit. (Fairhope *Courier,* December 8, 1922.)

Shortly after the incorporation of the Town of Fairhope, and in the face of much opposition, the colony sold the building which had been used by the public school to the organic school. In addition to furnishing a liberal amount of well located land, the colony for many years contributed to the organic school in the same proportion it assisted the public school—by paying the incidental fees of children living on colony land. In later years as the colony prospered materially and the organic school finances became more urgent, the Fairhope Single Tax Corporation made liberal appropriations to its maintenance.

Mrs. Johnson's School of Organic Education aroused the interest and admiration of educators and parents throughout the United States. One of the reasons for this was the many successful lecture tours she made. Professional educators, among whom were Dr. Charles H. Henderson of Minnesota and Professor John Dewey of Columbia, came to Fairhope for first-hand study. These and others were extravagant in their praise of the new school.

Mrs. Johnson early established within the school a department for the training of teachers. As a result she not only could staff the school at Fairhope with teachers trained in her methods, but she was able to help staff an organic school which she founded at Greenwich, Connecticut. This second organic school resulted from a summer course Mrs. Johnson conducted on "Organic Education" at Greenwich. A "Society for Organic Education" had been formed in the East as a result of her inspirational lectures and persuasive personality in private conversations, and this organization invited her to teach the course. (Fairhope *Courier,* June 13, 1913.)

A strong cult of organic education developed in the East. A "Fairhope League North" was formed and made appreciable contributions to the Fairhope school. Upon the founding of the school at Greenwich, Mrs. Johnson was placed under pressure to confine her activities to the lecture platform and to the Connecticut school. As a consequence a "Fairhope League South" was formed in 1917 to raise funds for the Fairhope school in areas not served by the "Fairhope League North." In 1920 the "Fairhope Educational Foundation" was organized to relieve Mrs. Johnson of money-raising efforts and to underwrite the $25,000 annual school budget.

It became increasingly difficult to finance the organic school in Fairhope. For a time in 1924, it was questionable whether the school would find the funds to reopen, but funds were somehow forthcoming and the school flourished until Mrs. Johnson's death in 1938.

During the more successful years the school obtained teachers of a variety of crafts and arts (including dramatics and folk dancing) for nominal salaries. This was possible because well-trained, competent, and dedicated teachers were anxious to obtain experience working with Mrs. Johnson.

Some residents of Fairhope believe the organic school was just as much or even more responsible for the growth of Fairhope as an intellectual and cultural center as were the single tax policies of the colony. However this may be, it is safe to say that not many small, new and comparatively poor communities in the year 1907, possessed the kind of intellectual climate that would both welcome and support such an innovation in the field of education.

In recent years the organic school has declined in prestige. Mrs. Johnson has been sorely missed although some of the many directors following her have been both competent and faithful in her methods. Mrs. Johnson steadfastly refused to attempt an accumulation of a permanent endowment. Recently, financing has become more and more difficult and the school long has been suffering from a grossly inadequate budget. These conditions coupled with the growth of "progressive education," which embodies some of Mrs. Johnson's notions, and the great increase in the support of the public schools of Alabama, have led many within the Fairhope community to question whether the organic school should be continued.

xïi

ADOPTION OF THE SOMERS SYSTEM

On March 31, 1914, a meeting of corporation lessees unanimously adopted the report submitted by W. A. Somers and recommended that the assessment of rents for 1914 be made in accordance with the recommendations contained therein. Thus for the first time since 1895 when rents were assessed for the year 1896, did the executive council have the advantage of a systematic and logically consistent method of making the annual rent appraisement.

Mr. Somers' report is presented verbatim except for the maps referred to.

It is with pleasure that I herewith submit a report of the application of the Somers System of valuation to the rent ratings of your lands, both the lots in Fairhope and the outside farm lands.

The work has been very interesting and somewhat difficult because the Somers System is based upon the theory that the only foundation for the valuation of land is its use and the specific value can only be determined by comparison and that the only reliable measure for making this comparison is community opinion.

I recognize that the common habit of modern times has, and does hold, that land is worth what it can be sold for, but this is only a speculative fallacy and the only foundation for this price is an estimate made by someone that it may, at some future time, be sold at a higher price, or it is based on an estimate of what the actual use of the land is worth from year to year.

In old communities, where business habits are comparatively staid and fixed, there is generally a well defined community opinion which can be used to compare the advantages of different localities and conditions and thus arrive at a satisfactory comparative value of the usefulness of different sites, but in new settlements, or where from any cause the conditions are unstable or changing, community opinion of land value does not and cannot exist.

Fairhope, partly because of its newness, but more on account of the rapid development of the agricultural possibilities of the surrounding country during the last few years, belongs in this last mentioned class. It was therefore necessary to develop a community opinion of comparative values before a rent rating could be made.

This has been to a degree accomplished by some ten or twelve public meetings and by the work of many committees who have freely given of their time and attention to the subject and as a result of this work I herewith submit two maps, one showing the lands and lots in Fairhope and the other showing the lands outside of Fairhope, owned by the Corporation. On each map is marked, in the streets, what are called street units of value, indicating the rental value per year for one foot front by one hundred feet depth and on the farm lands and the unsubdivided lands within the town limits is marked the acre unit values.

The proportionate units were arrived at and determined by the leaseholders after much discussion in some ten or twelve public meetings and many committee meetings in which I think it is safe to say that a majority of leaseholders participated.

These units were first fixed as a proportion or comparative value starting with the most valuable inside lot as 100; then a center lot on each side of every block was marked as a proportion or comparison of the first lot until the markings extended to every block in the town. The same method was adopted for the farm lands, that is, the best or most valuable tract outside the town lines was marked 100 and from this every other tract was marked proportionately. Then, at a general meeting, the units of the outside lands were connected with the inside units by comparing the 100 outside unit with the nearest inside unit and it was decided that a fair comparison would be to call the outside unit 5/6 of the inside unit.

At a general meeting it was determined to fix the gross rent for the year 1914, at $6,500. A calculation was then made and it is found that the street units and acre units, as marked on the maps before referred to, will, after deducting allowances for physical conditions as reported by the committees, produce the following rents:

Division 1	77 leases	$2,172.45
Division 2	68 leases	1,551.28
Division 3	17 leases	293.72
Division 4	75 leases	1,224.88
Total Town	237 leases	$5,242.33
Farm Lands	69 leases	1,258.74
Grand Total	306 leases	$6,501.07

The units as marked on the map and which are the basis for the rent of $6,500 are exactly the same relative proportions of each other as the original units recommended by the committees and adopted by the general meeting above referred to.

As a part of this report and a record of the work, there is submitted what is called a calculating card for each lease holding, on which is shown a description of the land, the proportionate unit from which the rent is calculated and the process of calculation. There is also a report of a committee as to the deductions for physical conditions. These records are arranged in envelopes, one envelope for each block of the different divisions, and the farm lands are arranged in the same manner by sections.

The street units marked on the map indicate the rent per year in cents for one foot front by one hundred feet deep. The units marked in white circles on the farm lands indicate the rent in dollars per year per acre.

The adoption of the Somers System for the relative appraisement of colony lands marked one of the periods when the lessees generally were in closest accord with the colony. In point of fact the lessees in this first application of the system played the major role, both in the determination of relative values, and in the adoption of one of the few formal expenditure budgets ever used by the colony. The use of such a budget was essential in this first application of the new system because Mr. Somers could not possibly measure the absolute economic rent from colony lands. His system, and competing systems, can only arrive at values of specific sites in terms of the "one hundred per cent" location and other measurable factors.

For two reasons the Somers System did not put an end to the problem of fixing annual rentals. First, it scarcely would be practicable for the lessees generally to busy themselves with so many meetings every year in determining relative values. The element of judgment as to *changes in relative values* remains a responsibility of the colony appraisement committee. Second, the underlying principle upon which the colony land system is based contemplates taking all of the economic rent each year. Any expenditure budget approved either by lessees, or by members only, would not necessarily be such as to equal the total economic rent. The colony appraising officials, therefore, cannot escape responsibility for exercising judgment on this point.

Thus, a change in the amount of rents annually assessed on colony lands is a function of three variables: (1) the algebraic sum of increases in some street unit values and decreases in other street unit values; (2) changes in the level of the general demand for colony lands; and (3) the amount of colony land actually under lease. For these reasons it would be impractical to present a detailed history of the changes in the *rate of increase of the level of colony rents*. Such an undertaking would necessitate using street value maps for each year in which any change was made in the frontage value of any street as well as a tabulation of changes in the "multiplier," *i.e.,* the across-the-board or general variable which presumably changes in proportion to changes in the general demand for colony land. Scarcely a year passes without some changes in street values—mostly upward. Changes in the multiplier in either direction have been much less frequent; in a rapidly growing community this may indicate a deliberate policy adopted for reasons of public relations, or it may indicate that the appraising authorities do not possess either the data or the understanding to keep the general level of colony rents moving precisely with changes in the general level of demand.

It may be significant that since 1914 the colony has not seen fit to seek out general lessee opinion on relative street values. Nor has it sought the assistance of any experienced appraiser or appraisal company in checking the relative street values as they now exist forty years after the lessees, in co-operation with W. A. Somers, first fixed them. Conceivably this could signify several things including one or more of the following: that rents in general are too low; that lessees trust implicitly either in the judgment of colony officials or in a system that is "mathematically sound" (given the data on the relevant variables); that lessees simply are indifferent to their rents or are careless in failing to make inquiries; that colony officials are confident that the values they have set are sound ones; or that colony officials simply prefer "to let sleeping dogs lie."

On balance it is evident that the introduction of the Somers System had the effect of reducing, if not wholly eliminating, one of the perennial sources of friction between colony and lessees. Without question the lessees felt that with this system they had attained some degree of authority in the fixing of rents and in colony expenditures. For a period this was substantially the case. Again, on balance, the lessees displayed a sense of responsibility with respect to annual rentals. On more than one occasion they urged the colony to increase rentals in order to finance certain street improvements desired by them.

The system as installed by Mr. Somers remains in effect. With the exception of a few years during the 1930's when the use of the corner influence was suspended in appraising residential lots, the system has been followed essentially as it was introduced. In 1947, however, an improvement was effected in the form of method to spread the total relative value of the corner influence, as determined by Mr. Somers, over two or more leaseholds affected thereby.

$\cdots$
xiii

"ARE YOU A KICKER? THE COLONY LAUGHS AND WILL RAISE YOUR RENT. ACT OR STOP KICKING!" Such was the heading on an invitation sent out by Alexander J. Melville to "kickers" to attend a meeting at Wheeler Hall. Forty of those invited attended the meeting held in December, 1913. The main purpose was to develop community sentiment to "approve and sanction an appeal to the courts, to dissolve the Fairhope Single Tax Corporation and define the rights of the lessees." Only ten "accredited" votes were cast and three of these were in the negative. Of the seven voting approval of an appeal to the courts only two were singletaxers (Melville, a member, and Wolf, a non-member); five were socialists.

The preamble and resolution presented to the meeting follows:

WHEREAS: The "Colony Plan" in operation at Fairhope in no manner illustrates the working of the single tax but repels converts and delays its popular acceptance.

Through the mismanagement of the Corporation and its failure as trustee to administer the Trust in the manner designated by the lease contracts, the situation of the lessees has become intolerable.

The rent fund, created by the lessees, has been expended in violation of the leases—for salaries and expenses of officials, for taxes on unleased land and for costs of administration not authorized by the leases and not for the exclusive benefit of the lessees.

There does not exist the democratic equality and cooperation between the members and their associates, the lessees, contemplated by the constitution and the charter. The lessees are denied voice and power in fixing of rents and expenditures.

The Corporation has abandoned its agreement to base rent upon land values, and has substituted therefor in practice the wholly new and unauthorized principle of making the Rent Fund equal to the expenditures which it alone determines.

This violent change in the basis of rent has removed the only protection enjoyed by the lessees against exorbitant rents and its continuance threatens to confiscate their properties.

Fairhope possesses two conflicting forms of government, one organized under the Municipal Code of Alabama and the other the Fairhope Single Tax Corporation, which constantly advocates and attempts the control of the town government. Hence we suffer under one of the most objectionable features of landlordism, interference with the rights of citizens and the growth and development of their town. By the single tax Henry George sought to destroy this pernicious phase of landlordism, while in Fairhope it has become paramount.

Every protest against these usurpations has been disregarded by the Corporation and all attempts to secure redress through constitutional means have been defeated. Repeated trials have demonstrated that it is impossible to amend that instrument.

Therefore BE IT RESOLVED that: As a last resort we approve and sanction an appeal to the courts to dissolve the corporation and define the rights of lessees. This appears to be the only means to correct the evils under which we suffer, prevent the impending confiscation of our property and compel the restoration of monies which have been illegally collected from us and expended without our consent by the Fairhope Single Tax Corporation. (Fairhope *Courier,* December 19, 1913.)

Mr. Melville, who offered the above resolution, joined the corporation in 1909 on a membership certificate he purchased for $70. In 1912, he was elected trustee but resigned from this office in August, 1913. Some of his previous proposals and judgments had been quite acceptable to the Fairhope "old guard." For example, he had opposed a proposition made by certain members to amend the constitution in order to discontinue the payment of taxes on improvements and personal property owned by the lessees, and instead to use the proceeds from rents for streets and other similar purposes. He also was on record as having opposed a recommendation to limit tax refunds to any lessee to the amount of rent paid by that lessee. (Fairhope *Courier,* May 22, 1914.)

On the other hand, Mr. Melville's resolution offered at the annual meeting of February 5, 1913, was not appreciated by many members. This resolution was one of approval for a rider to be prepared and attached to leases providing that rents be calculated at five per cent of the capital value of land. The suggested rider also provided that capital value would be determined by arbitration under certain circumstances. The meeting adopted a motion to put this suggestion in print for circulation among the members. (Minutes.)

In discussing Melville's activities in 1913 and 1914, Gaston characterized his principal thesis as one of "more democracy" for the lessees, and acknowledged that several members agreed with him (Melville) in part. This judgment is borne out by the content of constitutional changes subsequently proposed by Melville.

On April 2, 1913, the members met in special meeting to discuss some amendments to the constitution which were suggested by Melville. In particular, he urged changes designed: to provide for equal participation of lessees with members in determining annual rentals, and in the spending of the rental income; to abolish the privilege of husband and wife voting on one membership; to make the constitution amendable by a three-fourths affirmative vote of resident members; and to commit lessees to pay sufficient rents to meet taxes and other charges for services provided for in the leases. These proposals were generally discussed to the end that the membership unanimously approved a motion made by Gaston that the sense of the meeting was "that the constitution should be made amendable by an affirmative vote of three-fourths of those voting on the issue." None of Mr. Melville's other proposals received sufficient support to warrant submitting them to a referendum of the members.

A referendum on the question of so changing the amendment

provision of the constitution was held on June 6, 1913. Although the vote was sixty-six for to eighteen against, the amendment failed because with one hundred fourteen voting members it was necessary to have eighty-six affirmative votes. Parenthetically, it may be noted that this "gateway" amendment succeeded of adoption almost twenty years later.

Mr. Melville and Mr. A. J. Wolf circulated a petition among the members for a July 15 referendum on an entire revision of the constitution. To further their objective they established a paper called the *Monitor*. The proposed revision contained many changes but the more interesting related to membership, jurisdiction, and land. Under the proposed constitution any individual over eighteen with $100 could become a member *without the express approval of the executive council,* provided that upon petition of ten per cent of the membership filed within thirty days after application for membership, the applicant might be voted on by the entire membership. The proposed membership article did not contain any provision for subsequent expulsion of a member.

The proposed constitution would separate governmental jurisdiction into two bodies: "The Corporation," which would have jurisdiction "over all purely corporate affairs;" and "The Community," the jurisdiction of which would extend "to all matters relating to the administration of purely community affairs and shall include determining, fixing and collecting all rents . . . and such other income as the land and other property of the Corporation shall yield, the disposition of all revenue and the management of public utilities." Resident members would have supreme authority in *corporate* affairs; resident members and all lessees who had signed and agreed to support the constitution would exercise supreme authority in *community* affairs.

Somewhat surprising, however, in view of allegations subsequently made by Melville, was the provision under the article dealing with the leasing of land, namely: "But in no case shall the total rent be less than a sum sufficient to pay the taxes on all the land of the Corporation, leased or held for lease, and on the public utilities maintained by the Community, together with all taxes on the property of the lessees for which it is obligated, and such reasonable sums as may be needed for the protection of the Corporation's land and its title thereto, the exercise of its right of eminent domain, the payment of salaries to officers and deficits in the cost of operating public utilities."

The vote on the revised constitution was: for, 22; against, 38; defective, 1; number entitled to vote, 112. This vote apparently convinced Mr. Melville of the futility of attempting to alter colony actions by amending the constitution. Despite the clear failure of the proposed general revision, the twenty-two affirmative votes must have been interpreted by him as indicative of a comparatively large dissident element among the members who might be willing to see the single tax corporation dissolved. At any rate he organized the "kickers meeting," after which, despite his discouragement with the negative results from this meeting, he proceeded with his plans for a court test of the legality of the Fairhope Single Tax Corporation.

In May, 1914, Melville filed his bill of complaint in the Chancery Court at Mobile. He asked that the Fairhope Single Tax Corporation be dissolved. Melville's "Bill" contained the following points:

The complainant was both a member and a lessee. The legal history, charter, constitution, leases and landholdings of the corporation were recited. At the time of the suit the corporation owned four thousand acres, "mostly donated," with only about one-third under lease, the remainder "vacant, unimproved and unproductive." Melville alleged that rentals had been increased from year to year "as its necessities for money have increased until now all rentals are many times what they were in the beginning." He complained that: "These increases are out of all proportion to any increase in the value of the land, or to the value of the use thereof and have been made openly for the purpose of raising the amount necessary to pay the company's obligations and without regard to actual rental value." According to him, the corporation was charging all of its tenants far in excess of the true value of the use of the land.

Melville complained particularly against the operation of the corporation's "flimsy telephone system" which served only a few lessees. He characterized the water system as primitive and in bad repair. He complained that the corporation ". . . pays from its general revenues the taxes upon all of its lands and also all property taxes of its lessees . . . and in so doing claims to be following and demonstrating the single tax theory, notwithstanding the patent *absurdity* of such claims."[1] (Emphasis supplied.) Since much of the land is located in the Town of Fairhope, the Single Tax Corporation pays all municipal taxes and assessments for improvements out of the general fund. In addition to these tax payments, Melville complained of other colony expenditures. The highway work he thought of little value and he questioned the payment of $161.50 for the organic school which ". . . is of no value, to any one except those who wish to delve into unapplied theories of government."

In an over-all evaluation of the activities of the Fairhope Single Tax Corporation, he concluded:

There is not, and never has been, in the said company's activities any application of the single tax theory, or of any principles of co-operation having substantial effect or benefit, or of any economic principles resulting in any good to those concerned. On the contrary, the net result of the said activities has been to cause those who do not use telephones to aid those who do use them . . . to cause those who do not live in the Town of Fairhope to share much of the public burden of those who do live therein.

Melville contended that the corporation had always failed and must continue to fail to carry out any of the purposes for which it was organized. He stressed that the term single tax means . . . "taxation under which all of the expenses of government are to be borne by the land and all other forms of taxation forbidden." He stated that any attempt to apply this theory ". . . in this jurisdiction . . . [is] not only impossible of accomplishment, but absurd." Most surprising, in view of his

---

[1] Mr. Melville, his attorney, and many others who have contended against the Fairhope colony, were prone to make their cases in part by a rather extensive use of the terms "absurd" and "ridiculous."

earlier views, was his objection to the practice of the corporation paying taxes on all lands and taxes on lessees' improvements out of corporate funds raised from land rentals only.

Melville actually resorted to the hoary "mansion and hovel illustration" in his Bill of Complaint. His version of this widespread objection to the single tax was not uncommon. He asked the court to picture two adjoining lots rented at the same price. On one lot was a hovel and on the other a mansion. On the first lot total taxes would be a fraction of the rent; on the second lot taxes would be many times the rent. Therefore, the occupant of the mansion will have all taxes paid on his carriages, autos, pianos, silverware, etc. In Fairhope, therefore, the system is an actual application of the principle: "Unto every one that hath shall be given, but from him that hath not shall be taken away even that which he hath."

Melville further contended against the practice of refunding property taxes paid by the tenants on practical grounds. He asserted that rents were thereby raised to excessive levels, and that the practice had forced the corporation to discourage the location in Fairhope of factories and great mercantile establishments. He contended that as a result of this, improvements simply had to be discouraged. He questioned the "non-profit" character of the colony asserting that ultimately the members must benefit from the acquisition of the valuable landed estate ". . . for there is no one else to take the same when the inevitable dissolution comes." He visualized that profits would be increased to the extent to which improvements would be acquired by the colony when tenants would abandon their leases because of excessive rents. He asserted that tenants cannot establish credit and are therefore deprived of a chance to finance by mortgages because the improvements were on leased land. Therefore, he contended, progress was retarded.

Melville concluded his bill of complaint by asserting that lessees simply could not be the recipients of any benefits under the Fairhope plan because ". . . they are nothing more nor less than the tenants of a private landlord, with no hope for independent ownership and no assurance against oppressive demands . . ." He saw no future for the tenants other than increasingly burdensome rents. In his view the colony expenses and rentals must increase rapidly but the actual use value of the ground will increase slowly ". . . because in the locality under consideration there are hundreds of thousands of acres of unoccupied lands altogether as good as those owned by the corporation and affording a supply which will not be exhausted for many generations to come."

Melville sought a definitive relief—*dissolution* of the corporation. This, he contended, would not be unfair either to nonmember tenants or to members. Lessees could obtain title to the land they occupied by paying actual value of the land exclusive of improvements. Members, who at most had paid $100 membership fee, would receive many times this amount upon dissolution.

Melville characterized himself as "an earnest advocate of the single tax," but reiterated that he thought it impossible to demonstrate the single tax under the laws of Alabama.

The brief filed by Melville's attorney (Thomas M. Stevens, of Stevens, McCorvey and McCloud, Mobile) elaborated upon the contentions in the Bill of Complaint. The two alternative theories presented were:

1. That the statute authorizing the formation of corporations for an application of the single tax theory is unconstitutional. That any organization attempted thereunder is but a partnership, therefore should be dissolved upon the death of a member (*i.e.*, Joseph Fels).

2. If, alternately, the Court finds the Single Tax Corporation to be a corporation, it should be dissolved because it is legally impossible for it to accomplish in this jurisdiction the one purpose of its organization.

In support of the first contention counsel for the complainant offered a highly technical argument. Counsel argued that "the only possible purpose of the absurd statute" is to authorize the organization of corporations with the power "to radically and fundamentally change the existing tax laws (of Alabama) but also to abolish the existing system of federal taxation."

Counsel stressed the *literal interpretation* of the *purpose* of the Fairhope Single Tax Corporation as stated in the Declaration of Incorporation: "The purpose of said corporation is to demonstrate the beneficiency, utility and practicability of the single tax theory with the hope of its general adoption by the Governments of the future." Counsel interpreted this to mean the application of the single tax which it contended would be altogether "ridiculous" because: "To apply the theory [of the single tax] necessarily involved the abolition of all federal taxation and all state and municipal taxation, except the ad valorem tax on land . . ." In addition to finding such a statute "absurd and ridiculous," counsel argued that it conflicts with "a settled constitutional policy, both federal and state . . . to obtain revenues for . . . governmental purposes from sundry established methods of taxation, besides the taxation of real estate, and any statute which is offensive to a purpose and policy so declared and established is violative of a necessary constitutional implication and is void." Further: "Under our institutions, there can be no such thing as a corporation existing for the sole purpose of demonstrating, or even teaching, that the established constitutional policy, federal or state, is wrong and should be abandoned."

The "established law" underlying the alternative theory as understood by Melville's counsel is: ". . . where a corporation has failed of the purpose and objects of its creation a single stockholder may maintain a bill in equity for the dissolution of such corporation and a distribution of its assets." Therefore, since the one purpose of the Fairhope Single Tax Corporation was to demonstrate the single tax theory, it should be dissolved because: ". . . if an application in any degree or to any extent of single tax principles be legally impossible in this jurisdiction, it must follow that the said organization has never attained and never can hope to attain the one purpose set forth in its declaration of incorporation." Mr. Stevens asserted that the practice of returning part of the rental by paying taxes of the tenants as an application of single tax theory was *"wholly absurd."* Indeed: "If all of the rents should be returned to the tenants, or be spent for their use and benefit, there would still be nothing in the situation touching or relating to any matter or question of taxation, but only a donation by a land owner, of the use of his land—a mere private transaction in no wise resembling or relating to an exercise of the public or governmental function of taxation in any form."

The burden of the argument of the counsel for the complainant seems to have been that no method of demonstrating the beneficiency of the single tax theory is possible, or at least legally admissable, short of a literal or actual experiment by a government exercising the sovereign power of taxation.

The Fairhope Single Tax Corporation was represented by James H. Webb, of Webb & McAlpine, Mobile, and H. F. Ring, of Houston, Texas, as associate counsel. They offered twenty-two demurrers to the complaint but the Chancellor overruled all of them. Appeal was then taken to the Supreme Court of Alabama.

This ruling of the Mobile Chancery Court stirred many singletaxers to action. Many prominent single tax lawyers volunteered their services, among them: Judge A. B. Pittman, Alex Y. Scott, Bolton Smith and Robert S. Keebler, of Memphis, who joined in filing a brief as friends of the court. Fiske Warren of Boston brought with him William H. Dunbar, a law partner of Louis D. Brandeis. Mr. Dunbar acted as consultant and also filed a brief. The Joseph Fels Estate employed G. L. and H. T. Smith, of Mobile, to appear in both oral and written argument.

Before reviewing the decision of the Alabama Supreme Court, brief note will be taken of the reactions of the officers and members of the single tax corporation to the suit. Apparently they did not take the threat of the suit seriously at first, nor, when the complaint actually was filed, did it appear that officials of the colony were worried. It was more that they were chagrined that a fellow member should bring such an action. E. B. Gaston, secretary of the colony and editor of the *Courier,* wrote in the May 22, 1914, issue: ". . . a lawyer will hardly be necessary to convince a court that a private corporation, abso-

lutely without governmental powers, acting under a charter
from the state conferring upon it . . . the power which it exer-
cises, which is simply that of administering the land to which
it holds undisputed title, according to contracts voluntarily
entered into by and with individuals, providing for the payment of all taxes levied by the civil authorities and otherwise
complying with all of the laws of the state is not an illegal body
and should not be dissolved."

As editor Gaston saw it, the colony plan was sound in principle and successful in operation; the vital issue, therefore, *was
the single tax itself.* He declared that the dominant motive
behind the suit was hostility to the single tax. To Gaston, the
complaint inferentially denied that the colony fulfilled the
condition indispensable to the single tax of abolishing all other
forms of taxation. The vital issue, according to the *Courier,*
was whether the single tax, if applied by law, would reduce the
public revenue by approximately the amount now received
from sources other than land value taxation. If it would not
(as singletaxers maintain), the results would be the same as
those acomplished under the Fairhope plan. In either case the
total taxes would be the same (or even larger) and the "man-
sion-hovel" situation would necessarily prevail, but in either
case, a "first and most important truth" would be implemented,
namely: "All men are equally entitled to the use of the earth."
Taking the full rental value would eliminate land speculation,
it would discourage the non-use or the under-use of land.
Gaston argued that the colony had kept land under its control
open upon equal terms to all. "The corporation's land has been
offered to whomsoever would take it, without purchase price
and under pledge that the annual rental value, necessarily
taken to preserve equity, would all be expended for the benefit
of those paying it."

As would be expected, the *Courier* categorically denied many
of the allegations made by Melville: the colony had benefited
the lessees in many ways, through liberal reservations for parks,
sites for schools and wide streets. Dwellings had been built
from resources which would otherwise have been required to

pay for sites. All of this, and more, had been accomplished without permitting any individual to profit without labor from the growth of the community, and without encouraging any person to withhold land needed for use. Nor had the system retarded progress and created stagnation because "Fairhope has notoriously outgrown every other settlement on the eastern shore." Mr. Gaston denied that rentals were unreasonable and pointed out that for the last three years they had been fixed by the tenants themselves. Only one tenant in years had been dispossessed for non-payment of rents and this one was holding at least five times as much land as he was actually using.

As for the charge that the colony had a policy of deliberately discouraging improvements and especially the location of factories or large mercantile establishments, the *Courier* stated: "Experience of nearly twenty years has demonstrated that no one will put up great factories or mercantile establishments, until the population and facilities reach a state to make such enterprises profitable and when that point is reached, the land value will have risen to easily take care of the taxes on such enterprises."

Finally, as to the allegation by Melville that the rents were fixed in response to revenue needs, the *Courier* stated: the corporation has always insisted that, as provided in the leases, the rents should be the real rental value. Where any consideration has been given to the needs of the corporation in connection with fixing rentals, it has only been by way of convincing lessees that proposed rentals were not unjust because necessary "to meet payments which the corporation was paying for them, which, if they themselves were the owners of the land they would have to pay for themselves; such as taxes upon the land, etc." In regard to taxes which the corporation had to pay on its unimproved and unleased land—payments objected to by the complainant—". . . the records show that, taking one year with another, such taxes have not been paid from rent funds, but from the income derived from such land." Other relevant considerations in this connection were that the unleased lands included the parks which were freely available to the public, and the fact that the business of the corporation required a reasonable reserve of unoccupied lands.

Upon appeal, the Supreme Court of Alabama sustained the legality of the Fairhope Single Tax Corporation.

The court readily conceded "that any legislative attempt to apply or to enforce the 'Single Tax System' would be absolutely void under the Constitution of Alabama." After discussing the Henry George Single Tax, the court declared that the enactment of 1903 ". . . does not contemplate or attempt the application or enforcement of a Single Tax System. It does not effect a change in any degree of tax systems or tax provisions . . . The taxable property of an incorporation created by that authority and all property taxable as that of individuals, who are members or lessees of the corporation, are subject to the same system of taxation, as far as the government is concerned, that any other property is subject to in this State. So, the enactment affords no possible basis for a conclusion that it is invalid in consequence of an effort to actually institute a tax method or system offensive to constitutional provisions, Federal or State." What, however, of the question put as follows: ". . . is an enactment offensive to the constitution which authorizes the creation of a corporation to apply—as between individuals and the corporation and without denial or violation of, or infringement upon, any governmental rule or mandate—principles of taxation that if attempted to be translated into a rule of or mandate for governmental actions would offend the organic laws?"

The court answered this question clearly and emphatically in the negative. It rejected any notion that the fundamental laws are immutable. "Freedom of Speech, the Right of Assembly and Petition, and the orderly processes designed to effect the revision or amendment of the constitutions are among the provisions . . . emphasizing the idea that these fundamental instruments were not established as the immutable expressions of supreme law. So it is trite to say: the right to change necessarily presupposes and recognizes the even higher right, to be ever lawfully exercised, of the governed, or of any part of the governed, to convene, to discuss, to consider, and to experiment—

without offending or violating established law or personal or property right. . . . So the organic laws cannot be regarded as condemning or restraining, or inviting the restraint or condemnation of individual conception, propaganda, or the illustration or demonstration of ideas which offend no valid prohibitive or regulatory laws, or invade or violate no personal or property right of another. Except as forbidden or restrained by organic law particularly applicable to the artificial entities called corporations, it would seem to be the assertion of a selfevident truth to say: that which an individual may lawfully do with or about his own possessions a corporation may be created and authorized by law to do with its own possessions."

Although not necessary to its argument the court remarked upon a marked kinship between the Single Tax system as proposed by Henry George and what the Fairhope Single Tax Corporation appeared to be doing. The court expressed the common principle as follows: ". . . the corporation, though owning the land, holds it as if the land was the common property of the lessees; exacts annual individual rentals upon this basis, and as before described, pays from the common fund the taxes laid by existing tax laws upon the lands and the property of the tenants; and devotes the remainder to the common benefit of the lessees."

Having decided that the Fairhope Single Tax Corporation is a corporation *de jure,* the court turned to the alternate theory that the corporation should be dissolved because it "has failed and must fail of its purpose. . . . " With respect to this theory it held that ". . . it cannot be affirmed or denied that the stated purpose is impossible of approximate attainment. . . ." Whether a demonstration or illustration following the exercise of lawful powers "has been, is or will be successful" in proving certain economic principles, ". . . is purely a matter of deduction from a premise of fact. . . ." One individual might conclude that the exercise of the powers ". . . would conduce to no possible demonstration or illustration of the principles. . . ." Another individual might conclude ". . . with equal certainty of immunity from having his conclusion refuted that the lawful exercise of the lawful powers conferred had already made a real object lesson confirmatory of the soundness and practicability of the theories predicated on the principles sought to be illustrated. . . . There is no standard—nor can there be—by which the justification or correctness of these opposite deductions may be determined." It is evident, therefore, ". . . that the court cannot register a judgment that the *purpose* in authorizing the incorporation has or will fail any more than it can register a judgment that the *purpose* in authorizing the incorporation has or will succeed."

Finally, the court justified the payment of taxes on unleased lands and concluded that the righting of any alleged wrongs, such as confiscatory rentals or unwise use of corporation revenues, first must be sought within the organization—that the power of the court cannot be invoked except upon a showing of futility of appeal to the corporate authorities.

In view of the outcome of the Melville suit many members of the colony felt that the suit was one of the better things that had happened. The consensus was that the publicity was altogether good and that much benefit derived from the opportunity presented to the colony singletaxers to rally against a common foe. One immediate result was the receipt of an application for membership, the first in several years, the applicant saying that his principal motivation was a desire to help the colony. (Fairhope *Courier,* January 8, 1915.)

With its legality firmly established the colony was free to work out its manifold problems in moving toward maturity. As the people of the town of Fairhope came to look more and more to the municipality for the satisfaction of their public needs, the colony gradually turned its attention to perfecting the functioning of its underlying single tax or land tenure policies. Its immediate problems in this area were the perfecting of the Somers System of land appraisal and the financing of public improvements to streets, including curbs, gutters and sidewalks. Although the next decade was not to be completely uneventful, the colony experienced no serious crisis necessitating a change in policy until the somewhat even tenure of its ways was interrupted by that madness known as "The Florida Land Boom."

xiv

ATTEMPTS TO NEUTRALIZE THE EFFECTS OF THE FLORIDA BOOM

THE decade of the 1920's produced several eras of speculation in farm, urban, suburban and resort lands, in real estate mortgage bonds and in common stocks. Among the more spectacular of these was the Florida land boom which reached its peak in the winter and spring of 1925-1926. It was not until the boom neared its peak that it seriously affected the northern gulf coast region (including the Fairhope area). In the fall of 1925 its effects became noticeable in the vicinity of Fairhope and land "values" rose sharply. Quite understandably the tiny enclave of only four thousand acres could not remain isolated from the effects of a strong general compulsion among those on the outside to acquire and to speculate in land.

This condition posed a dilemma for the officers of the single tax corporation. The "law of supply and demand" operating in the market for Fairhope leaseholds was resulting in the offering of high "bonuses" to lessees for their leaseholds. Probably no reasonable and knowledgeable person would deny that the only basis for such rapidly rising "values" was the premise that the speculative period would continue for an indefinite time. At any rate it was becoming quite common to trade, deal or dabble in Fairhope leaseholds as speculative investments instead of seeking them solely for use. This condition threatened to undermine the basic justifications for the existence of the Fairhope colony. Speculation in leaseholds would necessarily lead either to the non-use or the under-use of colony lands; it would cause those using such lands to pay more than could be justified for current use; and it would divert unnecessarily large payments from the users of land to individual pocketbooks.

No Simple Solutions

It appeared to the officers and members of the colony that there could be no wholly satisfactory solution to this situation. If left unchecked, speculation in leaseholds would destroy the Fairhope plan, because it would be made clear to all that an enclave simply could not demonstrate the benefits flowing from an absence of land speculation. Increasing colony rentals sharply, so as to absorb all of the speculative values, necessarily would have imposed extreme hardships on many lessees who were employing their leased lands to normal usage, and who had little or no intention of realizing an unearned increment by transferring their leaseholds. Warnings, appeals to reason or programs designed to inform present and prospective lessees of the true nature of the Fairhope plan, and of the likelihood that speculation in such leaseholds would prove abortive, appeared to offer little promise. At best too many people are slow to learn and to apply reason to their decisions, and anyone who has experienced a boom will understand that virtually all resolutions to follow the dictates of reason tend to disappear. Any person touched by the fever to speculate has a most difficult time maintaining contact with reality. There was no way to immunize the people of Fairhope against such a fever, and there is ample evidence that several members, as well as non-member lessees and professional real estate operators, ran rather high temperatures, and steadfastly resisted all warnings and appeals made either to their reason or to their sense of justice. Finally, any program designed to tighten or to narrow the selectivity of lessees, or to recapture illicit bonuses through penalties, would have obvious dangers and unpleasant connotations. Any program which would narrow the market for Fairhope leaseholds would be prejudicial to the tenant who, in good

faith, wanted to sell only his improvements. More fundamentally, such a program would hamper attainment of the
objective to maintain the freest possible access to Fairhope
lands.

The entire situation was an unhappy one for the colony
faithful, but they foresaw the danger and made sincere efforts
to ensure the survival of their demonstration.

COLONY WARNING TO PROSPECTIVE LESSEES

The Fairhope *Courier* sounded an alert a full year before the
speculative fever hit Fairhope with its greatest intensity. In the
November 28, 1924, issue, there appeared a lead article headed:
"DON'T PAY 'BONUS' FOR LEASEHOLDS."

We take occasion to do, as we have done before, to warn people
against paying more for property on Colony land than the improvements are worth. Do not pay anything for "location," because you
are supposed to pay the full value of location in the rent you pay
to the Colony. If the rent does not now take the location value it
may be adjusted when rents are considered again, to do so. And the
fact that you pay a "bonus" for location, will leak out and be taken
as proof that the rent is too low and it will be raised.

Need for revenue is secondary in determining rents. The main
thing is to keep people from getting wealth without earning it.

The Colony might be agreeable to keeping rents down and running its affairs on the most economical basis possible, but if confronted with facts indicating that advantage was being taken of its
low rents to collect "bonuses" from others would be practically
compelled, in duty to its principle and lease contracts to advance
rents.   In this sense bonus collectors may be seen as enemies of
lessees generally, tending to cause raises in rents of all.

No great point was made of this problem, either by Fairhope
leaders or by the *Courier,* until almost a year later when the
situation threatened to get out of hand. Writing in the *Courier,*
on November 13, 1925, Gaston expressed some personal observations. He questioned whether, in view of the Florida
boom, the methods which had been sufficient, and which would
continue to be sufficient under normal conditions, would be
adequate to meet these abnormal conditions. Might it not be
necessary to adopt new methods to meet the new conditions?

Changes in the Land Application Form

Mr. Gaston, for one, did not want Fairhope to become a boom town; ". . . but are we justified in assuming that it is possible for us, with an infinitesimal bit of land in a world administered on the contrary plan and with people flowing into our community from the world filled with all the desire to get 'something for nothing' by land speculation, as they see being done elsewhere, to depend wholly upon raising rentals, to protect us from being overwhelmed by the land speculative wave?" He concluded that the only recourse open—namely the annual rent appraisal—would be both ineffective and unfair. A speculative demand for land, not for use but for resale, would tend to push land values far beyond any productive use of which it was capable. Accordingly, the *Courier* suggested a change in the "Application for Land" and the incorporation of the change in the lease. "Let those who are wedded to land speculation, go to others who cherish the same idea for their land and not expect us who are organized to destroy the institution to furnish them land free of purchase price for the purpose."

The application for land in use from November, 1905, was a short, simple document. In addition to describing the land sought, the applicant declared his understanding of the colony plan of taking the full annual use value in rent and the uses to be made thereof. The applicant pledged himself not to oppose the full application of the principles set forth in the application and contracted in the lease.

At the meeting of December 7, 1925, the executive council recommended a general ten per cent increase in town rents. Th council decided against an exclusive reliance upon raises in rents to check the current speculation because this would "penalize those who are holding land for use only." Other measures would be taken to combat the violation of the principles of the colony and its lease contracts.

High among these other measures was the adoption of a new application for land. In signing the new form the applicant asserted that he understood the purpose of the colony to be to prevent anyone from profiting from holding its land, other than through bona fide use. He agreed that he would "neither ask nor accept anything from another person for the transfer of the same in unimproved condition, nor an excessive price, out of any fair relation to the value of the improvements for its transfer if improved." He agreed that the corporation might forfeit his lease if he violated the agreement with respect to unimproved leaseholds, and that the corporation might refuse to approve a transfer of an improved leasehold if the consideration was excessive. In the event a transfer was effected for an excessive consideration without the knowledge of the corporation, the corporation would have a right of action against him for recovery of the excess. The amount recovered would go into the corporation's land fund.

The application, adopted December 7, 1925, was in use for only fourteen days. The feeling was widespread that this form was much too drastic; that the colony should devise another means of preventing speculation rather than exercising its right of action after transfers involving excessive considerations were concluded.

Still a third application for land was adopted December 21, 1925, a form which remains in effect to this day. (See Appendix C.) The last application stresses the two factors of value making up an improved leasehold: "improvements" which belong to the lessee, and "land" which belongs to the corporation. The application clarifies the meaning of improvements. These include anything of value which results from the efforts of lessees or from lessees' initiative or expenditures ". . . such as the good will of a going business, the exercise of taste in planning improvements or the making of grounds attractive, or the element of time and care in growing an orchard or shade trees or making land more productive by improved methods of farming, or increment of value due to increasing cost of building . . ." as well as all buildings.

The two revised applications for land both stipulated that the provisions contained in the applications became as much a part of the lease contract as though they were printed therein.

Further, both recently revised applications provided that any attempt to obtain a bonus for the transfer of unimproved lease-holds would be sufficient cause for forfeiture of the lease. With respect to bonuses asked or received for improved leaseholds, the two applications differ substantially. The short-lived form adopted December 7 contained a "right of action" against the lessee to be exercised within six months of approval of the transfer by the executive council, "for the recovery of the excess charged above a fair valuation. . . ." The form approved on December 21, and still in effect, sought to prevent any bonus before the transfer was authorized. Under it the applicant for colony land agrees to "advise the Corporation, before a transfer of an improved leasehold shall be effective, of the exact consideration for the transaction and that the Corporation, if it believes the consideration to include in fact a profit for the transfer of the land which belongs to it, shall be entitled to examine me and the prospective purchaser as to the elements of value in the consideration and if satisfied that the consideration is in part for the possession of the land above the value of the improvements, may refuse approval of the transfer. . . ."

This revised application aroused strenuous opposition from many in Fairhope, including several colony members. Some of the members opposed the revision on principle—or at least they so asserted. Some, however, merely desired to share in the material rewards of those successful in speculation. It was not that they approved of speculation *per se*—it was more that temptation was omnipresent and, for many, omnipotent.

Opposition to Revised Application

The opposition took two main forms. First, many members more or less constantly agitated against the new application in membership meetings and caused at least one referendum on the issue of its discontinuance. Second, some of the professional real estate operators colluded with leaseholders, and with would-be investors in colony lands, to circumvent the enforcement of the new provisions. This latter manifestation of opposition may be treated briefly. The following sketch is based

on copies of letters exchanged among real estate men, individual "investors" in colony lands who believed they had been
defrauded, and the secretary of the Fairhope Single Tax Corporation.

In response to a letter from an outraged client who had paid
what he considered to be an excessive price for improvements
on a colony leasehold, and who subsequently "discovered" that
colony land could not be "sold," the real estate agent replied
in part:

Yes, I made a good profit on the property I sold you—I would not
have sold it to you otherwise, *and you bought the property in order
to make a profit yourself and for no other reason.*

You knew at the time of your purchase that the Colony objected
to property being sold at a profit in Fairhope—that they have tried
to stop it since the beginning. I explained to you several times that
people who deal in Single Tax property *simply took an assignment
of the leaseholds and ignored the Colony.* This is done by most of
the people who dabble in Colony lands. For instance, the
_____has been owned for the past fourteen years by the
present owner and still the lease has never been assigned and not
as yet run through the Colony. I am holding several pieces of
property under the same condition and for the same reason. To
run a lease through the Colony at this time means that you have
to accept one of their new forms of leases and agree not to sell at a
profit, *and this people are unwilling to do.* This is common
knowledge and any business man here will tell you the same. I took
the assignment from_____on the property and hold the
lease in that condition and gave you a contract calling for the
assignment of the lease when you have completed the payment
called for, ... This property is in the name of. . . . . .on the
books of the Colony *but is very much in my name on the lease* and
this procedure has been advised by very good attorneys and followed
for several years in many cases . . . . (E. B. Gaston files.)

The leasehold referred to in the above communication apparently was one having a small improvement. It appears that
·the agent had purchased the improvement for $575 and had
taken an assignment of the lease. He sold it to the subject client
for $1,800. The purchaser had paid about $1,200 but balked at
paying the remaining $600. Unwilling to sue the agent for
misrepresentation, he sold back the property and leasehold

assignment for $700. Files of correspondence in the offices of the colony disclose many instances where "purchasers" of colony leaseholds, or the improvements thereon, subsequently complained to the Fairhope Single Tax Corporation. In response to such communications the secretary usually wrote a letter of condolence, attempted to lighten the load of misery by recounting other and more horrendous instances of allegedly "fraudulent" behavior on the part of agents, and concluded by stating: "The Colony has made every effort to acquaint people with its policy and feels no responsibility for Mr. _____'s representations, though greatly regretting the loss to you or any one else by the same."

HIGHWAY WARNING SIGNS

In asserting that the colony attempted to inform the public of its policy the secretary was eminently correct. One of the devices used was to post signs or billboards on all highways leading into Fairhope. These read: "WARNING: DON'T BUY ANY COLONY LEASEHOLDS UNTIL YOU CONSULT WITH THE SECRETARY." This effort was not appreciated by many in Fairhope. Writing in the *Baldwin County News* of Robertsdale, on August 1, 1929, R. F. Powell asserted that these signs were the equivalent of calling all lessees crooks and that all non-colony associations in Fairhope had asked that the signs be removed.[1]

Mr. Powell's statement that the colony in erecting these signs was implying that all lessees were crooks, cannot of course be sustained. That many residing within the colony were willing to pocket some unearned increment scarcely can be denied. During the campaign on the June 1, 1929, referendum on the discontinuance of the revised "Application for Land," Mr. Gaston offered a few illustrations of "violations of the Colony's principle that land should be held only for use, and that no one should be required to pay another for the use of land apart from improvements upon it." Among the instances cited, were:

[1] The late Mrs. Anne B. Call told the authors that these signs were discussed a full year before their erection, and that Mr. Gaston at first was opposed to their use.

1. "The collecting of $1,000 many years ago *by a member* for transfer of a vacant lot on the bay front.

2. "The payment or agreement to pay $2,000 for transfer of another bay front lot, from which the dwelling had burned, leaving only improvements of small value.

3. "The 'sale' of three *unimproved* lots, at $100 each, to a visitor." (Fairhope *Courier,* June 3, 1929.)

It would be erroneous to conclude that wholesale evasion through taking assignments of leaseholds, "and ignoring the Colony," wholly emasculated the revised "Application for Land." Numerous as such instances may have been, they amounted to only a small fraction of the total transfers of colony land. Whether the much more general practice of transferring leaseholds "through the colony" was due to the reluctance of most people to resort to subterfuge, or the uncertainty as to the legal position of one holding possession merely through an assignment of a lease, is of small importance in terms of the effectiveness of the new form. The persistence of the attempts over a period of three years to have the new application suspended is excellent evidence that it was effective, when combined with the highway signs and the *Courier's* constant preachments against speculation in colony lands.

ATTEMPTS TO RESTORE OLDER FORM

The last concerted attempt to restore the lease provisions in effect from 1905 to 1925 took place in May-June of 1929. The referendum held on June 1, 1929, sustained the revised application by a vote of forty-nine to thirty-five. Interest in the question among the members was intense, as evidenced by the size of the vote. The ten days prior to the referendum witnessed some of the most determined campaigning that ever took place in Fairhope. To influence the minds of the corporation members, the protagonists issued several documents worthy of brief mention. The chronology runs as follows:

1. A petition was presented to the executive council May 20, 1929, calling for a referendum election not later than June 1 on the following proposition: "Shall the present form of appli-

cation for lease be discontinued and the old form of application which was in use for approximately twenty years, prior to December 1, 1925, be readopted?" Fourteen members signed the petition. (Minutes.)

2. The council called the requested election for June 1, 1929. (Minutes.)

3. On May 24, the secretary formally notified the members of the referendum. The notice also included this paragraph: "You are further notified that President William Call has called a meeting of members for discussion of the question to be voted upon . . . at which time the signers to the petition for the referendum are particularly requested to appear and give their reasons why their proposition should prevail and the attendance of all members is hoped for that the question to be voted on may be understood by all."

4. Minutes of the members meeting, May 28, disclose there were only twenty members in attendance. Mrs. Anne B. Call suggested that, "as there had been one meeting for discussion of a similar proposition, when no one in favor of the proposal appeared to present the reasons for same, that if any favoring was present he, or they, be given first opportunity to be heard." The members adopted this suggestion.

Only one petitioner was present and he was reluctant to discuss the matter, stating that the petitioners thought it already had been thoroughly discussed and the thing now was simply to proceed with the vote. This view did not satisfy the members present (particularly Mrs. Call, a trustee) who pressed him to defend his position. Apparently, this petitioner was reluctant to testify and was content to make a brief general statement to the effect that the dissatisfaction was general; that the old lease had worked very well for twenty years; and that it was neither legal nor proper to change the contracts with lessees without their consent. The petitioner in question then withdrew before discussion developed on these points.

Inferentially, this reluctance of the petitioners to discuss their points in open meeting seemed almost to outrage the officers and members present. In a later personal statement sent to "selected members," Mr. Gaston observed: "The campaign has been a secret one. The proponents have refused all invitations to come out and present their reasons for favoring the change, where their arguments could be analyzed, counter arguments presented and mis-statements of fact, if any, corrected. Such methods are utterly devoid of the real Fairhope spirit, which is one of fairness, of openness, of willingness to 'lay the cards on the table,' a homely phrase, but one which means much."

The withdrawal of the petitioner from the meeting did not stop discussion of the issue among those who remained. In the ensuing discussion several points were made, *e.g.*, the revision made no attempt to change outstanding leases; every lease contained the provision that it was transferable *only to members and to others acceptable to the corporation;* the pledge required of lessees in the old application had proved insufficient to bind them, hence the changes in the new form which applied to new applicants only. The meeting also approved a statement by the secretary and directed that it be printed and a copy sent to every member.

5. In his statement, Gaston emphasized that the present form of application for land was needed to protect both the colony and those lessees who accepted colony policy in good faith. The pledge contained in the old form was signed by "all too many" with no real intention to observe it. The new form helped check the speculative boom in 1926, and "in protecting Fairhope from the evil results of that boom . . . ." Granting that the position of some of the members was that "although it was needed then, the boom has passed and it would be safe to return to the old form," Mr. Gaston said: "Unfortunately, however, the system which leads to land booms still exists and booms will again arise . . . and even Singletaxers pledged to fight the system sometimes prove unable to resist the temptation to take advantage of the same if opportunity is open . . . ." The new form had proved no bar to those "who would be desirable as lessees of a Single Tax Colony." He offered in evidence of this assertion the large number of new applications for land and trans-

fers of improved leaseholds, since the new form took effect. "It will be time enough to attribute to it a depressing effect on settlement and improvement of Colony lands when people in number greater than are taking and improving our land are taking and improving land outside, assigning the application as reasons for doing so; though even that would not be conclusive that the application should be changed, for the fact that the only way to get any sort of application of the Single Tax is through the Colony plan is conclusive that the vast majority of people are wedded to the system against which our whole effort is a protest."

6. The trustees issued a special communication to the members, the purpose of which was to call attention to some facts and situations relevant to the impending referendum election, as the trustees understood them.

The trustees deplored the refusal of the petitioners to discuss the reasons for their position. The argument the trustees chose to answer was that the corporation could make no change in its contracts without consent of the party of the second part. They pointed out the new contracts were not retroactive: "No one who has not signed the new application is bound by it but should be in honor bound by the spirit of the application which he did sign, but those who have signed the NEW application and have accepted the new leases are legally bound by them."

The phrase "should be in honor bound" was used advisedly, and unless the point was well taken, the argument of the trustees was only technically correct. While it is true that the new provisions did not apply to leaseholders under contract before December 1925, it also is true that these lessees could not transfer or assign their leaseholds to anyone not willing to sign the new application. If, therefore, the new form effectively reduced the market for *improved* colony leaseholds, then material damages might be suffered even by leaseholders who themselves were not attempting to collect bonuses. A consensus might be reached on the proposition that any leaseholder willing to collect a bonus in violation of his pledge would be standing on morally weak legs. But would there necessarily be uni-

versal agreement on the doctrine that the leaseholder's pledge
should extend to a refusal to transfer, without a bonus, to an
applicant unwilling to purchase improvements under the more
restrictive and effective provisions of the revised application?
To the extent that the new form was more effective than the
older one, it seems clear that it would tend to reduce the number of applicants bidding for improvements on colony land.
The case of the trustees and others who wanted to retain the
new form would have been stronger if they had admitted to this
tendency, however weak or strong it might be. It scarcely
would have hurt their case to concede that there might be
circumstances under which their moral position would not be
wholly tenable, and that the moral position of all who urged
that the new form be suspended was wholly untenable.

The trustees in their communication offered data to refute
the impression that the new application had had the effect of
greatly reducing land applications and transfers of colony leaseholds. They pointed out that there were two hundred and fifty-
four movements of land between January 1, 1923, and January
1, 1926, while from January 1, 1926, to about June 1, 1929,
there were two hundred and fifty-five such movements. The
two periods were roughly comparable in length "but the earlier
period was during the time that the application desired to be
reinstated was in use, when the Florida boom was at its peak
and when even speculation in Fairhope land was rife. The
latter period was that during which the new application and
leases were in use, when speculation in colony land had been
practically killed and when land values were depressed generally all over the country and especially in the boom centers."
The trustees reported on an examination they had made of the
records of building permits issued since January 1, 1926, by
the Town of Fairhope. The list compiled was impressive, particularly the permits issued for the year 1926. There was, therefore, some basis for the following judgment:

From the foregoing it would seem that our lessees only awaited the
passage of such measures as would curb speculative ventures to
embark on a large building program. Previous to the adoption of

the new application and new lease form the only method proposed to curb lease speculation had been to raise rents high enough to prevent it. With leaseholds on unimproved ground selling around $2,000 it is obvious that a rent which would prevent speculation in our leases would penalize the lessee who wished to make use of his holdings for business or residence purposes to the extent that he very naturally refrained from making any large improvements until he was assured that the rents would be calculated on the RENTAL value of the land for use and not for speculation.

7. Those favoring a return to the old application for land also issued a statement but sent it only to a portion of the membership. This statement was quite short and almost completely devoid either of argument or of fact. It consisted largely of such assertions as the one that the application in use is "so distasteful to everyone and so injurious to our progress and prosperity." The petitioners expressed the belief that "there is not a doubt but that the Corporation should return to the use of this old form and by so doing will materially aid in the prosperity of the community, and with the community prosperous the corporation will also be prosperous and successful." They offered the following as a "few of the reasons" for returning to the old form:

Most of the leases now outstanding are under this old form and while the council may have the right to change an agreement entered into with the leaseholders, without their consent, it is not generally considered right to make an agreement and then to attempt to substitute therefor a different one that materially detracts from the right of the other party to the agreement.

The Corporation had built up to a very large degree of public confidence by their long adherence to one policy and it is neither wise for them nor just to the rest of the community to destroy that confidence.

In order to continue the experiment, the corporation must receive revenue from its lands and therefore it is the height of bad judgment for it to do anything that would make the 'home builder' unwilling to erect permanent improvements on corporation land.

Since the change was made in the form of application, building has practically ceased in Fairhope and this has not been the case in the surrounding towns.

The result of the referendum in sustaining the revised appli-

cation by a vote of forty-nine to thirty-five indicated a deep
cleavage among the members—a cleavage that cannot be explained solely in terms of honest differences with respect either
to principle or to means—although without question some
among the thirty-five were motivated by a genuine concern
over the well-being of the colony. On balance it is clear that
the circumstances surrounding the adoption of the revised form
and the almost constant struggle to maintain it in effect, served
to unite those who were influential in the Fairhope demonstration from its inception, with those who joined later after acquiring an understanding and a faith in its basic principles.
Throughout the colony's history this has been the experience
within it. Whenever any situation threatened the survival of
the single tax aspects of the experiment, the "orthodox" Fairhopers buried personal differences and worked and fought in a
united effort to preserve the colony plan.

CONTINUING CONTROVERSY

The referendum of June 1, 1929, firmly established the land
application as revised December 21, 1925, but it did not restore
harmony among the members and residents of Fairhope. In
less than two months a bitter and excessively prolonged controversy broke out in the form of "letters to the editor" of the
Baldwin County News of Robertsdale. At least twenty-five
letters and other materials were published between July 18 and
November 7, 1929. The principal respondents and the number
of letters written included: Alex J. Melville, two, R. F. Powell,
six, E. B. Gaston, three, A. E. Schalkenbach, two, Mrs. Anne B.
Call, two, and one each from F. W. Beiser, Mrs. E. W. Schoaf,
Dr. C. G. Godard, Guernsey Clarke, and Dr. C. A. Gaston, all
of Fairhope. In addition some letters were written by non-
residents, including S. M. Dinkins of Selma, Alabama, and E.
Yancey Cohen, President of the Fairhope Single Tax Study
Club of Merriewold Park, New York. Melville, Powell, Dr.
Godard, and Mrs. Schoaf attacked the colony; the others defended or deplored the attacks upon it. (Source: A scrapbook
of clippings in the possession of Miss Helen Bellangee Call.)

Little benefit would be derived from a detailed recounting of this controversy. The issue over the contents of the application for land had been decided by the membership. Probably this explains why those who attacked the colony were so extremely personal, bitter, almost vindictive in their modes of expression, while those defending the official actions of the colony were, with a few exceptions, content to rely more on facts and on a more impersonal and reasoned presentation of their positions. The entire matter was unfortunate and served no useful purpose, especially since neither side was wholly correct or entirely incorrect in the position it took. The problem raised by the Florida boom was not resolved as satisfactorily as it might have been.

The architects and defenders of the colony policy to disallow transfers of leaseholds upon evidence of the payment of bonuses, were on morally sound grounds in wanting to protect the majority of their lessees from the effects of the Florida boom. Also, it would be difficult to find fault with their desire to protect the stranger who was ignorant of the colony plan from being "fleeced" by unscrupulous individuals who told him something less than the whole story in selling him an improvement. But an acknowledgment that there was moral soundness in the desired objectives does not necessarily provide justification for the means used in an attempt to achieve the desired ends.

Both groups found themselves in agreement on two points. First, the Florida boom did affect land values in the Fairhope community. The demand for lots was far in excess of the underlying need for building sites for immediate improvements. Evidence of this is the fact that a private subdivision in east Fairhope, developed in 1925 complete with sidewalks, only recently is coming into use through the construction of improvements. During the interim, nature took over and erased all physical evidence of sidewalks and curbs; however, these now are emerging, as lots are being cleared for homes. During the mid-1920's there can be no question but that the prices of urban real estate in the Fairhope area were greatly inflated

primarily from speculative demands. Bonuses were being paid
for colony leaseholds.

Second, both parties agreed that speculation in colony leaseholds could have been broken by a sufficiently sharp increase in
rents. Such a remedy was precisely the one proposed by
Powell and other dissenters. It was their claim that not only
would the boom be broken but that a free market in colony
leaseholds was necessary to a sound rent policy. In no other
fashion could the market value of the leaseholds be determined.
This group further pointed out that speculative values would
adhere to the benefit of someone and that they should be cap-
tured by the community. Spokesmen for the official colony
position based their argument largely upon a distinction between a speculative demand and a demand for use. They
pointed out that if the single tax were in effect nationally, the
full rental value would be the value of land for use, but that
since it was not in effect generally, the colony would not be
justified in raising rents to the level necessary to destroy the
speculative demand. These colony spokesmen wanted to protect the majority of their lessees from paying rents any higher
than they would have to pay if the single tax actually had been
in effect nationally.

Although the ethical values adopted by the colony seem ad-
mirable, it appears that the revision of the form for the application for land may have constituted one of the more serious
official mistakes made by the Fairhope Single Tax Corporation.
This particular remedy for an admittedly bad condition is
questionable on several counts, the most important of which is
that it is entirely out of character with the whole spirit of individualism so carefully nurtured in Fairhope. The official
policy essentially is one of paternalism, which of course is a
partial denial of the efficacy of individual responsibility in
making decisions. The judgment that the colony was in error
in its almost total rejection of the principle of *caveat emptor*
as applied to the transfer of improved colony leaseholds, does
not imply a positive judgment in support of the policy to increase the annual rental to the level justified by the principle

of "what the traffic would bear." The rental policy could have
been to fix rents at any place between what the subjective judgment of the executive council thought the true "use" value of
colony lands, and the value determined by the objective judgment of the market which would reflect the current speculative
demand. Quite possibly some increase in colony rents—perhaps
a rather sharp one—would have been proper.

If, however, the colony policy was to be one of great reluctance to increase rents out of deference to the majority of its
lessees who were not speculating in their leaseholds, it should
have exploited other remedies much more fully than it did
before resorting to a policy of restricting the free transfer of its
leaseholds. In retrospect it seems quite proper for the colony
to have erected the warning signs on the highways, and to have
attempted in every manner to inform the stranger about the
conditions under which colony lands might be held. If colony
officials urged prospective purchasers of improvements on
colony lands to inform themselves fully before making purchases, it would seem that no blame reasonably could attach to
the colony if buyers paid more than the market worth of the
improvements. *Caveat emptor* is not an unreasonable policy if
the buyer has full access to the facts needed before making a
purchase.

In addition to warnings and other attempts to inform those
seeking possession of colony lands that they were only lessees,
not owners, of such lands, the colony did have another remedy
which it ignored altogether. The literature of the period
clearly implies that some *colony members* were actively engaged
in speculating in colony leases. If this is the case, it would
seem that the membership was derelict in its duty in failing to
invoke Section 3 of Article III of the constitution. The section
states: "Any member against whom complaint of violation of
the spirit and purpose of the Corporation, or invasion of the
rights of its members, if preferred in writing by ten per cent of
the membership, may be expelled by the Executive Council,
after full investigation of the charges preferred. Such investigation shall be public, and the accused shall be entitled to be

represented by counsel." Certainly an attempt by members to profit by speculating in colony leaseholds would be in "violation of the spirit and purpose of the Corporation." If offending members had been brought to justice, *as members,* the colony could have taken no more effective action in convincing nonmembers of "sincerity of purpose"—an objective presumed to be the basis for the restriction on the transfer of leaseholds.[2]

AN EVALUATION OF THE NEW POLICY

In summary, it is here concluded that the colony adopted a questionable policy in interfering in the transfer of its leaseholds. A better policy might have been to remove a large part of the temptation to speculate by making a sharp increase in rents, in combination with an even more determined effort to explain to lessees and to prospective lessees the nature of the colony plan, and to bring to justice any member who demonstrably failed to live up to the colony code. This conclusion is reached in the full knowledge that "the innocent" would not be wholly protected from the evil effects of the general speculative fever, to the extent colony rents rose above the level justified by current use value alone.[3] It is submitted, however, that one

2 It is inconceivable that the colony did not in fact consider some such remedy in face of the action the executive council took on November 16, 1925, in amending the application for membership to read: "I hereby pledge on my honor, that I will, if a lessee, neither charge nor accept from any one, a bonus for the transfer of my leasehold in unimproved condition, nor an excessive price, for the transfer of same with improvement thereon. Also that I will not, while a member, buy any land for resale at a profit in the near vicinity of the Fairhope Single Tax Colony. And I hereby agree that the establishment of my violation of these conditions shall be cause for the forfeiture of my membership and without repayment of the membership fee."

3 This statement would not follow had the executive council adopted the remedy required in Section 6, Article VIII of the constitution, which provides: "If any lessee shall exact or attempt to exact from another a greater value for the use of land, exclusive of improvements, than the rent paid by him to the Corporation, the Executive Council *shall immediately* upon proof of such fact, increase the rental charge against *such land* to the amount so charged or sought to be charged." (Emphasis supplied.) Perhaps the reason the council did not follow this mandate was that the resulting rent structure would have been incompatible with the Somers System. Whatever the reason for non-compliance it is evident that the membership took no action either to mandamus the council on this point or to recall council members for such nonfeasance.

group of "innocents" cannot be fully protected against such a force without releasing an evil of a different kind (*i.e.,* without inducing a temptation to speculate by maintaining too low rents); further, that no one can measure "use" value and separate it out from a total "market" value which is inflated by speculation. If the results of the official policy were to trade one evil for another, and to compel those fixing rents to forego the evidence of objective data (such as bonuses) in favor of a wholly subjective judgment, then the policy was a poor one. Reluctantly, almost sadly, it must be concluded that the paternalistic policy was adopted because it was in the character of the colony management of that time to prefer the subjective over the objective. Such a preference, however, was more unconscious than conscious. The harsh epithets cast at certain colony officials, particularly at Mr. E. B. Gaston, were not deserved. Mr. Gaston had no desire to be a "Mussolini," as he was called by some; he was, however, very certain of the soundness of his own judgment and he quite openly exercised many of the wiles of the practiced politician in obtaining his own way. Without doubt he believed in the perfectability of man under conditions of freedom; but he found it easy to rationalize both that such conditions did not yet exist generally, and that man not yet perfected, needed, even deserved, some degree of paternalistic protection. Almost always he did get his own way and with few exceptions his way proved beneficial for the colony.

This attenuated sketch of Ernest B. Gaston is offered not only in explanation of the choice made by the colony in adjusting to the Florida boom, but as a partial explanation of a perennial complaint against the colony by some of its ill-wishers. The complaint is that some members negate by their actions some of their professions on behalf of the colony. Such a personal attack is not unusual particularly on the part of those who have lost out in a skirmish with a strong personality. It is therefore not surprising that in the course of the 1929 controversy, Mr. Gaston would be attacked through the person of one of his sons. One of the letters published in the *Baldwin County Times* made much of the point that Dr. C. A. Gaston was living in Fairhope on deeded land. Such behavior on the part of a member of the Gaston family was presumed to be reprehensible if not actually disloyal. The appearance of this charge prompted a letter of explanation. Dr. Gaston explained that he had built on a lot willed to him by his aunt, Dr. Clara Atkinson; that at the time he built, all colony lots available for homes were under lease; that lessees holding unimproved lots were asking bonuses for their release; and that his father had opposed his making his home on deeded land. A short time previous to this episode, Dr. Gaston had spent a year as acting secretary. Shortly thereafter he sold his lot to the colony for the nominal sum of $300, in realization of the fact that he could not properly take an active part in colony affairs without living on colony property.

In concluding his letter (published September 19, 1929), Dr. Gaston expressed the following opinion of some relevance to the Fairhope story: ". . . the greatest claim the corporation has to continued existence is in the exercise of its power to maintain freedom of access to unused or illused land." He went on to observe that formerly he had held to the belief that a free voice in the management should be extended to all lessees— "believers and non-believers alike"—but that he had learned by experience that he was wrong. His year of experience as acting secretary had convinced him that men do not look upon land in the same way as they look upon other property. Dr. Gaston expressed this opinion in a somewhat cryptic manner, but if it may be presumed that he meant that men cling to the institution of private property in land with more tenacity than they do to individual property rights in other types of property, then the task of propagandizing the single tax is indeed herculean. This makes it even more important that a colony attempting so to condition the attitudes of men should function as objectively as possible, and that the members conduct themselves in a manner beyond reproach.

The official action of the colony and the behavior of many colony members in the 1920's probably weakened the effectiveness of the Fairhope experiment. Officially the colony may have done the wrong thing for the right reasons, and the opponents may have advocated a better policy—some, however, for the wrong reasons.

XV

THE SINGLE TAX CORPORATION SUPERSEDES THE SINGLE TAX COLONY

*T*HE term colony never precisely described the Fairhope community. From the outset the non-members coming to the community outnumbered the members and the non-believers outnumbered those who were convinced singletaxers. Of greater significance was the fact that from the beginning every effort was made to integrate the new community with its larger environment; every attempt was made to minimize the extent to which those living in Fairhope were isolated from the outside world. If Fairhope ever was a colony the term must be used to describe certain modes of life, social overtones and community attitudes, directly attributable to the policies and practices of the Fairhope Industrial Association and its successor the Fairhope Single Tax Corporation. The principal reason for the existence of these entities was to administer land in a manner calculated to simulate single tax conditions. In practice there were numerous impurities from the point of view of singletaxers, not only in the use of scrip and the early association store, but in the direct provision of many essential community facilities and services. The decisions of the members of the private corporation necessarily and intimately affected the lives of a much larger number of local residents. It also was true that appreciable gifts of money and leadership resources were made by non-residents, particularly by Mr. Joseph Fels,

and always for the motive of furthering or glorifying the underlying land tenure policies or single tax features. With few exceptions the basic decisions were made by a small proportion of
the residents—actually the decisions came from a small number
of strong personalities within the membership who could and
did think, speak and act for the colony.

A Concept of Maturity

It will be recalled that the incorporation of the municipality
of Fairhope caused some to prophesy that the influence of the
colony in the community soon would disappear except for the
more impersonal effects flowing out of the peculiarities of the
local system of land tenure. This prophecy was not to be
realized in anything approaching a full sense for a full quarter
century or more. The single tax corporation retained its status
as a colony as long as it operated facilities or provided services
of direct significance to the community, and as long as the value
judgments of the small group governing it directly affected
community attitudes and mores.

If this concept of the Fairhope colony as an entity directly
responsible for significant non-single tax effects, both material
and social, is well taken, then the single tax corporation could
not mature until all influences, other than a purely impersonal
administration of its lands in a manner consistent with single
tax principles, actually disappeared. The test of maturity suggested for this particular venture is that the colonial features
must disappear entirely, leaving an impersonal corporation in
the twin roles of a landholding company operating on single
tax principles and an educational agency for propagating the
single tax doctrine. In every other respect the corporation
should be neutral within the community.

Viewed in this light it seems clear that the "colony" as distinct from the "corporation" was very much in evidence at the
onset of the depression. The revision of the application for land
in 1925 was reaffirmed in 1929, and was essentially the subjective action of a colonial group and not the result of an
impersonal corporation's objective decision. The single tax
corporation may have lost valuable ground in sanctioning this

violation of the spirit of freedom so fundamental to the doctrine it was organized to promote.

Nor had the single tax corporation entirely divested itself of all non-single tax operations by 1930. The corporation owned and operated the wharf, which it administered as a public utility; it owned and maintained almost all of the public parks within the municipality of Fairhope; it owned and maintained the cemetery and was the principal support of the public library. In addition it spent—on motion of the executive council—appreciable sums for road, street and other improvements to property and made contributions to various local institutions, particularly the organic school. It is significant that the form and terms of availability of these facilities and services depended on the value judgments of a few (*i.e.*, members who permitted themselves to be concerned) and the judgment of this small fraction of the total population affected the entire community. Quite clearly the single tax corporation was not yet a sufficiently neutral impersonal force within the community to enable an evaluation in terms of single tax considerations alone.

The adversities of the Great Depression resulted in the single tax corporation adopting expedients which, on balance, prodded the venture toward maturity as a single tax experiment. The controversy over the divestment of colony parks proved to be the last bitter difference of any significance, which in itself may be a compelling bit of evidence that the single tax corporation was approaching its destiny as an impersonal landholding company, and operating more in an objective as opposed to a subjective manner.

Generally speaking the officials of the Fairhope corporation kept abreast of current trends and were not delinquent in recognizing factual developments. At the pre-election meeting of January 15, 1930, (Minutes) the secretary alerted the membership to a hard reality. Cochrane bridge connecting Mobile with points east by highway was opened about the middle of 1927. This was followed by an improvement in roads and an inauguration of regular bus service. The opening of this bridge hurt Fairhope in a number of ways. It diverted much tourist business to the north and it quickly destroyed the Fairhope wharf as a commercial transportation facility. In the much longer run the bridge, together with the Bankhead tunnel and improved roads, was to help Fairhope to a rapid growth as a residential suburb of Mobile, but this eventuality did not mitigate the pains of the first few years. In his report Secretary E. B. Gaston directed the members' attention to the rapid falling off of net wharf revenues which the colony had been depending upon "to meet expenditures which really ought to be met from land rentals." The net wharf receipts in 1925 were $6,854; in 1926, $5,668; in 1927, $3,933; in 1928, $1,439; and in 1929, only $46. The members were told that future receipts possibly would not be sufficient to maintain the long wharf in a condition to carry heavy loads, and that in any case the corporation no longer could depend on net revenue from this source to meet taxes and other expenses. "We will have to depend on rent."

Rent receipts in 1929 were $31,422. Taxes paid were just under $25,000 which left only a little more than $6,000 for all other purposes. In 1929 the corporation paid $4,069 for roads including street assessments, $1,122 for library maintenance and insurance, and $1,500 for salaries. "We are brought up squarely against the real single tax proposition of paying the taxes we contract to pay for lessees and expenses necessary for our existence from ground rents."

TRUSTEES VS. EXECUTIVE COUNCIL

The incumbent trustees (Anne B. Call, A. E. Schalkenbach and Della K. Bancroft) apparently viewed the impending economic crisis as more of an opportunity and a challenge than as a threat—or perhaps they did not foresee any prolonged general depression. They warned: "If we are overcome with inertia and allow ourselves to drift along until the line of cleavage is slight between ourselves and the world in general, we shall lose a wonderful opportunity." The trustees noted that the treasurer was increasingly successful in the collection of rents but that his efforts "must not be abated." The theme of the 1930 trustees' report was that the colony should proceed in strict compliance with constitutional provisions and be most meticulous in the annual rent appraisement. They recommended once again a constitutional amendment "which will make it obligatory on the husband or wife of a member to satisfy the executive council of his or her fitness to become a member before he or she may sign the constitution." Finally, the trustees earnestly recommended "that the colony socials be resumed and that the colony entertain all who wish to come once each month, serving inexpensive refreshments and explaining our principles and policies." Although none of these recommendations are startling, they do disclose the genuine concern of the trustees that there be a strict compliance with the letter of the constitution; a concern that the annual rent appraisement be conducted thoroughly and systematically beginning in October; that the membership not be diluted by those either ignorant of or antagonistic to single tax principles; and that the single tax corporation function as a colony in a manner designed to preserve both its uniqueness and its importance in the lives of the community.

The trustees were justified in this oblique criticism of the executive council with respect to the manner of making the rent appraisement. Insofar as the official minutes are informative no action whatever was taken with respect to rents for 1930 until a special meeting held February 12 (Minutes) when the multiplier was raised from 2.42 to 2.66. At the regular meeting of February 18 the council increased rents on country land by five per cent and decided to leave the relative or frontage ratings undisturbed. In their annual report for 1931 (Minutes, January 21, 1931) the trustees were sharply critical of colony officials. After reaffirming strict adherence to the constitution they characterized the method of appraisal of rental values for the preceding years as being in direct conflict with the method prescribed by the constitution. "Was it done to relieve officers of unpleasant or untimely duties? We respectfully recommend that hereafter no such violation of the constitution shall be tolerated under any circumstances."

There is little reason to question the judgment of the trustees that single tax officials and members had become careless in performing such fundamental functions as rent appraisement and rent collection for at least a decade prior to 1930. Probably the corporation was slow to recognize that it had grown to a size which would justify full-time professional administration. In 1929 the salaries totaled only $1,500—a sum obviously inadequate to obtain full-time competent administrators and an adequate complement of clerical assistants. This, added to the deliberate decision to tilt with the windmill of general land speculation in the 1920's, seems sufficient to account for the relative failure to improve the administration of basic corporation functions, and to chart the ultimate destiny of the demonstration. In any event it seems probable (but cannot be proved) that the level of rents was too low in the 1920's, that relative or frontage values became distorted, and that there was a woeful lack of system directed at keeping rents currently collected.

The roots of the bitter and unfortunate break between the trustees and the majority of members who followed the leadership of the secretary, E. B. Gaston, cannot fully be explained in terms of relative failure in administrative matters. Basically the difficulty started as a conflict of value judgments among sincere and capable members. Mr. Gaston was a long-time, almost permanent, secretary and he came to identify the best interests of the Fairhope colony (indeed the entire community) in terms of his own values. He was a strong personality and except for two brief periods he proved almost omnipotent in colony politics, quite possibly because he was usually "right." Upon occasion, however, his opponents wanted merely to permit the decisions on policy and procedure to be decided in accordance with the constitution and to be debated on their merits. It is perhaps unfortunate but natural that the majority of the members frequently were not interested in debating a policy, nor were they interested in the manner of its determination and implementation.

The nature of the controversy of 1930-1932 between the trustees and the executive council and officers of the colony corporation may be made explicit by a summary of the more significant charges levied by the trustees in their report of 1931. The manner of expressing some of these complaints clearly indicates that the situation had deteriorated to the point where the trustees sometimes resorted to thinly disguised *ad hominem* arguments.

The trustees sharply criticized the manner in which the executive council granted a site on the beach for a community ball park. "We believe the issue of granting the lands was not deliberated upon as would be consistent with proper parliamentary procedure, having been granted at a special meeting attended by only three members. . . ." Apparently trees were felled and possession taken of the lands before any publication or notice could reach the members, thus leaving no opportunity for a referendum. "We submit that giving the free use of the lands and permitting the destruction of fine trees, are questions that our membership are entitled to be heard upon, especially since no such powers are conferred upon the council by the constitution." Closely related was the action of removing top soil from other lands to be used on the baseball diamond before any action was taken by the council, "a presumption that should not prevail in the management of a corporate body such as the Fairhope Single Tax Corporation should be."

The trustees charge that some of the advertisements of sales prepared by the treasurer, and sent to the *Courier* for publication, were not published. This was an apparent violation of a council action which had not been rescinded. The trustees could find no power invested in any one individual or group of individuals to nullify such an action of the council when lawfully convened; therefore, "it is self evident that the council has not been able to enforce its mandates."

The trustees charged undue laxity in the collection of rents, and indeed the problem of delinquency was a serious one. The total rent roll of 1930 amounted to $36,199.36, of which, in January, 1931, $15,130.17 was delinquent. The corporation paid out in taxes for lessees $21,697.34, or $705 in excess of rent collections for that year. The trustees stated they were

aware of the depression and did not desire to sell the improvements of anyone, "if satisfactory arrangements can be made for
payment of arrearages." They noted, however, that a bill becomes increasingly difficult to pay the longer it runs, and
meanwhile improvements are not kept up and become increasingly poor security. "We believe the law governing the collection of rents should be enforced uniformly; no one should be
favored to the disadvantage of paying lessees, who are entitled
to the benefits of the funds not collected. Therefore, the officers
should be required to perform their duties without favor."

The trustees strongly criticized the prevailing method of
refunding lessees' taxes. For years it had been the practice to
offset lessees' rents with receipts of taxes they had paid on improvements and personal property, and to make rebates in cash
in instances where the taxes paid exceeded the rents due. The
position taken by the trustees was that the lessees should be
required to pay their rents either in cash or in corporation
certificates before they were given any credit on their tax
receipts. Strictly speaking they wanted the corporation to
refrain from offsetting taxes paid against rent; the procedure
favored was for the lessees to pay their full rent and to receive
scrip to an amount equal to their tax receipts. The scrip would
be receivable by the corporation for any goods or services
rendered by it. In practice, in 1931, this meant the scrip would
be receivable on rents due the corporation.

As the trustees saw the matter, a change in policy would both
ease the problem of the corporation in finding cash to pay its
taxes and would achieve certain psychological benefits, such as
minimizing the tendency of certain lessees to over-value their
improvements for taxation. The sequence of the recommended
system would be as follows: (1) in a given year the lessees would
pay all rents due before they got any adjustment in the form
of rebates for taxes paid by them; (2) the corporation would
refund their taxes in scrip; (3) this scrip could then (a) be sold
to any debtor of the single tax corporation or (b) be retained
by the lessee receiving it and used in payment of rents the
following year. It is clear that the corporation would gain net

in cash receipts over cash disbursements *in the first year* of the recommended procedure, but it is difficult to understand how the new procedure would materially ease the problem of obtaining a cash income in succeeding years, unless it had the effect in practice of reducing rent delinquency, and of minimizing taxes paid by lessees by discouraging over-assessments of their properties.

The trustees, therefore, focused needed attention on weaknesses of policy and procedure which, in their opinion, directly resulted from a failure to follow the guidance of the constitution, the terms of the lease contract or orderly procedure. Their criticisms were well taken in the main and the judgment is expressed at this point that the single tax corporation could not mature until the annual rental appraisement was conducted in an objective and meticulous manner with continuous improvement in the techniques employed; until the policy and procedure for minimizing delinquent rents had been greatly clarified and improved; and until the corporation could take necessary action to control the liability for refunding of taxes on lessees' property, which means an effective control over the assessments on such property.

THE PARK CONTROVERSY

Another criticism of the trustees was directed more at the manner of taking an action still in contemplation. They said: "During the past year, a special meeting of the council was held to consider deeding the park lands to the town. One of your trustees presented this proposition to a noted attorney, together with the constitution of the corporation, receiving an opinion that the constitution makes the setting aside and maintenance of park lands mandatory; that before any such action could lawfully be carried out, the constitution must be amended by a referendum vote of all members. We think all of our members should be fully informed on this phase of the question."

The question of divestment of park lands had been discussed during 1930 and the membership was sufficiently informed to take some tentative steps toward this end at the annual meeting of January 26, 1931. The trustees must have known that the discussion had reached advance stages but, as will be seen, they were prepared to go to extreme lengths to block the transfer of park lands to the Town of Fairhope unless the entire membership authorized it via amendment of the constitution. In retrospect it seems clear that the trustees acted as they did only partly because they were convinced that the transfer would be unconstitutional unless the constitution were specifically amended. The trustees also believed that the colony, *per se,* would be weakened if it did not continue to perform some direct services to the community, and they further believed that the transfer would not be financially necessary if the corporation would improve its rent appraisement and rent collection procedures.

The constitutional issue may be described but scarcely could be resolved by any agency other than a court of law. As the trustees saw it the constitution put them virtually in the position of a court to decide on the constitutionality of a given policy. Their duty was to keep the constitutional conscience of the corporation. At any rate the 1931 trustees took a strong position to the effect that a divestment of park lands violated a mandatory provision of the constitution and could not be implemented without a vote by the total membership. The relevant provisions of the constitution follow:

Article IV—SUPREME AUTHORITY.

Sec. 1. Supreme authority shall be vested equally in the membership, to be exercised through the initiative and referendum as hereinafter provided.

Sec. 2. Each member not in arrears to the Corporation shall be entitled to one vote, and one only, at all elections involving changes in this constitution; but on election of officers and questions concerning local administration of affairs, only those shall be entitled to vote who are in person on the Corporation grounds on the day of election and who are not in arrears.

Article V—OFFICERS.

Sec. 8. The trustees shall have general oversight of all affairs of the Corporation, shall have charge of all elections, canvass the votes cast and declare the result thereof, shall act as committee to audit all accounts and review all reports of officers and employees, and shall annually and at other times in their discretion, submit reports

advising the members of the condition and needs of the Corporation's business in all departments. They shall have access to the
books and accounts of all officers and employees at all times. They
shall receive compensation only for time actively employed, and
shall hold no other office, either by election or by appointment.

Article XII—PARKS, LIBRARIES, ETC.

Ample provision shall be made in platting the lands of the corporation for land for parks and all other public purposes, and as
rapidly as may be, lands thus intended shall be improved and
beautified, and schools, libraries, public halls, natatoriums, etc.,
established and maintained at the expense of the Corporation for
the free use and enjoyment of the members and their families.

During 1930 representatives of the Alabama State Tax Commission, working in the course of a state-wide program to increase property assessments, proposed an increase in the assessed
valuation of colony land and improvements by $173,880. The
secretary reported: "By much effort and with considerable
expense, we succeeded in getting this down to an increase of
$25,000, which being altogether in town increased our tax for
1930 to $775, while our lawyers fee was $175." The combination of over-assessment of improvements and the increased
assessment of corporation lands made the colony areas "the
highest tax territory of equal area in the county necessitating
increases in rents and then decreasing ability of lessees to pay
their rents by decreasing business or loss of employment."
(Minutes, January 26, 1931.)

REFERENDUM ON PARKS AND WHARF

Solely as a result of the financial squeeze on the corporation
the secretary brought before the council an action taken at a
members' meeting on January 21, 1921 which had favored
deeding the park lands to the town in order to escape payment
of taxes on the same. In bringing this matter before the 1931
annual meeting the secretary stated that the town had in immediate contemplation the making of sewer and street improvements to be charged against the land affected using special
assessments. He maintained that a transfer of the parks under
adequate limiting safeguards would compel all who enjoyed
them to share in the expense of maintenance and that it would

do no violence to the colony constitution. The secretary proposed that the direction of the members meeting of ten years previous be carried into effect, the conveyance to be made duly protecting the land described for park purposes or to revert to the corporation. He expressed the hope that such action could be taken before October, 1931 in order to avoid another year's taxes. He expressed the same view with respect to the wharf because he saw no way to operate it at a profit and no effective way of confining its benefits to lessees.

The assembled members adopted two motions: (1) that the action of the annual meeting of January 21, 1921, with regard to the parks be reaffirmed except that Knoll Park be not included for the present; and (2) that the executive council take up with the town the matter of taking over the wharf.

The next move clearly was up to those who opposed deeding the parks to the town. With the apparent desire to clarify the constitutional issue, a petition was filed calling for a constitutional referendum on an amendment to Article XII. Section 1 was to be retained and the following to be added as a new section: " (2). If and when the lands of the Fairhope Single Tax Corporation are wholly or in part within a municipal corporation, should it be in the judgment of the executive council, to the advantage of the Fairhope Single Tax Corporation, to convey the park lands of the corporation, wholly or in part, to the municipality the executive council may make such conveyance provided that the terms of such conveyance are satisfactory to 75 per cent of the entire membership, as expressed by a referendum vote on the terms of each such conveyance." The petition was submitted for a vote on May 12. At the referendum, twenty-seven voted yes and fifty-two voted no.

At a regular meeting of the council, April 22, 1931, the trustees read a statement on the proposed transfer of the parks. The statement opened with a quotation of the underscored portion of Article VIII—LAND. Sec. 1: "There shall be no individual ownership of land within the jurisdiction of the Corporation, but *the Corporation shall hold as trustee for its entire membership, the title to all lands upon which its com-*

munity shall be maintained." The trustees stated that they wanted to be sure that the matter would be brought before the entire membership by means of a constitutional amendment, and that they had consulted two different attorneys each of whom rendered the judgment that a constitutional amendment would be necessary to effect the transfer. The trustees regretted that preparations apparently had gone forward to make the transfer without further authority and they thought additional advice should be sought. The trustees expressed the opinion that "the giving away of many acres of the most valuable lands, equally the property of the outside members . . . can by no stretch of the imagination be called 'local administration of affairs.' "

At a special meeting on the day following the referendum the council directed the president and secretary to consult the corporation attorney for his opinion upon the matter of park conveyance. Attorney J. H. Webb's opinion was that the corporation "could donate, with proper reservations, parks to the municipality and that the usual officers could make a valid deed to the corporation." However, this would first have to be authorized by the executive council and be subject to a possible referendum. Mr. Webb ruled against the necessity of a constitutional amendment and also against the need for a referendum of the entire membership. (Minutes, May 19, 1931.)

Upon receipt of this opinion the council resolved that immediate action be taken for the transfer of the parks, if acceptable to members, and that a committee be appointed to delimit such ground not already designated as parks, which in their judgment should be added to the conveyance, employing a surveyor to assist them in achieving an accurate description.

On August 6, 1931, the council met in special session further to consider the conveyance of the parks. With but one dissenting vote it adopted the following resolution: "That the president and secretary be directed to appear before the Town Council at its next meeting, inviting an expression from the same as to its attitude toward the proposed transfer of park lands, if in general favorable, inviting the appointment of a committee by the Council, or expressing the pleasure of the Council to consider with the Colony Council, the exact terms of such proposed conveyance." The resolution then detailed five general terms of such a proposed conveyance for the consideration of the Town Council, namely: 1. proper description; 2. that the use or uses of the land be expressed with a provision for reversion to the donor if not so used; 3. that no monopoly or special privilege shall ever be granted in or near such lands; 4. that the tender be contingent on acceptance before October 1, 1931; 5. that all assessments for street improvements against the land included in the conveyance hereafter falling due shall be assumed by the town.

Finally, the resolution provided for submitting the question to those members legally qualified to vote in the opinion of Attorney Webb.

The trustees countered by requesting that the council "take full responsibility for this action, not complicating it with anything requiring the cooperation of the trustees," *i.e.*, to omit the referendum to the local membership. On motion the executive council filed the trustees' statement. (Minutes, August 25, 1931.)

At the meeting of September 21, the council approved the description and the conditions of the proposed conveyance, which, upon approval by the Town Council, would cause the colony officers to make the conveyance. On September 23, an election was called in response to a petition on the question: "Shall the action of the executive council, Monday, September 21, 1931, relative to transfer to Town of Fairhope of park lands of the corporation be approved?"

The next day another special meeting was held to hear a communication from the trustees declining to conduct the referendum election petitioned for by more than ten per cent of the resident members. The trustees objected to sending out notices of the election on the grounds that they had not been consulted prior to their issuance and they requested that another notice be sent to the effect that the election would not be held. The secretary asserted that the notice had been sent in obedience to an action of the executive council, and that a form of the ballot had been sent to one of the trustees but that it had been returned without consideration. The council resolved that it could not "recognize any authority conferred upon the trustees by the constitution to set up their judgment of constitutional matters as final against the judgment of the executive council as guided by the considered opinion of the corporation counsel, nor to deny to members of the corporation the right to referendum." The council called the referendum and provided for election machinery in the event the trustees failed to appear and conduct the election.

The referendum was held on September 25 and the vote was: yes, 46; no, 3, and one ballot was spoiled.

On October 19, 1931, the president and secretary reported the tender of a deed to the Town of Fairhope for the park lands and its acceptance by the Town Council at a special meeting of September 29.

The actual tender of the park deed did not end the controversy. The three trustees involved either resigned or were recalled at an election of October 29. It is possible that this action would not have been taken except for the fact that some of those opposing the manner of transfer of the park lands were so convinced of its illegality that they proceeded to bring court action to get the transfer set aside. Suit actually was brought and the complainants lost out in the district court. Still unconvinced they at first planned an appeal but, being the responsible persons they were, and being most loyal to the colony *per se,* they decided against putting the corporation to the expense and uncertainty of a prolonged court battle.

Thus the Town of Fairhope came into ownership of its most valuable asset, the generous, well located and intensively used park system. Along with the decorative but otherwise little used Knoll Park, the town acquired ownership of a most adequate bay front acreage providing free public access to the bay and an unusually wide and well shaded shore for family outings. The advantage of Fairhope from the point of view of the general public lies in the accessible, but not otherwise notable, public beach. The colony was able to provide these parks because of the decision of the early settlers to set aside this abundant and well endowed recreational area for park purposes and to pay taxes and other costs for over forty years without any offsetting revenue. Had this reservation not been made, or had a prolonged period of financial stringency forced the colony to lease more of its park lands for revenue, Fairhope would be much less attractive today except for the fortunate few holding leaseholds or owning property giving them access to the bay. Included in the park deed were the gulleys and certain other lands which the city has had available for drainage purposes and for sites for such facilities as the sewage disposal plant. It is inconceivable that the Town of Fairhope ever would have decided that it could afford to purchase anything like the acreage within the parks which it received free.

LIMITATIONS IN PARK DEED

Free? Not completely free because certain strings were attached to the gift and upon occasion some of these conditions have produced a degree of frustration among town officials and some residents.

Some of the conditions included in the deed have caused no difficulties, *e.g.*, the naming of "Henry George Park" and the reservation of the right of the colony "to place and maintain at its expense suitable markers, (subject to approval of the party of the second part) setting forth that the lands on which the same are placed were donated by it to party of the second part for park purposes." The colony never has seen fit to erect such markers.

From time to time, however, local conflicts have arisen over the conditions embodied in the following paragraph of the deed, particularly the prohibition against the Town Council giving any exclusive franchise, indeed any concession for a period longer than one year. Without question this limitation has prevented any commercial development, no matter how desirable it might be, for the obvious reason that business men shrink from investing capital in a specialized and fixed form under such an uncertainty. In this connection it should be noted that the lease does not in any way prohibit the town from making capital improvements of a self-liquidating nature and, under the lease, the beach could be improved via public owner-ship but operated by private lessees who would have no invest-ment other than in supplies and other personal property. The deed provides:

That the property conveyed shall be forever used as public parks of the Town of Fairhope, according to general usage of public parks and according to the wishes of a majority of the qualified electors of the Town, provided that in such use there shall be no special privileges of any kind to individuals or organizations and no profit to individuals, but the latter shall not apply to use made of any concession which may be given by the Town Council or other body in which control of the parks may be placed, for the fuller enjoy-ment of same by the public and awarded for terms not exceeding a year, on a competitive basis; but, provided further, that the natural function of gullies included in conveyance as drainage ways for water from streets and other public and private lands, shall be recognized as a proper use of same in conjunction with their use as parks; also, that if in the future the Town decides upon putting in a sewer system and the Town Council and engineers agree that the best location for a disposal plant as an essential part of the sewer system is in or along the gulley north of the cemetery as now located, such use may be made of the needed land, with laying of such sewer lines leading to the same and pipe lines for carrying the effluent therefrom as may be necessary, but modern methods shall be made use of to render the same inoffensive.

Within a few months following the conveyance of the parks, the colony conveyed the wharf property to the town by a vote of thirty-four to one, (Minutes, May 2, 1932), and on Septem-ber 30, 1932, deeded the golf course to the town with a right of reversion to grantor after failure for two years to use the ground for the purposes mentioned. The grantor also reserved the right after ten years and not more than twenty years to re-purchase from the grantee for the amount of the original con-sideration. In this instance the foresight of the colony was fully vindicated. The municipal course was not overly popular and the subsequent growth of the community within twenty years demonstrated that a higher use of the land would be for residential sites. (Minutes, October 3, 1932.)

In his annual report for 1934, the secretary stated that the deeding of the parks, wharf and golf course effected a reduction of annual taxes of over $1,100 and relief from special assessments for sidewalks, curbs and gutters of $262, sums which were extremely important to the colony during those distressing years. It may, however, be questioned whether many members of the colony interpreted these divestments as acts necessary to the maturing of the single tax corporation. In fact there was an overtone of regret that such actions were necessary. The secretary came close to expressing a strong nostalgic sentiment when he reported against giving more colony land to the larger community to be used as a landing field. "Our officers feel that our corporation has been so generous in donations of land for parks, golf course, wharf, etc., that it is high time for others, with homes and investments here to come to the front with generous offers . . . there can be no thought of turning back the wheels of progress, no hope of regaining the strategic position we once held. . . ."

LIMITATION ON TAXES TO BE REFUNDED

If the actions of the colony in giving to the town lands which it had been using for general public purposes were consonant with the ultimate maturity of the single tax corporation, the corporation took another action which appeared defeatist and inconsistent with the expressed single tax objectives. On November 21, 1932, the colony council adopted a new rule limiting the receipt on rent of tax receipts for town taxes to the extent of the difference between the total rent due from the lessee and the tax receipts from state and county. On May 13, 1934, the membership voted to amend the constitution to limit the liability of the corporation to refund lessees' taxes to the total rent received during the year on leaseholds on which the improvements and personal property were located.

The roots of these actions go back to December 11, 1908, when the executive council, by resolution, decided to receive against rent (without limitation) receipts for town taxes against lessees' improvements and personal property. At that time few questioned this action either on grounds of policy or on the ability of the corporation to make such refunds and remain solvent. From time to time some would suggest that a limitation be placed on such refunds but the reaction from resident leaders of the colony, and from non-resident members of considerable influence, was that such an act would be unthinkable, almost horrendous, in its implications. The realities of the depression caused a change in thinking and this action was anticipated by the secretary at the annual members meeting of January 30, 1932. Mr. Gaston discussed at some length whether or not the corporation had tried to do more than was practicable in applying the single tax principle under existing laws. Apparently the executive council came to think that it had. It adopted the following resolution which, incidentally, was not challenged by a petition for a referendum.

WHEREAS, the constitution makes no provision for paying or accepting on rent, receipts for town taxes of lessees, nor do any outstanding leases provide for the same, and the practice for some time existing of accepting such tax receipts on rent is founded only upon an extra-constitutional order of the Executive Council and

WHEREAS, a danger has developed from a tendency of some lessees to over-assess their properties, or to fail to make such resistance as they might to over-assessment by the Board of Review, and

WHEREAS, there has developed a fear of some that the financial security of the corporation is or may be menaced by assuming payment or giving credit on rent, without limit, for taxes paid by lessees; but it is in furtherance of the principles of the corporation and in the interest of a majority of the lessees that their town taxes as well as state and county taxes should be taken from the rental value of the land, rather than rest upon them on the basis of their individual thrift and industry, to the extent that they can be safely assumed, therefore

RESOLVED, that the executive council order of December 11, 1908, relative to Town taxes, be rescinded and that hereafter receipts for town taxes of lessees will only be received on rent from any lessee to the extent of the difference between his receipts for state and county taxes applied on rent and the total rent due from him;

each separate parcel of land and the taxes upon the personal property and improvements thereon, to be considered together in the application of this rule.

Not only was this resolution acceptable to the members but they voted eighty-eight to nineteen in favor of the following amendment of Article VIII of the constitution: Section 1. "All taxes assessed against the Corporation shall be paid from the Corporation treasury. Section 2. Receipts for taxes paid by lessee to state, county, town or school district, upon his improvements and personal property held upon any leasehold, (money and credits excepted) shall be applicable upon the rent of such leasehold; provided that the corporation shall not be bound to accept such tax receipts to a greater amount for any year than the rent for that year on the ground on which such improvements and personal property are held." Section 3 of the lease form was amended to conform to this amendment and in 1954 only one of the older leases remained in force.

In his report of 1934 the secretary credited the new rule limiting the offsetting of town taxes paid by lessees with saving over $1,100 in 1933. He stated that the rule affected about fifty lessees out of approximately five hundred—about one in ten.

It will be noted that the new constitutional provision does not prohibit the corporation from paying all of the taxes of the lessees. It merely prohibits the corporation from being bound to do so by contract.

"Gateway Amendment"

The first amendment to the constitution since 1904 is popularly known as the "gateway amendment." Prior to its passage the constitution was extremely difficult to amend since such an action required the affirmative votes of three-fourths of the members. With the passage of time some non-resident members lost interest, and others had died, but were carried on the roll of voting members because the secretary was unaware of their deaths. Many attempts had been made to amend the constitution and while some of these attempts had received but few negative votes none had received an affirmative three-fourths vote of the entire membership. The matter of the amendability of the constitution thus became a question of grave concern to corporation officers and members.

On April 6, 1925, a petition was presented to amend the constitution by inserting after the word "member" in Article VII, Section 7, the word "voting." The petition requested that ballots be sent out by April 15 with a request that they be returned by July 1, and remain in the hands of the trustees unopened until the day of the election. The trustees were requested to furnish the secretary with the names of members from whom ballots were not received in order that further communication might be permitted. The results of the election were reported to the membership meeting of February 4, 1926. Ninety-one voted for and only twelve against, but the amendment failed because the membership roll indicated that one hundred thirty-two were eligible to vote; therefore ninety-three affirmative votes would be necessary for ratification.

At the annual meeting of January 20, 1932, a motion carried that another effort be made to pass a so-called "gateway amendment" and that the president appoint the trustees a committee to take the initiative in securing the submission of the amendment. This was done and a petition was filed on February 10, 1932, signed by fifty-three members calling for a special election on May 5, 1932, on the proposed amendment. This time it passed; one hundred twenty-four were entitled to vote and one hundred ten voted yes and only eight voted no. The amendment as passed was worded quite differently from the one which failed in 1926. The constitution still requires an affirmative vote of three-fourths of the membership but it provides that *non-resident* members shall not be counted members if, in response to election notices sent by registered mail, either the post office reports inability to deliver mail to any such member or no ballot shall be received from him at the election. In effect the constitution now may be amended by a three-fourths affirmative vote of *resident* members plus those *non-resident* members actually voting.

It seems probable that if the "gateway amendment" had been

in force in 1931 much of the bitterness over the park controversy might have been avoided. The issue of the manner of
approving the park transfer could have been resolved in a
practicable manner by means of a constitutional amendment.
Certainly there would seem to be little reason for any such re-
currence in the future; any difference among members over
convictions as to whether a policy is a constitutional matter or
one of local administrative import henceforth may be resolved
on its merits. This in itself reflects a trend toward maturity.

As the secretary pointed out on more than one occasion during the early years of the depression, the vital issue was one of
meeting the obligations the corporation had assumed for lessees
and preserving its financial standing. That the situation was
serious is evident from the ratios of total property taxes to rents
collected. For the period of the 1930's taxes averaged 83.44
per cent of rents collected, reaching a high of 96.04 per cent in
1933. Quite clearly this left a dangerously thin margin of
safety—in fact a negative margin after allowance for expenses
and commitments other than taxes. It is evident that sheer
financial necessity forced the corporation to the expedients of
divesting itself of the expenses in connection with the wharf,
parks and golf course, and in placing a limitation on the refunding of lessees' taxes.

MOVES TO CONTROL TAX ASSESSMENTS

Among the continuing frustrations encountered by the colony
were: (1) the persistence of over-assessment of lessees property
because of the carelessness, in some cases the vindictiveness, of
individual lessees, and (2) the inherent stickiness of assessed
valuations. For example, at the meeting of February 17, 1931,
the treasurer reported that one lessee had shown a large *increase*
in the assessment of improvements without apparent justification. The council moved that where the treasurer had reason
to think property had been assessed too high he might decline
to accept tax receipts on rent, and that the treasurer and the
president might select a committee to advise with the lessee and
"ask arbitration if they see fit." At the meeting on May 2, 1932,
the council directed that the president, vice-president and secre-

tary constitute a committee to investigate over-assessments for
1932, and to notify lessees in time to file objections so as to
secure a hearing before the board of equalization. The secretary indirectly reported on this situation in his report to the
annual pre-election meeting of January 23, 1933, saying: "Great
difficulty has been found in securing reductions in assessments
of corporation and lessees' properties comparable to the obvious
decrease in values."

It must be granted that the single tax corporation could do
little about the inherent tendency of tax assessments to lag
behind general changes in market values of properties. The
corporation like other taxpayers benefited from this situation
during the prosperous 1920's but failed to follow through in
increasing the level of its rents along single tax principles. The
average increase in rent collected for the decade of the twenties
over the previous period (1905-1919) was only two hundred
ninety-one per cent, whereas total property taxes increased by
over three hundred seventy-nine per cent. By no means all of
this increase in taxes could be attributed to investments in new
improvements and personal property because the taxes paid on
corporation land also increased more rapidly than did rent
collections. The colony, however, did face one situation unique
to it. Agreeing to reimburse lessees for their taxes or to credit
these on rents meant that the corporation, *per se,* necessarily
had to rely on the initiative of the individual lessees to protest
against any over-assessments. It must be clear that the lessees
found it easy to be indifferent or uncoöperative in this respect
because their self-interest would not be served through an
effective protest. In any event they would have their taxes paid
for them by the corporation. Since this introduced an unnatural factor in the matter of determining property tax
liability, the corporation could not mature and be judged in
its single tax aspects until it found some way to control the
assessments of lessees' properties; *i.e.,* to simulate the normal
protest most property owners will make whenever they believe that their property tax assessments are too high or that
they are unfair.

A New Secretary

No progress toward the objective of controlling assessments of lessees' properties was made until 1936. At the pre-election meeting of January 14, 1936, Mr. E. B. Gaston said he felt a need to retire and recommended the election of his son, Dr. C. A. Gaston, a recommendation found acceptable by the membership. This change in leadership proved quite significant. Mr. E. B. Gaston undoubtedly had been the central figure of the Fairhope Single Tax Corporation in many ways but he had not devoted full time to it. He had been at least equally interested in "colony" affairs as distinct from strictly land management or "corporation" affairs. He had continually sponsored "sideshow" ventures such as the colony-owned telephone system, water system, and colony subsidized or sponsored boats and railroad. Without in any way being disloyal to the single tax phases of the colony, he had permitted himself and the corporation to become involved in town politics, and related activities, which were entirely outside the realm of the single tax. Under these conditions there was little time or energy left for a more systematic analysis and procedure directed at a permanent cure of recurrent problems.

Changes in Procedures

The council made the position of secretary a full-time one. Thus the new incumbent was in a position to think through and to begin an implementation of procedures designed to improve the operations of the corporation as a unique land owner. During 1938 the new secretary inaugurated a service for the tenants of the corporation. In his annual report (January 16, 1939) he said: "Probably one of the most advanced and most radical steps of the year and of many years was the extending of an invitation to lessees, whose rent accounts were paid up, to bring their tax bills to the corporation treasurer for payment from rent funds already collected." He noted that already about one hundred fifty lessees were doing so, resulting in the corporation drawing checks for such direct payments amounting to almost $4,000. This relieved the tenants of the necessity of financing their own tax payments for several months and perhaps quickened to a degree the trade of Fairhope merchants. Within a short period almost all lessees were taking advantage of this service. The next step was for the secretary to extend the tax service of the corporation to include making property tax returns for the lessees from information furnished by them. For the past several years the secretary has returned virtually all of the tax assessments for its lessees. Thus the single tax corporation not only has obtained control over the assessments of lessees' properties, *i.e.,* control over the *returns,* and over protests before the board of equalization, but it can determine at the start of any fiscal year precisely what its total tax liability will be. Along with this, the secretary has for some time prepared annual rent lists of each leasehold along with the tax liabilities; hence, the corporation now is in a position to evaluate its financial condition to a much better extent than was formerly the case.

The extent of the financial squeeze experienced by the single tax corporation during the decade of the 1930's is reflected by the percentage increases in the average of rents collected, and property taxes paid as compared with the previous decade. The average percentage increase in rent collections was 39.31; in taxes paid for lessees, 58.27; in corporation land taxes, 41.48; and in total property taxes paid, 53.97. For the period as a whole, the total property tax payments made by the corporation averaged 83.44 per cent of the total rent collections.

In terms of total amounts handled, however, the decade 1930-1939 almost belies the condition of depression as opposed to the period 1920-1929. On the average the annual rent collections in the latter period were more than \$8,000 greater than those in the earlier period and total property taxes paid averaged over \$8,500 more. For the period as a whole, there was growth both in receipts and in tax disbursements—conditions which call for explanation.

One part of the explanation lies in the fact that the period opened with the previously noted increase in rent charges—an increase which probably should have been made several years earlier. Second, the trustees, in their reports of 1929 and 1930, stressed the moral obligation of the corporation to minimize lessee delinquency in the payment of rents, thus in maintaining rent collections for 1930 and 1931 at levels approximately equal those of 1928 and 1929. This was possible by collecting rents which had become delinquent in the 1920's. A third point is that the decade of the 1920's opened with rent collections of less than $10,000, whereas the annual amount collected for the decade as a whole was almost $21,000. The average for the earlier decade does not reflect the strong upward trend for the period. A fourth factor lies in an increase in rent collections caused by the need for more revenue to meet special assessments levied by the Town of Fairhope to finance improvement projects. Since these assessments are not included in the figures for property taxes paid, the financial squeeze on the corporation in the depression years was even greater than the narrowing spread between rents collected and property taxes paid. Fifth, the corporation ultimately took full advantage of the operations of the Home Owners Loan Corporation as a means of collecting delinquent rents; a means alternative to the harsher procedure of foreclosure and subsequent sale of improvements. Sixth, corporation officials did become somewhat more alert in enforcing rent collections. Seventh, a considerable recovery set in during the middle and late 1930's which was reflected in a marked increase in rent collections which raised the average for the period as a whole. For example, rent collections increased over thirty-four per cent in 1936 and remained at somewhat higher average levels in subsequent years.

OTHER CHANGES

Surviving the combined blows of the Cochrane bridge and the depression was not a simple matter, and in fact was met by making a large number of adjustments in addition to the more major ones of limiting liability for lessees' taxes and deeding away publicly used lands. The following chronicle of official decisions is merely illustrative of the kind of problem posed and of action taken during this period.

December 23, 1931: The council decided against changing the rents for 1932 but adopted a proviso. If the Town of Fairhope should order and complete any improvements during 1932 and assess the cost of such against street frontages, "the rent against the land affected shall be increased by an amount sufficient to meet one-half of the cost of the improvements upon the terms of payment fixed by the Town, the increased rent to be effective from the date upon which the assessment against the property shall become legally fixed." The motivation for this decision must have been at least two-fold. First, the corporation treasury and budget was such that it could not have financed additional assessments without an increase in revenues. Second, the provision that the additional rents would automatically be increased by fifty per cent of the cost, and payable within the relatively short period commonly used for amortizing the costs of such improvements, meant that the annual outlays of tenants would be somewhat larger than they would be if they were required to pay only the amount of additional use value added to their leaseholds by the improvements. That is, the use value of the improvements would extend over a much longer period than double the assessment period. This provision looking to a rapid amortization of the costs of the improvement may therefore have been motivated by a desire to put the lessees affected in a negative frame of mind toward proposed improvements. But whatever the motivation the action scarcely was consistent with the basic intent of the lease contract under which rent would be annually calculated to secure for the community as nearly as possible the entire use value of the leasehold without regard to the underlying reasons for such a value.

This method of financing public improvements was invoked in 1935 following an agreement between the Town of Fairhope and the Public Works Administration. The Fairhope Single Tax Corporation resolved against objecting to the public works projected under this agreement. In his report for 1935, the secretary noted that the increased liabilities would be hard for the colony to finance but the lessees wanted them. He also noted that the amount of rents due was ample but that collection would continue to be difficult.

On November 3, 1938, the paving charges as such were dropped and the council decided to increase the frontage rates on paved streets by amounts sufficient to reflect the benefits derived.

This sequence of events relating to the financing of improvements has a significance beyond the mere adoption of a financial expedient. It is an illustration of a pronounced tendency on the part of the corporation to compromise the inherently esoteric doctrine of collecting the full economic rent in favor of an exoteric policy of basing rents on budget needs with emphasis on concrete services performed.

SMALL ECONOMIES

Concern over the situation caused the council to become more aware of small economies. Illustrative of this were the decisions made on February 6, 1932, (1) to discontinue regular advertising in the *Courier,* and (2) to accept the offer of the secretary to assume the light charges on the council room, saving approximately $1.55 per month. Shortly thereafter the appropriation for the library was cut to $25 per month.

The council was not willing to follow the policy of a literal enforcement of the lease contract in collecting rents. Among other provisions Section 6 of the lease provides: "Upon failure to pay the rents, or any portion thereof, for six months after the same become due, the lessor is hereby authorized to sell at public sale the improvements on any leasehold . . ." Although the courts previously had upheld the corporation in the enforcement of the lease, such drastic action seldom was resorted to in enforcing rent payments even during more prosperous periods. Action taken on February 20, 1933, illustrates the council's reluctance to follow a strict collection policy. At a meeting on this date, the trustees were requested to act as an advisory committee on the question of rent collections and the treasurer was directed to be guided accordingly. It seems reasonable to generalize that the corporation was most considerate in enforcing its claims. It did force some sales of improvements upon occasion but the practice was not a general one.

TAX SALES OF IMPROVEMENTS

Early in the depression the corporation did intervene in the tax sales of improvements. On May 14, 1932, certain officers were directed to attend tax sales and to use their judgment in making bids on corporation account. The power to bid on their own judgment was reaffirmed at the meeting of July 5, 1933, and a fair number of improvements actually were bid in by the corporation—the consideration for at least one being in excess of the taxes and penalties. The number of properties bought in by the corporation has not been determined but it was sufficient to cause the erection of some movable signs offering improvements for sale. The extent to which the corporation found itself in the real estate business other than as a lessor is indicated by the amounts reported as receipts from the sale of improvements during this period: 1933, $359; 1934, $965; 1935, $828; 1936, $1,294; 1937, $3,057; 1938, $1,418. To some extent these receipts represent such things as the value of trees or other similar improvements paid for by the lessee prior to securing a lease, but they also represent considerations received for the sale of improvements lost by the lessees either at tax or at private sales and bid in by the corporation. It is impossible to tell from the annual reports whether these were gross receipts from the sale of improvements or simply receipts net to the corporation; in some cases the corporation returned to the lessee all proceeds in excess of its equity in the property.

GOVERNMENT LOANS TO LESSEES

The principal reason the depression period did not result in a much larger number of tax and forced sales of improvements must have been the availability of Home Owners Loan Corporation (HOLC) loans to lessees. The first action taken by the corporation to avail itself of this source of a more liquid income was at the meeting of August 28, 1933, when the council resolved to accept HOLC bonds for delinquent rents subject to an approval of each particular loan. Some members questioned the wisdom of this on the grounds that loans made by the HOLC would have priority over corporation rents. A few loans were ratified but after October 10, 1934, a much larger number of such loans were granted. On this date the council authorized the president and vice-president to sign any agreement reached with the HOLC.

The reason the corporation had to take notice of loans made to its lessees was that the mortgagor needed assurances on two points: (1) that the single tax corporation would refuse to approve a transfer of the lease without the consent of the mortgagor while the mortgage remained in effect, and (2) that in event of foreclosure of the mortgage the corporation would approve a transfer of the lease to said mortgagee. The first mortgage assent form was adopted by the executive council on April 18, 1927, for use by the Baldwin County Savings and Loan Association. Subsequently new forms of greater detail and somewhat different phraseology were adopted to meet the special conditions of the HOLC, the RFC and the Veterans Administration. In at least three instances it was necessary to obtain amendments in state and federal legislation to permit loans on improvements made on colony leaseholds. The extent to which the HOLC eased the problems of lessees and colony alike is reflected in the reports of HOLC bonds sold: in 1935 the colony sold bonds amounting to $1,539 and in 1936 the sales netted $1,032.

There is no record of the number of lessees who found themselves unable to use the HOLC but who did get some indirect relief through the refinancing activities of the RFC, or the extent to which the Bank of Fairhope found relief by using the facilities of the RFC. The number must have been significant because the resolution of April 19, 1932, intending to facilitate discounting by the local bank with the RFC, of paper secured by an assignment of improved leaseholds, refers to the "many leases" which had been transferred by the lessees to the Bank of Fairhope.

Despite the fact that the secretary could state as he did in his annual report of 1934: "The causes and the efforts at recovery are almost entirely at variance with the economic gospel for which we stand, and the outlook is darkly uncertain," the corporation was quite willing to co-operate with, and actively seek the benefits from, some of these efforts at relief and recovery.

FINANCIAL IMPROVEMENT

The first official sign that the corporation was getting well financially came with the decision of the executive council on August 4, 1936, to make a $5.00 contribution to the Fairhope Baseball Association in the form of a rent credit to its account! A few months later (November 4, 1936) the council authorized an advance payment of $1,000 to the Town of Fairhope for 1936 taxes. On February 15, 1937, it authorized the payment of $1.50 per regular meeting attended to the non-salaried council members, and at the same meeting it increased the appropriation for the library from $25 per month to $50. In 1937 the financial situation was so much easier that the treasurer was authorized to purchase warrants from the Town of Fairhope (July 8); to make a $15 monthly appropriation for five months to support the Fairhope Tourist Club; and to drop the paving charges by incorporating them into increased frontage rates.

The decade of the 1930's ended with a decision to keep the rent multiplier at 2.55 and without making any change in country land rents but with a decision to reincorporate in the rental calculations of residential lots the corner influence tables which had been dropped a few years previously. A review of the annual reports for 1939 will indicate the extent to which the corporation had changed during the previous ten years. Of considerable significance is the fact that all work done on the streets in 1939 was paid for in full ($2,637.51) in addition to meeting the annual installment on work previously done ($3,190.59). The secretary emphasized that in the latter case a considerable sum was for interest and legal and engineering charges which the corporation was able to avoid for the work done in 1939. Second, the corporation was becoming sufficiently prosperous to worry over its income tax liabilities and to advise that the corporation not only should spend what could be spent on deductible obligations but should make further efforts to secure exemptions from the income tax. Third, the failure of colony lessees to obtain loans under provisions of the FHA was noted and it was urged that an effort should be made to secure an amendment in the law such as was secured in the case of the HOLC. Fourth, the members were advised against liberalizing the provision for a transfer of the membership certificate as had been previously recommended. The argument used was: ". . . it is better to go along with a small group than to invite to membership those who had not enough knowledge or interest to seek membership." The rapid rate of decline in the number of members had concerned colony officials for many years but a new cause for concern was expressed in the membership meeting of January 15, 1940. Matters were just too harmonious! Local expressions of interest in either the activities or the policies of the corporation were at a low ebb. After discussing this relatively new phenomenon the members appeared to conclude: (1) the apparent lack of interest was due to the general satisfaction with the management; and (2) most reforms or advances had been activated by relatively small groups. Certainly there was truth in both these observations but perhaps what happened can be explained in still another way. The corporation had superseded the colony. The Fairhope venture was on the verge of attaining maturity but it had not yet thought through its destiny as a corporation and some of the members continued to think in terms of the past and longed for the good old days of colony socials and anniversary celebrations.

XVI

"MATERIALLY, THE COLONY IS DOING WELL . . ."

"MATERIALLY, the Colony is doing well. Educationally, it is getting nowhere." Thus wrote Trustee J. Francis Lemon in an article published in the Fairhope *Courier*, January 11, 1945. Mr. Lemon was by all odds the most active and responsible trustee of the colony in recent years. Finding it necessary to leave Fairhope, he wanted not only to declare "his complete confidence in the ability and honesty of the administrators of the colony's financial affairs," but to elaborate on his notion that: "The colony lessees should be organized, if not by the colony officials by the lessees themselves, forming an association or union—call it what you may."

Trustee Lemon asserted that the colony was becoming less democratic each year. The membership was shrinking and the power concentrating in fewer hands. In earlier periods there had been occasional active campaigns to keep the ranks filled with convinced followers of Henry George, and there had been periods when it was customary to call lessees' meetings to discuss rents and expenditures, and sometimes non-member lessees had served on corporation committees.

"Now," he wrote, "rents are raised without any opportunity for previous public discussion, without any previous notice to lessees, members or trustees." Calculation of rents on the basis of the Somers System would lend itself very well to a co-operative consideration of rents because this system is based on public opinion as to relative land values within the community. The lessees should have an association through which they could study the Somers System, "and demand its full use." Mr. Lemon concluded: "There is no better way of educating people in the economics of rent and single tax than by getting them together in meeting and discussing their own rent problems. Modern education demands more than merely reading books and listening to talks. There must be active participation in doing things. Here in Fairhope is the greatest opportunity to educate people in the principles of single tax economics—by having them take part in the administration of a single tax system. The Fairhope colony should be made a true organic school of single tax education."

Mr. Lemon could not remain in Fairhope for the annual membership meeting held January 19, but his last report stimulated much discussion. The members in attendance thought the judgment that educationally the colony was getting nowhere was a bit extreme. They did agree that the educational accomplishments left much to be desired and that "plans should be considered for greater effectiveness in that field." To a degree the attending members reacted as though they had been placed on the defensive; they argued that "education has to be preceded by a desire to become educated and that the educational accomplishment of paid churchmen in tens of thousands of churches throughout the world also left much to be desired." Nonetheless, "public meetings, social gatherings and study classes were discussed but no action taken."

Twelve members attended this 1945 annual membership meeting.

That the period beginning with 1940 was one in which the single tax corporation was "doing well" materially is amply borne out by the data in Table III. Although the corporation keeps its books and makes its annual reports on a cash rather than an accrual basis, which permits rather large fluctuations from year to year because of variations in rent delinquencies and in tax payments, the trend definitely was in the direction of widening the margin by which rents collected exceeded taxes paid. The average annual percentage increase for the period 1940-1953 in rent collected was 69.88, as compared with an annual average increase in property taxes paid for lessees of 34.15 per cent, and an actual decrease in taxes paid on corporation property of 2.42 per cent.

TABLE III.   FAIRHOPE SINGLE TAX CORPORATION
PART I.   RENT COLLECTIONS AND PROPERTY TAXES
PAID, ANNUALLY, 1905-1953

Year	Rent Collected	Taxes Paid for Lessees	Taxes Paid on Land	Total Property Taxes	Per Cent Lessees Taxes of Rent	Per Cent Total Taxes of Rent
1905	$ 2,294	$ 641	$ 265	$ 906	27.94	39.49
1906	2,142	640	297	937	29.87	43.74
1907	(3,025)	n. a.	n. a.	(1,561)	——	51.60
1908	3,195	1,351	362	1,713	42.28	53.61
1909	(3,500)	n. a.	n. a.	(2,223)	——	63.51
1910	3,907	2,000	619	2,619	51.19	67.03
1911	4,458	2,319	546	2,865	52.02	64.27
1912	5,665	2,736	882	3,618	48.77	63.87
1913	5,891	2,170	1,241	3,411	36.84	57.90
1914	5,992	2,569	268	2,837	42.87	47.35
1915	7,064	2,878	1,555	4,433	40.74	62.75
1916	6,203	2,533	998	3,531	40.84	56.92
1917	7,151	2,844	1,519	4,363	39.77	61.01
1918	8,014	3,877	2,783	6,660	48.38	83.10
1919	7,478	3,402	1,464	4,866	45.49	65.07
Total	$ 69,454	$ 29,960	$ 12,799	$ 42,759	43.14	61.56
1920	$ 7,834	$ 4,200	$ 2,730	$ 6,930	53.59	88.42
1921	10,624	5,792	2,732	8,524	54.52	80.23
1922	13,007	6,952	2,845	9,797	53.45	75.32
1923	19,234	9,687	2,993	12,680	50.36	65.92
1924	22,587	11,942	3,503	15,445	52.87	68.38
1925	20,633	11,607	3,287	14,894	56.25	72.19
1926	24,650	14,777	5,658	20,435	59.95	82.90
1927	28,414	15,495	5,654	21,149	54.53	74.43
1928	30,573	17,565	5,709	23,274	57.45	76.13
1929	31,419	18,974	5,655	24,629	60.39	78.39
Total	$208,975	$116,991	$ 40,766	$157,757	55.98	75.49

TABLE III.   FAIRHOPE SINGLE TAX CORPORATION
PART I.   RENT COLLECTIONS AND PROPERTY TAXES
PAID, ANNUALLY, 1905-1953 (CONTINUED)

Year	Rent Collected	Taxes Paid for Lessees	Taxes Paid on Land	Total Property Taxes	Per Cent Lessees Taxes of Rent	Per Cent Total Taxes of Rent
1930	$ 32,532	$ 21,694	$ 6,396	$ 28,090	66.69	86.35
1931	30,561	21,074	4,599	25,673	68.96	85.01
1932	28,106	20,840	2,030	22,870	74.15	81.37
1933	26,734	18,986	6,689	25,675	71.02	96.04
1934	27,030	17,319	5,514	22,833	64.07	84.47
1935	26,589	15,356	9,630	24,986	57.75	93.63
1936	34,621	19,669	6,462	26,131	56.81	75.48
1937	24,711	15,100	5,829	20,929	61.11	84.70
1938	33,232	20,994	5,330	26,324	63.17	79.21
1939	27,021	14,125	5,285	19,410	52.27	71.83
Total	$291,137	$185,157	$ 57,764	$242,921	63.59	83.44
1940	$ 31,102	$ 17,667	$ 5,291	$ 22,958	56.80	73.82
1941	35,517	18,940	5,269	24,209	53.33	68.16
1942	38,434	20,139	5,268	25,407	52.40	66.11
1943	38,396	19,509	5,268	24,777	50.84	64.53
1944	37,354	20,653	5,257	25,910	50.51	69.38
1945	40,892	19,931	5,271	25,202	48.74	61.63
1946	40,758	19,345	5,287	24,632	47.46	60.43
1947	53,221	24,871	6,000	30,871	46.73	58.01
1948	56,681	27,006	6,027	33,033	47.64	58.28
1949	61,687	29,526	6,008	35,534	47.86	57.60
1950	61,991	30,403	6,078	36,481	49.04	58.14
1951	63,108	31,396	6,038	37,434	49.75	59.32
1952	66,437	36,186	6,098	42,284	54.47	63.65
1953	66,889	32,182	6,098	38,280	48.11	57.23
Total	$692,467	$347,754	$ 78,898	$426,652	50.22	61.61

Table III does not necessarily demonstrate the single tax contention that the economic rent of land will increase with sufficient speed in a rapidly maturing urban community to permit an even larger revenue from land taxes alone than would be obtained from a uniform tax on land, improvements and personal property. On the other hand it is quite evident that the economic rent of corporation land (as determined by the subjective valuation of corporation officials) recently has tended to outstrip the tax payments from uniform rates on the

TABLE III.   FAIRHOPE SINGLE TAX CORPORATION
PART II.   RENT COLLECTIONS AND PROPERTY TAXES PAID BY PERIODS, 1905-1953*

A.   TOTAL FOR PERIODS

	Rent Collected	Taxes Paid for Lessees	Taxes on Corporation Land	Total Property Taxes	Per Cent Lessees Taxes of Rent	Per Cent Total Taxes of Rent
Period 1**	$ 69,454	$ 29,960	$12,799	$ 42,759	43.14	61.56
Period 2	208,975	116,991	40,766	157,757	55.98	75.49
Period 3	291,137	185,157	56,800	241,957	63.59	83.44
Period 4	692,457	347,754	78,898	426,652	50.22	61.61

B.   ANNUAL AVERAGE

	Rent Collected	Lessees Taxes Paid	Corporation Land Taxes	Total Property Taxes
Period 1	$ 5,343	$ 2,304	$ 985	$ 3,289
Period 2	20,898	11,699	4,077	15,776
Period 3	29,114	18,516	5,776	24,292
Period 4	49,461	24,839	5,636	30,475

C.   PERCENTAGE INCREASE IN ANNUAL AVERAGES

	Rent Collected	Lessees Taxes Paid	Corporation Land Taxes	Total Property Taxes
Period 2 over 1	291.13	407.77	313.91	379.66
Period 3 over 2	39.31	58.27	41.48	53.97
Period 4 over 3	69.88	34.15	− 2.42	25.45

D.   PER CENT LESSEES TAXES PAID TO TOTAL PROPERTY TAXES

Period 1	70.01
Period 2	74.07
Period 3	76.21
Period 4	81.51

* Does not include receipts from penalties, lease fees, or bonuses; property taxes paid do not include special assessments or direct outlays on roads, streets, curbs, gutters and sidewalks.

** Period 1: 1905-1919 except for years 1907 and 1909; Period 2: 1920-1929; Period 3: 1930-1939; Period 4: 1940-1953.

assessed values of property located on corporation lands (as determined by the subjective valuation of the assessing authorities). Since rents and assessed valuations rest upon the judgment of two separate groups of human beings, a conclusion as to whether exclusive taxation of economic rent would return as much or more revenue than a more general property tax must await an analysis of the taxes paid by lessees, and by the tenants of lessees, over and above the amounts paid for them by the corporation.

The principal reasons for the material well-being of the corporation during the early 1940's were: the more complete current collection of rents together with the collection of previous delinquencies; the cumulative effect of corporation control over the making of tax returns for lessees' improvements and personal property, together with an increased practice of protesting unfairly high assessments; the inability to make street and other property improvements during the war years because of shortages of material and labor; and the population growth which greatly stimulated applications for land, thus bringing more land on the rent roll. Nor was this increasing margin between rent collections and taxes paid absorbed by increases in salaries, property maintenance and other expenses. The corporation always has been quite careful in appropriating for its own employees, equipment, supplies and related expenses. Throughout its history the single tax corporation has leaned backward with respect to salaries in order to avoid any charge of self-interest being leveled against its leaders. Those who have served have been motivated at least as much by a spirit of dedication as by a desire for income. For example, the total salaries in 1941 were $3,051, and as late as 1953 the total salaries for two full-time officials and occasional part-time assistants amounted only to $8,523—approximately ten per cent of the total disbursements.

The material or financial well-being of the single tax corporation posed some fundamental questions of policy and created some new problems.

One of these was the policy with respect to the annual rent appraisement, with particular reference to the general level of rents, *i.e.*, the size of the multiplier. From a doctrinal standpoint the policy of the level of rents should have been fixed from the inception of the colony—as indeed it was in terms of the official utterances of the colony leaders who never wavered from the position that the policy should be one of taking all economic rent. In practice, however, it appears that most increases in rents were made at times when the need for revenue could easily be demonstrated, and from time to time colony officials explicitly stated that the policy should be one of an accurate determination of *relative* values to which a multiplier would be applied sufficient to bring in the needed revenue. As a rule, however, the rationalization of increased rents was two-fold: (1) an attempted demonstration that the use value of the land had increased, and (2) an attempt to show that the increased rent was justified on moral grounds. From its beginnings the colony leadership laid heavy stress on ethical considerations—the wrongness of taxes levied on individual effort and the rightness of the community taking for its own purposes that which it created. Although colony spokesmen explicitly recognized the adverse effects of speculation in keeping land unused, or under-used, there was a definite emphasis on the idea that private speculation in land was morally bad.

The observations just made are not intended to imply that the prophets of the Fairhope colony were unaware of the virtues of discriminatory land taxation to encourage the utilization of land, because they manifestly were not. What may be inferred from these observations is that, with the principal exception of the bay frontage from the beginning, and some commercial locations within a short period, there was neither an absolute scarcity of land in and around the colony, nor was there for many years any appreciable relative superiority of some locations over others. If rents were too low to impel all lessees to make the most economical or intensive use of their respective leaseholds, the practical difference was small. The colony possessed much unleased land on which newcomers might settle with but slight disadvantage as to either location or fertility. As long as the differential advantages among locations were small, the colony could fulfill its humanitarian purpose of providing improvident but ambitious individuals with sites for subsistence farming, or for homes, without the necessity of accumulating funds for outright purchase, and it could and did leave them almost absolutely free to use their leaseholds as they wished. Of course the colony did differentiate among locations, and it did increase the general levels of its rentals upon occasion to such an extent that those sites the community decided were the most valuable were improved more and more intensively. The illustration of Henry George of the appearance of economic rent concurrently with that of a few settlers forming a neighborhood in the midst of an un-bounded savannah of uniform fertility, was clearly borne out in the Fairhope experience. On balance, however, it does seem that the motivation behind the policy of periodic rental in-creases for the first thirty-five years was more to meet a revenue need and to achieve an ethical objective than it was to maxi-mize the productivity of labor and capital within the com-munity.

By 1940 conditions had changed radically. The corporation did not need more revenue to meet its contractual obligations. The community had grown so large with a population com-posed overwhelmingly of non-members, of non-believers, and of those wholly ignorant of or entirely indifferent to the ethical bases of the single tax doctrine, that rationalizations of an ethical nature had lost much of their practical significance. It must be observed further that the membership, never ex-clusively single tax in its composition, became both smaller and more indifferent to the historic objectives and philosophical considerations undergirding the Georgian rent policy. By 1940 the single tax corporation badly needed a restatement, if not a revision of its *raison d'être*. It is also evident that the justifica-tion would necessarily have to emphasize the material well-being of the community and of the individual lessees, with ethical considerations relegated to a supporting role.

For a few years after 1940 the general level of rents was not increased. At first the policy was one of "wait and see." In his report for 1940 (Minutes, membership meeting, January 23, 1941) the secretary said: "Country lands are very largely under lease but there is some question if some of the leased lands are being put to the most productive use. However as pressure of demand develops the proof should result." In this statement there is a clear implication that the secretary was aware of the function of the corporation as being one of com-pelling the most productive use of land. However, rents were not increased and the decision of the council in 1942 was not to change rents for 1943.

At the membership meeting of January 27, 1944, Trustee Lemon reported on a partial inspection he had made of country lands. He stated that in some cases misuse could cause serious erosion. He suggested a sustained inspection of those lands where the corporation had granted an allowance or discount of rents for physical defects. If, upon inspection, it was found that the lessee was not making use of compensatory treatment (proper terracing or confining use to pasture or wood lots) he would be penalized by a charge of full rent. In this suggestion there is evidence of a desire to conserve the inherent productivity of corporation lands but no discernible concern with respect to keeping these lands accessible to those who would use them most intensively. At this same meeting, however, the secretary reported that all of the country land was under lease and that "we will soon have to give consideration to further subdivision of some of the larger tracts of land inside the town. In doing this consideration must be given to the most economical and practical extension of streets and public services." Quite possibly this explicit recognition of the increasing scarcity of unleased corporation lands may have supported the decision of the council to increase rents for 1945; the frontage rates of several streets were increased, the multiplier was increased from 2.55 to 2.70, and the rents on country lands were increased six per cent. (Minutes, December 7, 1944.) This was the first increase in the general rent level since 1930.

In the light of the rapid rate of increase in Fairhope's population and the war-time prosperity, the 1944 increase in rents was indeed a modest one, a judgment clearly demonstrated by the excessive prices paid for improvements in the transfer of leaseholds. The executive council met in special meeting on November 28, 1945, to consider reports of excessive prices being asked for the transfer of leaseholds. The meeting resulted in an apparent agreement on several points. 1. The higher prices asked and paid during war-time were due to increased building costs and scarcity of buildings because of restrictions. 2. The high prices paid during war-time were therefore for improvements and not for land. 3. This conclusion is borne out because throughout the war period the corporation had land available for lease without any purchase price. 4. This condition has changed; the corporation no longer has enough available unimproved land to prevent lessees from adding a land value to the prices asked for improvements. 5. Adding an increment for land value would defeat the purpose of the corporation, *i.e.,* to prevent anyone from profiting from holding its land other than by use, and would create an artificial demand, one not for use but for resale at a profit. For some undisclosed reason the council was reluctant to raise rents across the board, but resolved "that endorsements on instruments of transfer state the exact consideration of the transfer." If the consideration of the transfer was excessive the council would not approve, as provided in the lease contract. Thus, in 1945, the council decided to rely on the procedure adopted in 1925 to combat speculation in corporation lands.

At its meeting of December 20, 1945, the council decided that 1946 rents would be figured at the same street frontage rates and that there would be no change either in the multiplier or in acreage rates.

During 1946 the speculation in colony leaseholds became quite noticeable. At its meeting of October 3, 1946, the council took cognizance that the considerations asked and paid for the transfer of improved leaseholds were reaching even higher levels. It decided that the prices were excessive on any basis of normal demand, and normal supply and replacement costs. Major factors were the war-time growth of Fairhope, restrictions on building, and high building costs. However, "some part" of the present high prices might have been a too low level of colony rents, a factor which "should receive consideration in rents for 1947." The council nevertheless repeated some of the arguments of the 1920's, particularly that a local application of the single tax could not overcome general speculative forces. Therefore, "there is no effective means available to the corporation to protect those who must or will buy or build now, from the loss in price sure to come when the country reaches a balance in supply and effective demand." As a partial solution, however, the corporation made extensive changes in its street frontage rates, increased the multiplier from 2.70 to 3.0, and increased acreage rates by fifteen per cent. (Minutes, December 19, 1946.)

Fairhope continued to grow and to prosper. The amount of unleased corporation land within the urban community shrank rapidly toward the vanishing point. As a result intensive margins of use of more centrally located lands demanded an increasingly intensive development, and a noticeable growth of improvements on privately-owned lands took place—a growth which checked the upward trend in the annual use value of lands owned by the corporation which, after all, accounted for only twenty per cent of the area of the Town of Fairhope. The demand for colony-owned land continued to increase and the council reacted by making frequent changes, mostly upward, in street values. General increases, however, continued to be made infrequently but were sufficient to keep a considerable pressure on excessively large holdings and on under-used lease-holds. The result was an appreciable number of partial and total surrenders. With the forfeitures, these enabled the corporation to satisfy some demands for building sites through acceptance of applications for land as opposed to transfers of existing leaseholds. It was, however, quite apparent that the colony soon would exhaust these sources of land; hence, it took steps to enlarge its supply by (1) exercising its option to recover possession of the golf course for subsequent subdivision, and (2) subdividing acreage hitherto unaccessible by financing the extension of public services to these areas.

The pressure of circumstances was forcing the corporation to adopt all alternative expedients to meet the rapidly growing demand for land within urban Fairhope. How the corporation has attempted to do this, and with what results, is treated in Chapter XVII as a special problem. It is a foregone conclusion that the present day problem of making land accessible not only is quite different from the one of the first forty years, but is one which must be met increasingly by reliance on the impersonal force of carefully calculated annual rentals.

Another problem to be resolved was how to dispose of the "surplus" of receipts over contractual obligations and recurrent expenses. In theory corporation revenues were to be spent for the benefit of the lessees, with a high priority given to a refunding of property taxes paid by lessees for the purpose of simulating a single tax situation. But, aside from tax refunds, how should the excess revenues be spent? How is the question of maximum lessee benefits to be determined? Who is to determine it? Who actually makes the decisions and upon what bases?

These questions have attracted surprisingly little attention in the last fifteen years and only the last question, and that only partially, can be answered off-hand. There can be little question but that the decisions of how and when to spend were made by the officers and the executive council. Lessees long since have stopped attending meetings of the council to say nothing of ceasing to have meetings among themselves and of making suggestions to the corporation. Even the general membership turned indifferent toward corporation problems. The range of attendance of members at recent annual meetings has been between eleven and twenty with a median attendance of about fifteen. The matters concerning those few members in attendance, for the most part, were not those of expenditure policy, except in minor matters such as cemetery maintenance and library improvement and service. There have been a few exceptions. At the meeting of January 20, 1942, a question was raised concerning the propriety of the corporation's making appropriations for the aid of the organic school, but the minutes disclose neither an animated debate nor a consensus. At one of the better attended membership meetings (January 20, 1949) Mr. R. L. Rockwell suggested, "that all members be giving consideration to how such income might be expended to most effectively and specifically benefit the corporation's lessees, thus accentuating lessee advantages over others." There is no evidence that a single member other than officers expended much if any energy in a positive response to this plea.

In practice most of the margin of receipts above expenses and contractual obligations was disbursed for improvements such as roads, streets, sidewalks, curbs, sewers and extensions of utility services. Also, as a matter of practice, most such expenditures have been made within the urban community. Since the bulk of single tax corporation disbursements have been made within the municipal limits, and since the city lands owned by the corporation are to a degree intermingled with privately-owned lands, some problems of practical co-operation and some intra-community tensions have resulted.

On April 12, 1947, the executive council authorized the town to make certain street improvements at the corporation's expense. The town council decided to make extensive improvements in 1948 and adopted the special assessment method of financing some of them. Approximately $77,000 was spent on improvements, of which $32,765 was paid by the colony and $44,258 charged against deeded property. The corporation paid its share immediately, thus lowering the total interest charges but probably not reducing the legal and engineering charges, which presumably were spread evenly over all property affected. An undetermined amount of the improvements made in 1948 were made at the volition of the single tax corporation and the nature of the improvements actually was determined by corporation officials. Where improvements are entirely on colony land it is practicable for the initiative to be taken by either party, and for the Town Council to agree that the colony might hire the contractor and pay him directly and even draw up the specifications. This arrangement has not always been entirely satisfactory to the town officials who point out that sometimes the improvements have been too extensive—too cheap—therefore imposing on the general fund of the town an undue expense for re-sealing. This complaint may or may not be well taken but the criticism does exist, and it is quite possible that the corporation has followed a "poor man's" psychology in its decisions to spread its improvements over as large an area as possible.

The Town of Fairhope also undertook major improvements in 1949 in the form of widening Highway 89 (Section Street) and constructing sidewalks from Section Street to the bay. This was done by the town which was reimbursed by the colony, and by the owners of deeded property affected, all of the latter being located within two blocks. In the 1949 improvements the city contributed only about $2,000 to cover the cost of widening an extensive fill by twenty feet. In Fairhope, it is customary for the general fund of the municipality to pay only a small part, usually that caused by some preparatory ground work.

The financial well-being of the corporation in recent years has permitted extensive improvements abutting its own lands which has stimulated similar improvements on adjacent privately-owned lands. It has also caused some misunderstandings within the community. Some residents on deeded lands find it difficult to understand why they cannot get improvements. The explanation is a simple one. First, the special assessment procedure requires over fifty per cent agreement among the property owners affected. Second, bonds cannot be marketed unless the issue is at least $25,000. This means that the improvement must be approximately a mile in extent. There simply is no effective way for the city to finance small improvements. To do so it would have to have the money available in its general fund. There also would be a basic question of fairness involved in the city making some street improvements out of general funds while financing most of them out of special assessments.

The cash disbursements of the corporation for "lands, highways and property expense" since 1947 have been: 1948, $37,763; 1949, $24,038; 1950, $10,915; 1951, $2,870; 1952, $21,880; and 1953, $34,408. The great bulk of these have been made directly by the corporation on its own specifications and arrangements with contractors with, of course, the full knowledge and consent of the town authorities. Whether the very best co-operative arrangements have been worked out between the town and the single tax corporation has not been determined, but it can be asserted that the little town of Fairhope appears to have far more such improvements than almost any similarly populated city, unless it be within those areas where per capita incomes are very much larger. Fairhope always has been a community of lower middle-class income families; its high relative rank in the matter of street and related improvements must be attributable to the fact that so much of the annual value of its land has been made available for such projects. The example set in this respect by the single tax corporation may have forced private developers of land to undertake more such improvements in the course of making their developments than they otherwise might have done. The colony definitely has performed a yardstick function.

Aside from the increased tempo of spending for street and road improvements, the development of the expenditure pattern of the corporation since 1940 has not been remarkable. Upon occasion relatively large sums were spent for library expansion and cemetery maintenance, and most of the usual expenses gradually increased in dollar amounts. The only change of any degree took place in the disbursements for "civic contributions." These were: 1944, $345; 1945, $346; 1946, $445; 1947, $522; 1948, $385; 1949, $416; 1950, $373; *1951, $3,075; 1952, $2,310;* and *1953, $2,540.* Most of these contributions were to the organic school which long has benefited from the single tax corporation in several ways. The school occupies free of all charges nine of the more valuable acres in town. In addition, the corporation owns the school buildings which the school uses free of charge.[1] The total contribution for civic

---

[1] During one of the periods when the school was in financial distress, the buildings were mortgaged to an individual for $10,000. The school could not retire this debt and the colony purchased the mortgage at a discount. When the school again experienced financial difficulties, the colony came to its aid but took in consideration a bill of sale to the colony covering all the physical properties of the school. The school has free use of the buildings and land but is responsible for maintenance.

purposes currently is fairly large, but it is too concentrated to suit the taste of many residents of the community. Those who complain may have a point if they are lessees. Non-lessee residents of the community may have cause to question the judgment of the single tax corporation. In theory the rental revenues are to be disbursed for the benefit of the lessees. Morally, they would appear to be analagous to a special trust. Although the sums are not large in an absolute sense, the ratio of direct contributions to this private school is relatively large —approximately 2.5 to 66.8. Quite aside from such questions as to whether the school any longer is an "organic" school as Mrs. Johnson conceived such a school, or whether even a true "organic" school is needed under present conditions, there remains the underlying question of *who* should make the decision as to what is in the lessees' general interest.

It is difficult to disagree with Trustee Lemon's judgment that materially the colony is doing well and educationally it is getting nowhere, or at least not very far. The membership is appreciably smaller and older than it was in 1944 and the extent to which the general membership and the lessees actively participate in colony decisions is almost nil. The corporation is well administered and its influence is great even though it is neither understood nor appreciated generally, even among the lessees. Do the colony leaders want it this way? Or are they disturbed that their doctrinal influence has fallen to such a low stage that the municipality in very recent times has (1) started on a program of business license taxation, and (2) adopted a city zoning ordinance? According to single tax doctrine neither of these two steps would be necessary or desirable.

With respect to Mr. Lemon's recommendations of reinaugurating lessees' meetings, judgment must be reserved. Before maximum good could be accomplished thereby, the corporation members and officials need a much clearer notion of the present-day role of their venture. In particular they need to decide whether a collection of the full economic rent under present-day conditions in Fairhope serves a useful purpose. As previously stated, this purpose largely must be one of acting as an expedient to assure maximum productivity for Fairhope capital and labor. They also need to decide whether they should resume a more liberal policy of paying taxes for lessees and the tenants of lessees. This problem is analyzed in Chapter XVIII. Only after decisions are made on these two points would it seem possible for the corporation to make a mature judgment on the desirability of more formal community education, and of a resumption of efforts to tie the lessees into the colony on a more active basis.

xvii

ACCESSIBILITY OF FAIRHOPE
SINGLE TAX CORPORATION LAND;
SOME PROBLEMS OF POLICY

D*URING* 1944 the colony leased the last acre of its country lands and many applicants for such lands have since been turned away. The corporation still possessed some unleased land in town but none that was immediately available "has access to the essential public utilities, water electricity and good roads." (Annual report for 1945.) Much of the practically inaccessible urban land, as of 1945, has since been opened for lease. Within a short period the colony will not have any land not under lease. Thus the Fairhope Single Tax Corporation now must answer a question which has been raised many times over the years: what will be the future of the colony when all of its land is under lease?

The present secretary, Dr. C. A. Gaston, long has been among those who have looked upon this condition as a problem of land shortage. He sees three possible solutions. "One is to buy undeveloped land that has access to existing streets and established utilities; present inflated land prices discourage this course. Another is to clear and develop new streets and secure the extension of utilities into our nearest unleased areas, which is now contemplated. Still another is to provide additional public improvements in nearby sections where low rent encourages larger holdings. In such areas within the corporate limits of the town there are single leaseholds of from one to ten acres, and one of twenty acres, with correspondingly large utilization of street frontage, where utilities are already established." (Annual report for 1945.) The secretary explains that the improved facilities *will justify* higher rents, which, in their turn, will encourage the lessees of these larger tracts either to put them to higher uses or to share them with others— through the process of surrender, forfeiture, or transfer.

Dr. Gaston's argument should not be interpreted too literally. He would be among the first to protest premature or overly costly improvements solely for the purpose of justifying higher rents with a view to forcing a more intensive use of the lands affected. The general demand for the land must be such that the higher usages are economically justifiable; well-planned public improvements may facilitate or even hasten a higher land utilization but they seldom, if ever, would be an independent causative factor.

A TEST OF THE FAIRHOPE PLAN

One test of the soundness of the Fairhope plan is whether colony-owned land is used more or less effectively than the same or similar land would be under the more usual system of land tenure. From the point of view of the community, do colony policies facilitate, or retard, the maximum improvement of a land site justified at any given time? Do they facilitate shifting the use of land from an inferior to a superior use over a period of time? From the point of view of an individual, does the colony plan unduly discourage expensive or specialized improvements? Does it tend to handicap a growing business in acquiring additional land? Or, from the point of view of the several neighborhoods making up the community, does the colony policy of according complete freedom to its lessees with respect to their improvements, make for uncertainty over the future character of the neighborhoods and hence over the values of existing improvements. In short, is the Fairhope policy superior or inferior to individual ownership of land in achieving an optimum balance between sometimes conflicting individual interests and rights, and those of the community as such?

Too frequently such questions as these must rest upon argument alone. With respect to Fairhope, however, it is possible to contrast actual land usages of colony property with the land usages in other organized communities in Baldwin County, and with the usages of privately-owned land adjacent to colony leaseholds within the municipality of Fairhope. Although it is never possible to control a social experiment and thus definitely prove or disprove a social theory, the results of the Fairhope colony experience appear to these observers as quite superior to those observable in comparable areas. The values accepted in reaching this judgment are those of the community as a whole, as opposed to the values of individuals as speculators or as seekers after absolute privacy, irrespective of the costs to them or to the group. It is, of course, impossible to define community or social values with as much precision or universality as might be desired. In a general sense, however, optimum community land utilization would include a continuing highest use of all sites, serving as many people as possible with access to the best lands for employment of their labor or for their homes, and without forcing users to pay exorbitant prices. An exorbitant price would be one "appreciably higher" than the capitalized value of the net income from land on the basis of its most productive usage. In a rapidly growing community it is probably inevitable (even in the Fairhope colony) that late-comers pay some premium to current possessors for the privilege of using certain lands. A "reasonable" premium, therefore, might be one which does not prevent land from being used in the most effective manner. Implicit in the values herein accepted is a rejection of paternalism in any degree. The community values are conceived to be those *accepted* by individuals, not those imposed upon individuals by any oligarchy, whether official or unofficial.

RAPID GROWTH OF FAIRHOPE

Over the years the Fairhope colonists have made much of

the fact that Fairhope grew steadily and more rapidly than any of her sister communities in Baldwin County, particularly those communities similarly situated on Mobile Bay such as Daphne, Montrose, Battles Wharf and Point Clear. All of these are much older, some of them having been established village centers for more than one hundred years before Fairhope was founded. Daphne formerly was a county seat and had the further advantage afforded by the presence of a normal school. None of these communities enjoyed any protection whatever from land speculation, which, from the point of view of a singletaxer, is a "retarding and growth destructive influence." As Dr. Gaston put it, the Fairhope (or single tax) plan for community collection of the increase in land values (due to the community itself) protected "Fairhope from land speculation." As a result of such protection ". . . many who had desired to, but could not economically secure sites on the shore, came to Fairhope." Besides finding Fairhope sites accessible, without the necessity of paying speculative premiums, the ". . . collection of the socially created economic rent of its lands gave it a locally controlled public fund with which to provide improvements of its own choice and its own direction." (1947 annual report.) The relatively rapid growth of Fairhope as contrasted with the much slower growth, or even the long-term stagnation with some retrogression, of other Eastern Shore centers, may, with considerable certainty, be attributable to the colony plan.

Before adducing any further considerations in support of this conclusion, it may be well to dispose of a misunderstanding current among some of the non-colony residents of Fairhope. Some are inclined to dismiss out-of-hand any basis for the contention that the single tax features of Fairhope have had any bearing upon the relative growths of Fairhope and the other Eastern Shore communities. Discounting those who would discredit colony accomplishments either out of human perversity or because of enmity toward the single tax, many Fairhope citizens honestly misunderstand the nature of the claim. They think the colony is attempting to take full credit for the *absolute* growth of the community. This, of course, simply is not the case. Colony leaders fully understand that the recent quite rapid growth in Fairhope is due primarily to the recent growth of Mobile together with improved highways. They understand that the future of Fairhope depends to a great extent on developments on the outside, and particularly in Mobile. They maintain solely that Fairhope developed earlier and faster, and has enjoyed more public services financed out of its own resources, for a much longer period of time, than have any of the neighboring communities, and that this *relatively* superior experience is attributable to its underlying system of land tenure.

If this is not the explanation then what can it be? What advantages has Fairhope had over the older settlements? It is difficult to find any.

Fairhope agricultural land is inferior in several respects to much of the hinterland of Daphne. Nor was Fairhope as favorably located for water transportation as several of the other communities.

Did Fairhope attract a superior type of resident? Possibly but not probably; at least it would be gratuitous so to claim. Certainly members of the colony make no such claim. In his annual report for 1948, secretary Gaston wrote: "Baldwin County is largely a product of colonies. In the beginning few occupied as small an area or had as little capital as did the half dozen Singletaxer families that came to Baldwin County in 1894. . . . The other colonists, Italians at and near Daphne, Scandinavians at Silverhill, Greeks near Loxley, Germans at Elberta and many lesser groups and the immigrants from northern states who settled Foley and Magnolia Springs, *composed no less ambitious and industrious men and women than were those who came to Fairhope.*"

Was Fairhope subsidized by wealthy friends to a greater extent than comparable communities? The answer here must be yes, but no inference can be logically drawn that these subsidies were of major importance in accounting for Fairhope's superior development. The most important gifts received by the colony were those of land or money for the land fund. Obviously gifts of land merely changed its ownership from private to colony; in no wise did they add anything to the economic foundation of the community, save as colony policies made land more accessible to those who would use it. The gifts to the library and the organic school contributed to the cultural life of Fairhope and undoubtedly were influential in attracting some residents. Gifts of this type, however, scarcely were unique with Fairhope; quite possibly outside friends of other colonies based on ethnic or religious considerations made some such contributions to them. Outside contributions to the wharf were fully and quickly amortized, and the outside money lost on the ill-fated steamer *Fairhope* and on the People's Railroad Company scarcely gave any permanent advantage to the little community. Mr. Fels and others did make personal loans to the early colonists which enabled some of them to remain in Fairhope.

Did Fairhope grow primarily because of the superb advertising it received? Quite probably the nation-wide, even world-wide, advertising of the young colony did attract some of the earlier arrivals. Almost from the outset the community possessed cultural advantages which attracted some. Its intellectual aliveness, its friendliness toward the reformer, and its general cosmopolitan characteristics brought many who were not single-taxers. Even granting that the advertising (much of it free) stimulated many to visit and some to remain in Fairhope, the nexus is not wholly removed from the single tax features of the place. Let it never be forgotten that singletaxers are individualist in their philosophy, and as such appreciate individuality in others. If the general intellectual and cultural environment was such as to bring outsiders in, this may have been due to the spirit of freedom so characteristic of the singletaxer.

ASSESSED VALUATIONS

A rough comparison of the relative growth of Fairhope and other communities in Baldwin County is afforded by the assessed valuations for property taxation. The comparison must be imperfect because although the law contemplates uniform treatment of all property wherever located in the State, in prac-

tice property located within the colony or in the Town of Fairhope may be over or under-assessed in comparison with property located elsewhere in the county.

Recall that in 1894 the land on which the colony located was
wholly unimproved and was virtually without value except for
a nominal speculative value. Ultimately the colony acquired
about four thousand acres of which about four hundred acres
are within the municipality of Fairhope, about twenty per cent
of the area. The total acreage within Baldwin County is one
million forty thousand. The colony therefore owns only about
one two-hundred and sixtieth (1/260) of the county. Table IV
clearly shows the relatively high concentration of assessed valuations of Baldwin County and in the Town of Fairhope on
colony land.

TABLE IV.   1953 ASSESSMENT COMPARISONS

	Individuals	Corporations	Utilities	Total
Baldwin County	$21,874,800	$1,775,980	$3,216,800	$26,867,580
Colony	1,126,770	328,010		1,454,780
Assessments in the Town of Fairhope:				
Total for Town	1,766,870	352,830	66,560	2,186,260
Colony	1,000,870	287,490		1,288,360
Non-colony owners	766,000	65,340	66,560	901,550
Assessments on property in Bay Minette	1,644,535	36,640	253,404	1,934,570

Assessments, Exclusive of Utilities, Against Property

In Town of Fairhope	$ 2,119,700
In Town of Bay Minette	1,681,175
In urban portion of colony	1,288,360
In Baldwin County	23,650,780

It thus appears that, exclusive of the assessments against railroads and utilities, the total assessed values of property located
on colony lands is 60.82 per cent of all taxable property in the
Town of Fairhope and is 6.1 per cent or one-sixteenth of all
taxable property in Baldwin County. It also is apparent that
the assessed valuations within the municipality of Fairhope
exceed those in Bay Minette and account for 8.96 per cent or
one-eleventh of all assessed valuations in the county, again

exclusive of utilities. Exclusion of utilities is justified largely
because the Town of Fairhope owns all utilities operating
therein except the telephone; Fairhope does not have any railroad. Whatever the cause, "Stapleton's pasture" was developed
much more rapidly than any other comparable area within
Baldwin County. As the remainder of the county continues its
belated growth, the relative significance of the limited colony
acreage must decline.

Although it seems certain that the development of other parts
of Baldwin County will decrease the relative significance of
Fairhope and the colony in population, volume of business and
assessed valuations, it is equally certain that the colony will
continue to grow in an absolute sense and the rate of its growth
very well might continue equal to that of many other comparable areas. In addition to such general factors affecting the
development of the Eastern Shore such as continued prosperity,
especially in Mobile, additional improvements in highway
transportation, a municipal government sensitive to the needs
of Fairhope, and a resolution of such problems as the threatened pollution of Mobile Bay and the maintenance and improvement of the beach parks, two factors will determine the
rate of intensive development of colony lands. These are: the
rate at which "deeded land" in Fairhope is made available for
use and the terms thereof; and the success with which single
tax principles continue to work on colony lands. There is
considerable unimproved privately-owned land within the
municipal limits—and much of it is well located. If this becomes
available on reasonable terms the effect will be to reduce the
intensity of the demand for access to colony sites, and will therefore tend to retard increases in colony rents. If, however, Fairhope should continue its recent rapid increase in population
at a rate exceeding that at which privately-owned lands are
made available on reasonable terms, then there will be an intensified demand for colony land. How will this be likely to
work out in practice under the colony plan?

Perhaps the proper place to begin is with a review of the

current status of colony leaseholds and the extent to which they have been improved.

DATA ON COLONY LEASEHOLDS

As of January 1, 1954, the Fairhope Single Tax Corporation had ninety rural lessees and six hundred thirty urban lessees. It had ninety-nine country leaseholds and seven hundred eighty-eight urban leaseholds.[1] Of these, eighty-eight or about ten per cent contained no taxable improvements for the assessment period of 1953. It would, however, be grossly misleading to conclude that ten per cent of corporation leaseholds were unimproved. Of the eighty-eight, seventeen were country leaseholds, all of which were improved and in proper use as a part of larger farming units against which improvements were assessed.

Of the seventy-one urban leaseholds against which there were no 1953 assessments for improvements, twenty-six represented applications for land affirmed during 1953. Most of these new leaseholds were located in a Fairhope suburb, Magnolia Beach, and were in process of improvement by the middle of 1954. Of the remaining forty-five urban leaseholds without taxable improvements in 1953, twenty are being used to some extent or are in process of being improved. Remaining are twenty-five leaseholds wholly unimproved and with no apparent prospect of improvement. (This judgment rests solely upon inspection

---

[1] Of the seven hundred twenty lessees, only twenty-three are members of the colony. Of the eight hundred eighty-seven leaseholds, members hold only forty-nine. Six resident members have no leaseholds. Several of these are elderly and have given up both active business and the maintenance of independent households. Two members without leaseholds fall into quite a different category; they are officers of the colony and are living on deeded property. Another colony officer holds leaseholds for business purposes but is living on deeded property. Although there are explanations for each of these situations, the condition is embarrassing to the colony. Of the forty-nine leaseholds held by members, fifteen (nearly one-third) are held by two colony officers who are contractors by profession. Another businessman member holds seven leaseholds. The over-all picture clearly is one in which the members of the colony are unimportant to the corporation, as lessees. In only two or three cases are colony members currently enjoying preferential status in obtaining access to colony land. Possession of several leaseholds is not conclusive evidence of preferential treatment of members because a few non-members likewise are multiple leaseholders.

of the sites; the lessees have not been queried concerning their intentions.)

Although twenty-five wholly unimproved leaseholds out of a total of eight hundred eighty-seven (less than three per cent) is not a large number, it does demonstrate that the single tax principle as applied in Fairhope has not worked to perfection. Perfection in an absolute sense has not been attained, but in a relative sense the ratio of unimproved colony leaseholds to total colony leaseholds is very much smaller than the ratio of unimproved lots in almost any growing city to the total lots available. But why not absolute perfection? Is the single tax theory inadequate to assure optimum land utilization?

LIMITATIONS OF FAIRHOPE PLAN

A pondering of the Fairhope experience leads to the conclusion that singletaxers would be unwise to argue that their system would assure perfection in the use of land. Perfection could result only under two assumed conditions: first, that the tax (or land rent) actually equalled the full annual use value of the land; second, that the fictional "economic man" of the classical economists actually existed universally and in a pure state. That is, any private receipt of income from land as such must be prevented in order to destroy all incentive to withhold land from its highest use, and individual landholders must be fully aware of the situation and must be motivated by no consideration other than a nice calculation of material gain primarily from the point of view of a producer.

The Fairhope version of the single tax failed to achieve absolute perfection because of a partial failure of both assumptions. First, although there can be no definite proof, the colony probably never collected the full economic rent for more than a few short periods. As a result, lessees seldom were put under full economic pressure either to improve or to surrender their leaseholds. Second, a few lessees failed to respond in the indicated way to whatever pressure was exerted through increasing rents.

In one instance, however, there may be a rational explanation for the fact that the lessee continues to hold unimproved colony lands. A lessee, who is also a member of the colony, has been holding unimproved two business sites for anticipated expansion of his business. In part he is financially able to do this because his rent is an allowable expense for income tax purposes. Notwithstanding this mitigating circumstance the behavior of this member-lessee raises a serious question in connection with the Fairhope plan. The issue may be stated hypothetically: how, under the Fairhope plan, can an individual who has an assumed greater need for a particular site than that of any other, obtain possession of the site in question? And if the answer is that he cannot, is this a fatal weakness of the single tax theory?

In discussing this problem let it be understood that under no system of land tenure would it be physically possible for all who might desire to use a particular site to have access to it. The almost universal system of private ownership of land under more or less general property taxation may have a slight advantage here. Under the usual system it may be presumed that any particular individual may obtain access to any site he wants if there is no practicable limit to the price he is willing to pay. In most situations a business can obtain a suitable site by paying something in excess of a reasonable capitalized value of the *current use value* of the land. This it may be most willing to do on the assumption that the value of the site for use soon will equal or exceed the speculative value paid for its possession. In too many cases, however, the business either must pay an unreasonable premium or use an inferior location. The special case under consideration is one where the site seeker is willing to pay almost any price for a given location. Under the usual situation he can almost always be accommodated.

Under the Fairhope plan an individual with an exaggerated desire for a particular site may not be satisfied, particularly if the site desired is an improved leasehold. A would-be lessee of colony land must obtain his leasehold either from the colony direct or by transfer from a lessee. Again, the colony can come into possession of land for lease only through purchase, gift, forfeiture or surrender. Any appreciable additions to colony landholdings through purchase or gift is most unlikely. It is unlikely that the colony will come into repossession of any considerable number of its leaseholds through forfeiture for non-payment of rent, except in the unhappy circumstances of another serious and prolonged depression. Surrenders of un-improved leaseholds or portions of leaseholds not used by the lessee will be received in limited numbers for a limited period. If, however, Fairhope should enjoy a prolonged period of rapid growth, the colony could come into possession of a large amount of urban locations through surrender of lands now used for farming.

The principal source of a leasehold today is that of transfer of leaseholds by lessees to individuals willing to purchase the improvements thereon. However, since December, 1925, the colony has reserved the right to disapprove of particular trans-fers unless the executive council determines that the considera-tion paid for improvements is not excessive. As long as this provision is contained in the application for land and, by refer-ence in the lease, there is a practical limitation which might prevent an individual wanting a site very much indeed, from obtaining this site through payment of an indirect bonus to the present leaseholder. Whether the colony should discon-tinue this method of guarding against the effects of speculation is a serious policy matter.

Some of the unimproved leaseholds have proved rather costly to certain lessees. For example, consider the amount of rent paid over a period of years by four lessees. Lessee "A" has paid $428; lessee "B", $386; lessee "C," $330; and lessee "D," $305. Since these lessees have not occupied these sites or otherwise used them there appears to be no rational explanation for their holding on at a considerable cost. Nothing has been deter-mined as to their motives for continuing to pay rent without any present return. There have been recurrent rumors that in three of these cases the leaseholders have been contacted by people seeking to use these locations and that the lessees have solicited bonuses for transfers. There may or may not be any foundation in fact for these rumors but colony officials are alerted to the possibility and it seems unlikely that any such transfer would be approved by the council.

TYPES OF LAND TRANSACTIONS

The following data demonstrate the maturity attained by the Fairhope Single Tax Corporation in the sense that activities in corporation land are overwhelmingly in the form of transfers rather than in approved applications for land in possession of the colony. The data on transfers overstates the number of separate leaseholds changing hands because in every year some are transferred two or more times. For example, in 1946 two lots changed hands three times and twenty-one others twice. Thus the net number of leaseholds transferred in 1946 was one hundred forty-two rather than one hundred sixty-nine. The data also show that the principal source of lots leased under new applications in recent years has been the subdividing of colony acreage previously withheld from lease. The total number of surrenders and forfeitures is insignificant. One reason for this is that many lessees have "improved" their total leaseholds with trees or shrubbery; hence, when higher rents caused them to decide not to hold all of the land, they sold the improvements and affected a transfer rather than a surrender. However, the data do demonstrate that surrenders and forfeitures have some correlation with increases in rents. This was

TABLE V.   LAND TRANSACTIONS, 1944-1953

Year	Approved Applications	Surrenders and Forfeitures	Approved Transfers
1944	48	10	72
1945	60	5	112
1946	8	3	169
1947	7	9	116
1948	8	3	88
1949	12	4	90
1950	11	2	101
1951	15	8	91
1952	18	2	80
1953	26	0	69

Source: Annual reports of the Fairhope Single Tax Corporation.

particularly true in 1947 following the rent increase of 1946.

As the population and income of Fairhope increases, some additional demand will be felt for colony lands. Rents will increase and the land will be put to a more intensive use in one of several ways. Some lessees will expand and modernize their improvements; a steadily decreasing number of lots will revert to the colony through surrender and forfeiture to be released to applicants who can afford the level of improvements consonant with the higher rents; but the great majority of land transactions resulting in more intensive use of land will take the form of transfers, most of them carrying a consideration in payment for improvements. (A few transfers carry no consideration, *e.g.,* leaseholds transferred in the settlement of estates.) This outlook raises the three following questions of policy: 1. Should the executive council make an even greater effort to keep rentals fully abreast of increases in economic rent? 2. Should the officers of the colony become even more sensitive to the occasional special case where the incidence of loss to a lessee from much higher rents caused by a rapid community development is unusually severe—perhaps taking the form of a considerable discount in the market value of his improvements? 3. Should the colony abandon its attempt to control "bonuses" paid to transferors of improved leaseholds by any means other than charging full economic rent and fully informing the transferees of the nature of their lease contract with the colony?

Inadequacies of Appraisal System

The Fairhope Single Tax Corporation is completing its fortieth year of experience with the mathematically precise system of land appraisals as developed by Mr. W. A. Somers. The heart of this system is the assumption that the community places relative values on different street frontages and on corner and alley influences. Once these relatives are determined for a standard unit (usually one hundred foot squares) by a judgment as to community opinion, and standard depth tables are developed, it is then possible to determine mathematically the value of any lot whether standard or non-standard in depth or in shape. The system as originally installed by Mr. Somers was quite sufficient for the time, but one feature gave the colony continuing difficulty until 1947. Mr. Somers constructed corner tables reflecting the values added by a corner and his appraisal of the total value of the corner remains in use. He did not, however, work out a method for distributing the total or gross values of a corner among the one hundred foot squares. In 1914 this was not necessary as practically all corner leaseholds contained all or very nearly all of the frontages on each street influenced by the corner. However, as the business leaseholds were divided by surrender or transfer, the time arrived when the customary situation was for several leaseholds to be within the corner influence. Mr. R. A. Calhoun, a mathematics instructor at the School of Organic Education, worked out a means of distributing the corner influence among the leaseholds affected.

Although something like the Somers System is indispensable in the equitable appraisal of land, it by no means does away with the continuing need to develop and exercise judgment. Every year it is necessary for the colony to do two things: first, to review all street frontage rates; and second, to decide whether the gross annual use values of colony land have increased or decreased during the year and to estimate the extent of the change. The rental of a given lot, of course, may change either because the street frontage value has changed relative to other street frontage values, or because land has changed in value generally throughout the community, or both. How do colony officers charged with the annual appraisal perform their task?

Ostensibly, the appraisal committee of the executive committee and the secretary make their judgments in the course of an actual inspection of all colony lands. Actually this inspection simply is a last precautionary step taken before a final decision on changes in street frontage values already largely decided upon. Inspection, of course, throws little or no light on the necessity of making a general increase or decrease in rents which is effected through a change in a "multiplier" applied universally to all lots.

The process of determining rent appraisals is a continuous one in the sense that the officers of the colony, and particularly the secretary, have been pondering the effects of changes in many variables, perhaps for several months. Fundamentally, all decisions on street frontage rates and on the multiplier are value judgments; these of course are not arrived at during the course of an automobile ride. What considerations govern these decisions? What information is taken into account and how is it weighed?

Both from published reports and extended conversations with the present secretary, it has been concluded that the appraisal committee decides upon any change in street frontage values largely in terms of the value added to the several locations by any increased public services such as paving, curbing, or extensions of utility services. In fact the only rule of thumb followed in changing relatives is that "center strip paving" is worth seven cents per front foot to urban lots and two cents per front foot to rural lands.

CHANGES IN DEMAND FOR LAND

The second factor considered in the annual review of relative street frontage values is a complex of factors causing changes in the demand for the different types of land (*i.e.,* changes in land usage). How to determine whether land in a given location is shifting from one use to another and how to measure the effect or degree of this change is difficult. It would, of course, be unreasonable to expect any appraiser to explain fully how he arrives at judgments on these points. It must suffice to report that colony appraisers do not attempt any systematic quantitative solution of this problem by gathering data and measuring changes and rates of change. Necessarily, there results a lag in time between any actual change in the usage of a given location and a reflection of this change in the street frontage rates. One effect of this probably is to reduce the cost to a transferee from buying and razing improvements he does not need, because he is able to reap the benefits from a higher usage of the land for whatever period is needed for colony officials to determine that the change has taken place. An even more difficult theoretical question is how the colony appraisers can measure changes in the *intensity* of the demand for land when there is no change in the type of usage? How, in other words, can they attempt to measure any relative increases or decreases in the most valuable business (or exclusive residential) areas? It would seem that too large a degree of reliance on the value inducing effects of street and utility improvements might lead to a too great narrowing between the street frontage values of residential neighborhoods and those of business locations. There is a high probability that this has taken place; it was given official recognition on more than one occasion during the 1920's and 1930's, upon the appearance of questions as to whether business rents were not too low. The problem is an inherently difficult one and relevant data are necessarily scarce. There is no present disposition to be adversely critical of any partial failure here, except as it may or may not be true that colony officials have not looked upon this problem with sufficient concern.

With respect to changes in the multiplier, the problem is somewhat different in that it is a bit easier to isolate and obtain data on some of the variables to be considered. The factors pondered by colony appraisers include: population growth; changes in market prices of privately-owned lands in comparable neighborhoods; considerations paid for the transfer of improvements; number of transfers, applications for land, inquiries, surrenders and forfeitures; and the rapidity with which leaseholds are developed. These were listed in the order of their significance according to the judgment of the secretary. Population growth is given far and away the greatest weight but is not used as an exclusive factor. The rapidity with which leaseholds are developed is of almost no significance because undeveloped leaseholds are too few and too scattered. Perhaps the only tincture of adverse criticism warranted here is that the colony does not keep a systematic tabulation of data relevant to a measurement of these variables. Nor has it been actively concerned with any attempt to improve, clarify or otherwise formulate a theory of valuation in this unique situation.

As a matter of fact subjective considerations continue to be important both in the fixing of relative rents and in changing the multiplier or general rents. A quite laudable sentimental consideration long has retarded increases in the street frontage value on one side of one business block but the degree of subsidy involved has not been so great as to be objectionable to the community generally.

The importance of subjective considerations in determining whether general rents shall be changed may be demonstrated by quoting some excerpts from the 1944 and 1945 reports of the Fairhope Single Tax Corporation.

From the 1944 report:

In fixing the rents for 1945 consideration was given to the obviously increased local demand for land and to the fact that there had been no general increase since 1930 when the multiplier was increased 10 per cent from 2.42 to 2.66, an increase that remained in full effect only through 1933 after which the multiplier was reduced 4.2 per cent to 2.55 at which figure it has remained for the past eleven years. Considering the very apparent increase in demand resulting from a very nearly trebled population since 1930, and the greatly increased value of the public service that has become available in the past fifteen years, it was decided to raise the multiplier approximately 6 per cent to 2.70, *only about one and one-half per cent greater than it was in 1930, and at that time there was not a paved highway in this section of Baldwin County.* (Emphasis supplied.)

From the 1945 report:

The increasing demand for land in Fairhope and the almost total exhaustion of our supply that is immediately available to meet such demand, probably justified an increase in 1946 rental rates. However, no such increase was ordered by the council. . . .

It was decided that a rent increase this year, following last year's general six per cent increase, *might produce some discontent and a feeling of insecurity in those not sufficiently well informed to appreciate the true nature of rent and the beneficent influence of its public collection.*

There can be little doubt that there was in 1945, an actual increase in the rental value of our land. Also there can be little doubt there will be an added increase in 1946. (Emphasis supplied.)

RENT APPRAISAL POLICIES

In deciding against its better judgment (single tax judgment, that is) not to increase rents for 1946, the council took note of the almost certain result that this would "tempt some lessee owners to add this publicly created, but uncollected, value to the selling price asked for the sale of improved leaseholds." In order to minimize this anticipated inflation of the prices for improvements, the council "decided to put to fullest use its control over lease transfers as provided in the lease contract. It is now required that the exact amount of the consideration be declared in all endorsements or instruments of transfer. By 1947 we hope to have accomplished a considerable amount of public improvements *to give a substantial physical support for the full collection of the rent."*

Granting that no social organization can be completely objective it does seem that the executive council of the colony frequently carried subjectivity to an extreme. Manifestly it is impossible to demonstrate either that the single tax would be more conducive to the maximum utilization of land than the prevailing system, or that there would be a truly beneficent influence from the public collection and spending of economic rent, if substantially all of the economic rent is not to be collected. If the demonstration is to succeed in influencing the minds of men with respect to the desirability of the single tax, the colony must both perfect its appraisal procedures and minimize the subjective considerations in the annual appraisements.

The reason given for the 1945 failure is well taken. The lessees do not understand the principles behind the colony plan, and not understanding would feel insecure if rents were increased either rapidly or frequently. It may be significant that this frank explanation of the decision not to increase rents came just one year after Mr. J. Francis Lemon made his last official report to the colony.[2]

If the basic integrity of the Fairhope plan is to be upheld and if the accomplishments of its operation for sixty years are to become known and understood generally, then some program of education of lessees and many members is a must.

The second question of policy arising from this aspect of the inquiry is: to what extent should colony officials be influenced

2 See Chapter XVI.

by the possibility that justifiable increases in annual rentals might cause considerable financial loss to certain lessees, and what could be done about this? The question is a touchy one because basic to the philosophy of the single tax is a maximum faith in individual freedom—a dislike of bureaucratic or paternalistic advice and control. The question is touchy in still another respect. Singletaxers are prone to argue that changes would not be so rapid but that reasonably prudent investors in improvements on land would be aided, rather than hurt, because of changing demands for land.

Indeed, it may be granted that the colony would not need a policy with respect to this problem (*i.e.,* that there would be no problem) if two conditions existed, namely: a full understanding of colony principles and policies by all lessees; and a not too rapid change in either the community growth or the relative demands for certain locations. The point has been made that the lessees generally do not understand the plan. It is also almost axiomatic that some individuals will contemplate either the wrong type or an improper quality of improvements for a given location. The colony has no arbitrary rules to govern this situation but both E. B. Gaston and C. A. Gaston made it a general practice, if given the opportunity, to advise an applicant against making a contemplated improper usage of a site and against taking more land than would be necessary for his purpose. Further, they have been most patient in explaining the colony plan to new applicants and to transferees, and urging them to study the lease contract and other documents carefully. No reasonable criticism can be directed against the colony on the score of not attempting to inform the lessees as individuals making applications for colony land. All prospective lessees have ample opportunity to obtain an understanding. The stubborn fact remains that the colony principles are quite difficult to understand. There is, therefore, a great need to inaugurate a sustained program of community-wide education in the underlying principles and procedures of the colony.

Occasionally, however, events move so fast that higher rents destroy the value of improvements that were quite justifiable and economically sound just a short time previous to the change. A familiar case in point concerns the transition of rural property first to suburban, then to urban demands. The values of such lands are quite different; there would be a real problem under the single tax of smoothing the transition without an undue period during which the land would be either idle or under-used because of fear that improvements would lose value.

A UNIQUE AGREEMENT

In 1950 this problem presented itself in a form sufficiently exaggerated to prompt the colony to enter into a unique agreement with one of its lessees. The agreement is self-explanatory and, despite its length is reproduced in full partly because it could serve as a model or prototype for the guidance of those who conceivably might encounter similar problems under any system of exclusive or even discriminatory land taxation:

This Agreement entered into this 5th day of March, 1950, by and between Fred Ingersoll and Sadie M. Ingersoll, parties of the first part, and Fairhope Single Tax Corporation, party of the second part, Witnesseth:

That whereas the parties of the first part hold a 99 year lease from the party of the second part covering the $N\frac{1}{2}$ of $N\frac{1}{2}$ of $SE\frac{1}{4}$ of $NE\frac{1}{4}$ of Sec. 17, Division four (4) of its lands in the Town of Fairhope, Alabama, as per its plat thereof filed for record Sept. 13, 1911, and the subsequent moving of the North line thereof 10 feet to the South to provide additional street right of way, and

Whereas demand for this land for residence occupancy has caused the rent to increase so that it is no longer profitable to hold it for the purposes for which it was originally leased, and

Whereas the parties of the first part listed their improvements on the land for sale at $5,000.00 in 1948 when the rent charge was $164.40, and in 1949 when the rent charge was increased to $384.54, they offered to sell for $4,000.00, and they have been unable to make any sale thereof, and

Whereas, as a result of a conference of both parties hereto, it appears that a part of the land should be subdivided into lots and the improvements thereon offered for sale separately, and a plan has been made subdividing the North 150 feet into eleven lots with the valuation of improvements thereon separately valued as follows, numbering from West to East: Lot 1, 97 feet more or less $150.00;

Lot 2, 97 feet more or less $200.00; Lot 3, 120 feet $350.00; Lots 4 to 10 inclusive, 120 feet per lot, $300.00 each; Lot 11, 125 feet more or less $300.00, and

Whereas the parties of the first part believe they were unjustly injured by the 1949 increase with which they were charged while unable to dispose of their improvements at a price they consider to have been reasonable, and they believe such injury will continue and be increased by requiring them to pay the 1950 rent charge on the subdivided North 150 feet, while the lots thereon are being offered for transfer on purchase of their improvements at the prices agreed to, the parties hereto agree to the following:

1. The party of the second part agrees to amend the 1949 rent charge by reducing it to the rent charge for 1948, on the entire leasehold, and to reduce the 1950 rent charge on the above described Lots to $5.00 each per annum until leased so long as this agreement remains in force.

2. The parties of the first part agree that as fast as purchasers are found for the improvements on the lots herein described, at the prices set forth, they will make transfer of their lease rights to such lots if the prospective purchaser is acceptable to the party of the second part, and that their refusal to do so will void this agreement with respect to the lots they may refuse to transfer.

3. The parties of the first part agree that upon demand they will release to the party of the second part, without charge therefor, all of their leasehold lying South of the North 300 feet thereof to be used for a street right of way and in consideration therefor the party of the second part agrees to make no rental charge for the use of such land unless or until it abandons its plan to make such use of the land.

4. The parties of the first part agree to maintain the value of the improvements now situated on the land and the party of the second part agrees that in addition to the rent consideration herein made, the parties of the first part shall be entitled to all of such compensation as may be derived from the harvesting of all crops produced on the lands that have not at the time of harvest been transferred to others.

5. Whereas both parties hereto recognize that time and circumstance may alter the prices herein agreed to for sale of improvements, such prices may be changed from time to time by mutual agreement.

6. This agreement may be terminated by the party of the second part at the end of any annual rental period, and may be terminated

by the parties of the first part by written notice filed with the secretary of the party of the second part and payment of all rents due and unpaid.

7. The parties of the first part agree that, if they do not pay the rents due as provided herein the party of the second part has full authority to proceed as provided in paragraph (6) of its regular lease contract, and in that event all rent concessions allowed in this agreement will become cancelled and the amount due the corporation shall be considered to be the full rental charge on the lands at that time held in possession of the party of the first part as heretofore or hereafter figured.

FREEDOM TO TRANSFER LEASEHOLDS

The third policy question is whether the colony should continue the practice of withholding approval of transfers of improvements and leaseholds to non-members until it has satisfied itself that there is no hidden "bonus" for the land buried in the consideration for the improvements. The origin of this practice and the prolonged controversy it engendered has been explained. Mention also has been made of the intention of the executive council in 1945 to take full advantage of this right in an endeavor to keep down any unwarranted inflation of prices for improvements flowing from a failure to increase colony rentals. Recalling that the practice originated in the most unusual circumstance of the Florida boom of the mid-1920's, together with the understandable reluctance of the colony to rack speculative rents to the unwarranted discomfort of the majority of its lessees, it seems reasonable to inquire whether colony purposes best are served by continuing the practice thirty years after the proximate cause for its inauguration.

Careful pondering of the factors involved leads to the conclusion that this restriction upon the transfer of colony leaseholds should be discontinued *provided:* first, that an effective educational program has been in operation for a sufficient period fully to inform lessees of colony principles and policies; and second, that rental appraisement procedures are improved and rents are fixed to achieve the objective purposes of the colony and are not governed by subjective considerations.

This conclusion is postulated upon four considerations:

1. There is considerable doubt that the executive council is able to ascertain whether or to what extent the price agreed upon for improvements contains a hidden bonus for the privilege of occupying the land.

2. If the discussion in the early pages of this chapter is sound, proper land utilization under the Fairhope (or any other) plan necessitates an occasional payment of a premium in order to obtain access to land. Officers of the colony will admit that business firms must pay something for additional land even if only in the form of buying and razing improvements they do not need.

3. A more accurate appraisal of annual use values for land requires more data than are available to colony appraisers. After all, the level of rents in general can be appraised only in terms of the results. One of the significant results would be the effect on the prices of improvements relative to the prices of comparable improvements in other comparable localities, or relative to the cost of reproduction. An absolutely free market (*i.e.,* free of restrictions imposed by the lease contract) for improvements on colony land would be a valuable guide to the propriety of the current general level of rents. Such data also would be most useful in appraising changes in relative values of land on different streets.

4. A negative consideration is the fact that the colony has attempted absolutely no control over the charges made by lessees to their tenants. Since many residences and business buildings are owned by others than the occupiers, the owners of the improvements which are rented have just as great an opportunity to reap an unearned increment as those who sell their improvements. Why attempt to lock one stable door and leave another one wide open?

As the secretary wrote in 1950 (annual report), "a quite natural result of our policy" is that the colony would have no unleased land where sites are most desired. "In 1900," he wrote, "the colony had no unleased land on either side of Fairhope Avenue, from the bay front to Section Street, and beyond.

This did not mean that the future growth of the community would have to be on other lands." To drive this point home, he recounted the history of the first colony leasehold to be occupied, that of his father, Mr. E. B. Gaston. This consisted of all the land in Block 12, Division 1, the block on the south side of Fairhope Avenue, extending from Section Street, on the east to Church Street, on the west, and contained two and one-half acres. This leasehold was taken for subsistence homestead purposes and the rent for the entire two and one-half acres was $5.95 in 1896. This first lessee made an error in assuming that business would not want this location. By 1906, transfers to others had reduced the size of his leasehold to one-fourth of an acre, on which he paid an annual rent of $20.05. By this time he had given up any notion of holding any part of this location for subsistence and utilized most of what he retained for his business. Ultimately another transfer was made leaving him with less than one-fifth of an acre, the rent on which in 1950 was $214.56. The total rent on the original leasehold in 1950 was $3,022.47, a product obviously of an intensified demand for business purposes. Without question this process will continue in Fairhope and, despite some imperfections, it will continue more completely, and more smoothly than would be the case if colony policies did not exist.

FREEDOM TO DEVELOP LEASEHOLDS

In conclusion two further observations may be of interest. First, colony land utilization has developed without benefit of any municipal zoning ordinance and without colony restrictions on any improvements the lessees might decide upon. The motive for making improvements has been wholly that of the self-interest of the individual lessees. There have been very few exceptions. Once, in the early days a petition by members successfully blocked a land application where the intention was to erect a livery stable. In recent years, on two occasions, a petition of member and non-member lessees caused the executive council to refuse an application for a corner lot to be used as a filling station. In time, however, this objection disap-

peared; on the third attempt to lease this site for this purpose
no petition was filed against it. Let it be emphasized that
throughout the history of Fairhope members could have compelled the executive council to place restrictions on the type or
quality of improvements to be made on colony land. Since
1905, non-member lessees have had the privilege of so petition-
ing the executive council, and there is little doubt but that any
general dissatisfaction over a specific improvement contemplated on any leasehold, would have received a sympathetic and
responsive hearing. This great respect for the right of petition
and the willingness to resort to referenda on the part of the
colony, and the fact that few petitions and referenda were used
in objecting to proposed land usages, is rather compelling evidence that colony land was developed in a manner acceptable
to the residents.

The second observation is not wholly unconnected with the
one just made. Fairhope was founded by people of very modest
means and it attracted many with limited resources. Largely
for this reason, plus the fact that the land had little value in the
early days, expensive improvements would have been out of
character. The colony always resisted placing any qualitative or
other restrictions on improvements. Colony land literally was
easy and cheap of access to the relatively poor. There are many
living there today in quite comfortable and attractive homes
who started with a "trailer cabin" or worse, but who added to
and improved over a period of time, until they now own quite
valuable homes. Naturally, this kind of development offended
some who could afford expensive homes and who sometimes
became petulant over what they called a lack of protection for
their own investments. In almost every instance their fears
turned out to be groundless. The conditions they objected to
were soon corrected. There is much truth in the colony claim
that their principles lead to an economically and otherwise
properly balanced land utilization, without formal restrictions
or zoning ordinances. The second observation is that the type
of person who made up the bulk of the Fairhope colony, the
person with little means, no longer will find a haven on colony

land, not, at least, until it becomes feasible to subdivide some of the more remote country lands. In the municipal limits of the present Fairhope, residents with the psychology of the $20,000 to $40,000 residence may put aside their fears of having their views spoiled by a shack. Economic nature has taken care of this problem. But a Fairhope landmark has passed—a very nice landmark indeed.

xviii

FINANCIAL EFFECTS OF LIMITING PAYMENT OF PROPERTY TAXES FOR LESSEES

FROM the outset the founders of the Fairhope colony recognized that a private corporation could not apply the single tax directly; the best it could do would be to refund out of rent certain taxes paid by lessees. In practice not all taxes paid by lessees could be refunded; for example, there would be no way to reimburse lessees for higher prices paid because of federal customs duties. In 1894, however, the property tax was almost the sole reliance of state and local governments. Thus a close approximation of a "single tax" could be obtained by an arrangement shifting all property taxes to land. This the young colony undertook to accomplish by having its lessees assess their own improvements and personal property, pay the taxes thereon, then present their tax receipts to the colony for a refund payable, during most of the early period, in colony scrip.

Although there were many bitter struggles over the soundness of this policy and several self-professed singletaxers left Fairhope in protest, resident leaders, whose views were upheld by strong and articulate non-resident members, held firmly to the policy. They held to this policy because they believed it to be vital to the demonstration. Upon occasion they went beyond the existing contractual obligations as in the payment of poll taxes and in the payment of municipal taxes upon resolution of the executive council. In 1932, the depression caused the financially embarrassed colony to place a limitation upon the amount of lessees' taxes it would refund. The limitation (of contractual liability) was embodied in the constitution by amendment, making Article XIV—Payment of Taxes, read:

Section 1. All taxes assessed against the Corporation shall be paid from the Corporation Treasury.

Section 2. Receipts for taxes paid by any lessee to state, county, town or school district, upon his improvements and personal property held upon any leasehold, (moneys and credits excepted) shall be applicable upon the rent of such leasehold; provided that the corporation shall not be bound to accept such tax receipts to a greater amount for any year than the rent for that year on the ground on which such improvements and personal property are held.

Section 3 of the lease makes the following provisions with respect to the tax liability of the corporation:

In consideration of the agreement of said lessee to pay the rentals herein provided for, the Fairhope Single Tax Corporation will pay all taxes upon the land leased and will accept from the lessee on rent receipts of the County Tax Collector or Clerk of Town of Fairhope for taxes paid to State, County, School District, or Town, upon the improvements and personal property (money and credits excepted) *held by lessee upon the land herein leased;* or, if all rent due be paid, will give him a certificate in amount equal to such acceptable tax receipts remaining, receivable from bearer at face value on rent, or in discharge of any indebtedness to the corporation; *provided that said lessee will appoint whomsoever may be designated by the Corporation as his agent to return his property for taxation where permitted by law so to do; that in no event shall the Corporation be bound to accept tax receipts on more than a fair assessed valuation of the property, on the basis required by law, or to a greater amount for any year than the rent for that year on the land on which such improvements and personal property are held.*

Portions of the above provisions in the lease were italicized to clarify the contractual limitations governing the refunding of taxes. Two groups of "property" the taxes on which are non-allowable under the lease contract are. 1. taxes on the personal property of lessees' tenants (the contract specifically covers property of lessees only); 2. taxes paid by domestic corporations on their shares of stock. Under Alabama law the liability for this tax is placed on the shareholders but the corporations may make the payment for their stockholders and all of them do so. It is not, therefore, a tax upon "improvements and personal property (money and credits excepted) held by lessees upon the land herein leased."

Although the above quoted constitutional and lease provisions have been in effect for little more than twenty years they apply to all but one outstanding lease, because every time a leasehold is transferred a new lease is written and because many lessees voluntarily accepted the new lease in exchange for the old one.

The restrictions against refunding taxes unless the taxable returns either are made by an official designated by the colony or the assessed valuations are reasonable, are not of great practical importance today. Almost all lessees have concluded that it is a great convenience to have their property taxes taken care of through the corporation office. In earlier periods there were several instances where lessees sought to embarrass the colony by grossly over-assessing their property.

The financial difficulties of the great depression long since have disappeared. A series of questions arise almost automatically. 1. How much additional taxes would the corporation have to pay if it paid all which are allowable under the constitution? 2. Could it afford to remove the existing limitations? 3. Would it be good single tax or good Fairhope policy to do so? 4. Or could the beneficent results from the public collection of economic rent better be demonstrated *to the Fairhope lessees,* by using corporation income in other ways? 5. If the latter, how could colony expenditures be budgeted and what role should be accorded the lessees in formulating the budget? Some of these questions can be answered factually; others admit of honest differences of opinion.

The following data on assessments and on taxes paid were assembled in co-operation with the colony secretary from data he obtained from the office of the tax assessor of Baldwin County.

TABLE VI.   1953 ASSESSMENTS

On land, improvements, and personal property of the Fairhope Single Tax
Corporation, its lessees, and lessees' tenants. Assessed values of shares of stock of
domestic corporations are included. Excluded (because of non-availability) are
the assessed values of automobiles and trucks and that portion of the Southern
Bell Telephone Company located within Colony lands.

Assessments		*Assessed Values*	
Improvements of City Lessees	$832,060		
Personal property of City Lessees	200,360*		
City land of F.S.T.C.	145,740		
Personal property of F.S.T.C.	460		
Personal property of Lessees' Tenants	112,900**	$1,291,520	
Improvements of Lessees in Magnolia Beach	8,140		
Personal Property of Lessees in M. B.	8,340***		
Magnolia Beach Land of F.S.T.C.	900	17,380	
Improvement of Country Leases	66,280		
Personal Property of Country Leases	40,740		
Country Land of F.S.T.C.	38,860	145,880	$1,454,780

  * Includes $83,950 assessment against shares of stock of domestic corporations.
"Allowable" assessments, $116,410.
  **Includes $43,840 assessment against shares of stock of domestic corporations.
Subtracting this from the total assessment against lessees' tenants leaves $69,060,
which might become "allowable" if lease contract were changed.
  *** This apparently disproportionately large figure is accounted for by the
location in Magnolia Beach (as a home base) of earth moving equipment owned
by a lessee (Mr. Schneider), assessed at $8,000. This would be "allowable" under
the language of the lease but Mr. Schneider does not assess it through the
Colony.

It should be made explicit that the total allowable tax liability
of $40,599.98 exceeds the sums reported as having been dis-
bursed for taxes in 1953 by $2,319.77   This discrepancy is
attributable to differences in the bases of the two reports.   The
table (p. 282) of taxes payable by the colony is one of taxes *due*
in 1953 from assessments for 1953 taxes.   The financial report
of the corporation is on a cash rather than on an accrual basis
and some of the 1953 taxes were paid after the close of the
calendar year 1953.

The data presented on taxes paid by all parties on corporation lands provide a basis for a partial estimation of the addi-

TABLE VII.   1953 TAXES

Paid by Fairhope Single Tax Corporation, its lessees and the tenants of lessees on
land, improvements and personal property other than automobiles. Includes
taxes paid on shares of stock of domestic corporations. Does not include taxes
paid by the Southern Bell Telephone Company.

Taxes		*Amount*	
Improvements of City Lessees	$27,223.12		
Personal property of City Lessees	7,185.60		
City land of F.S.T.C.	5,263.20		
Property of Lessees' Tenants	4,064.40	$43,736.32	
Improvements of Lessees in Magnolia Beach	135.34		
Personal Property of Lessees in M. B.	175.14		
M. B. Land of F.S.T.C.	18.90	329.38	
Improvements of Country Lessees	1,102.11		
Personal Property of Country Lessees	855.40		
Country Land of F.S.T.C.	816,06	2,773.57	$46,839.27
Less "non-allowable" taxes:			
Paid by Lessee Corporations on shares of stock		$ 3,021.20	
Paid by Lessee Tenant Corporations on share tax		1,578.24	4,599.44
Total "allowable" or potentially "allowable"			$42,239.83
Less:			
1953 excess of Lessees' taxes over rents		$ 2,001.09*	
1953 taxes on Lessees' Tenants		2,486.16**	4,487.25
Total 1953 Corporation Tax Liability on above classes of property			$37,752.58
Add other taxes paid by Corporation:			
On Lessees' automobiles and trucks			2,740.50***
Poll taxes			106.92
Total 1953 Property and Poll Taxes payable by the Fairhope Single Tax Corporation			$40,599.98

* This amount was determined from an analysis of the 1953 rent roll. The
$2,001.09 is a sum of the excess "allowable" taxes over rents paid on seventy-two
leaseholds. Most of the excesses are quite small. The largest excesses were for
three or four business lessees. This figure does not include taxes paid by lessee
corporations on their shares of stock.

** Does not include taxes paid by lessee tenant corporations on shares of stock.
Under present terms of lease all taxes paid by lessees' tenants are disallowed but
the constitution would permit paying such taxes on improvements and personal
property held on colony land.

*** This figure does not include all property taxes paid on automobiles of
lessees and it does not include any such taxes paid by tenants of lessees. No
attempt was made to obtain a summation of such taxes omitted from the table.

tional cost to the corporation if it paid all taxes allowable under the constitution. Clearly the $2,001.09 would be allowable; almost equally evident in so far as the constitution is concerned is that the tangible property of lessees' tenants would be allowable, or an additional $2,486.16. Under the present provisions of the lease these taxes are not contractual liabilities of the corporation. The additional tax liability of the Fairhope Single Tax Corporation permitted by its constitution would be $4,487.25 *plus* an undetermined liability for taxes on the assessed valuations of automobiles and trucks owned either by lessees or by tenants of lessees. Assuming the additional property tax liabilities on such automotive equipment would be in the neighborhood of $1,000, then an outside estimate of the total additional tax liability if present limitations were removed would be about $5,500.

Could the colony afford to remove these restrictions in practice? Technically, the language of the constitution does not prohibit the executive council from paying all taxes on improvements and tangible personal property located on colony lands. It simply prohibits entering into a contractual liability to do so. A partial answer to this must be based on the report of cash receipts and cash disbursements for the calendar year 1953.

There can be no doubt but that the colony could pay all taxes allowable by the constitution and have enough remaining from rents, penalties and lease fees to pay all other expenses and charges, plus an appreciable sum for lands, highways, property expenses and contingencies. Nor would this judgment be reversed by data showing the trends of rent collections, expenses and taxes over the past fifteen years. The question of retaining the existing limits on the refunding of taxes otherwise allowable is one of policy not one of financial practicability.

Would the colony demonstration of the single tax theory best be served by a more liberal policy on tax refunds or by using the available funds in some other manner? To some extent this question is one of opinion; an answer does not neces-

FINANCIAL STATEMENT, 1953
RECEIPTS

Rent	$66,888.72
Penalty	359.22
Lease Fees	138.00
Sales Improvements, Etc.	2,671.72
Interest on Corporation Investments	125.00
Interest on Library Investments	87.50
Interest on Sales of Improvements	22.03
Membership Fee	100.00
Oil Lease	3,710.00
Refund Lessees' Taxes	120.22
Miscellaneous	766.75
	74,989.16
Cash on Hand January 1, 1953	19,522.71
	$94,511.87

DISBURSEMENTS

Taxes Paid for Lessees:	
State, County and City	$29,334.65
Car and Truck Taxes	2,740.50
Poll Taxes	106.92
Taxes on Corporation Land and Property	6,098.16
Social Security Tax	113.52
Federal Income Tax	307.89
Salaries	8,523.00
Corporation Office and Business Expense	1,438.39
Lands, Highways and Property Expense	34,408.23
Civic Contributions	2,540.00
Library Maintenance	1,800.00
Interest Transferred to Library	87.50
Cemetery Maintenance	400.00
Improvement Purchase Refund	75.00
Rent Refunds	332.34
Miscellaneous	307.71
	$88,613.81
Cash on Hand, December 31, 1953	5,898.06
	$94,511.87

sarily follow in terms of doctrine. When George wrote, and for a few decades thereafter, the doctrinal answer would have been clear; the first use of any income after expenses of the corporation and taxes on corporation lands necessarily would have been used to pay other property taxes (including any special assessments). Such a policy may be stated in unequivocal terms for that period, for it was a time characterized by relatively low total costs of government, a dominant position in government by local units and by the states, and an almost exclusive reliance on property taxation for state and local revenues. Under such conditions there was considerable force in the argument of singletaxers that land rents alone would provide liberally for government; therefore a total refunding of taxes on improvements and personal property by the colony would have resulted in a simulated single tax, and the incidence of almost all taxes would have been shifted to land alone.

The world moved away from Henry George and the early Fairhope colonists. Federal corporation and individual income taxes and a greatly expanded number of excises, together with a rapid development of state and local income, sales and business taxes, combined to push the property tax into a minor role as a tax source for total government in the United States. On the disbursement side, two world wars, a severe depression, Korea and a continuing cold war, together with an increasing propensity of people to look toward the government for an increasing variety of services, have combined to push tax requirements beyond any amount that reasonably could be obtained from land rents alone. Perhaps if Henry George had had his way on an international basis none of these events would have occurred, but this is highly conjectural. The Fairhope colony is too small to wag the world; it must accept conditions as they exist and adjust its policies accordingly.

It is here suggested that an analysis of this issue of policy may be approached by postulating a choice in the form of one decision that might be largely objective, and another choice which would rest largely on subjective considerations. A decision to use all "surplus" receipts in the refunding of taxes would be one in favor of a largely objective approach. It would be wholly routine (involving no judgment) to refund *all property taxes*. Beyond this, however, judgment must enter in, deciding which among the other taxes and charges imposed upon those on colony land would be refunded, or, alternatively, in deciding what improvements or other services the corporation as such would render.

On the other hand a decision against a more liberal tax refunding policy leaves the decision as to what to do with any "surplus" almost wholly in the realm of subjectivity or judgment. The ultimate objective would be the same, namely, to spend the income from land rents in such a manner as to *demonstrate* the beneficence of its collection and disbursements for public purposes. If it be granted that colony rents fall far short of an amount equaling all taxes and other governmental charges paid by those on colony land, thereby effectively erasing the word "single" from any current Georgian experiment, then land rentals should be spent as the *lessees themselves* would like to see them expended. Only one limitation would need be put on the scope of choices among which the lessees might choose. *Under no circumstances should any part of the rent collected be refunded. The colony must continue to attempt a collection of the full economic rent and it should do so on as objective a basis as is humanly possible.* This restriction is a vital one. The full rent must be taken to discourage speculation and to keep Fairhope land as freely accessible as possible. With this exception the choices lessees might make are almost limitless. For example, they might choose: higher grade street and property improvements; a more liberal tax refunding policy; a rebatement of monthly municipal garbage fees; a partial rebate of charges for other municipal services such as water, gas or electricity; giving more or less to the School of Organic Education; joining with the Town Council and/or other civic groups in rebuilding and improving the Fairhope wharf.

The above suggestion should not be taken as a firm recommendation to turn over to the lessees the complete responsibility for the disbursement plan of the colony. Present contractual commitments must be safeguarded and an adequate proportion of receipts for administrative and other expenses must be withheld. It is likewise probable that the executive council would want to establish a continuing fund for street, highway and property improvements, extensions and maintenance. Disbursements for these purposes quite likely would be understood among the lessees as essential. However, after making liberal allowances for such expenditures, the colony should have, in 1953, as a matter of policy, permitted the lessees to exercise a final judgment on the spending of from $5,000 to $10,000. The amount of the "surplus" so conceived will of course vary annually but it seems likely that it will increase as Fairhope grows.

xix

AN OPINION ON THE
SURVIVAL VALUE OF THE
FAIRHOPE SINGLE TAX CORPORATION

*T*HE present and future significance of the Fairhope Single Tax Corporation should be estimated with reference to its place within the existing social structure and in relation to discernible social trends. The corporation should not be judged entirely either on its past accomplishments and failures, or on its present importance to those directly affected —the members and lessees. If the single tax corporation is to have a *survival value*—as distinguished from mere survival, which many outmoded institutions manage to achieve for an indefinite period—its leaders, members and lessees must succeed both in identifying these qualities which are of lasting significance to the larger society, and in adopting consistent policies and procedures. At the risk of appearing presumptuous the authors will make some suggestions on each of these points.

The following are purely personal opinions about the past accomplishments of the Fairhope experiment—opinions which necessarily flow in part from information and personal experiences not all of which could be successfully detailed in the body of this study.

The urban community of Fairhope has outdistanced many small American cities both in material achievements and in those intangible, imponderable qualities which make a community worthwhile. Both sets of accomplishments should be related to the age and economic bases of the community. Underlying any judgment of Fairhope must be an explicit recognition that it is only sixty years old and that its economic foundations were and are relatively weak. When the community was first settled most of the lands were submarginal; only a small fraction had even a slight value other than for speculative purposes. Had the original colonists and the Fairhope Industrial Association been "well heeled," the present location would not have been chosen as the site for a single tax demonstration for the simple reason that the location and inherent inferiority of the land could not then provide a margin above going rates of interest and wages sufficient to sustain a community household. To be sure events of recent decades have provided more productive economic foundations but the proximate agricultural hinterland remains relatively inferior, and Fairhope has neither unearthed any windfall, such as striking oil, nor has it benefited directly from an industrial development in its immediate vicinity. The oil might come but a major industrial development is unlikely.

Even to the casual observer the evidences of *relative* material well-being within the Fairhope community are evident in the wealth of parks, the system of improved streets, an almost model sewage disposal system, public and private schools, a library, an adequate and attractive commercial area and the general tone of most of its residential sections. Again, relative to the generally low money incomes of the population of Fairhope, the real income in terms of consumption of food, general adequacy and attractiveness of dwellings, percentage of ownership of residences, and the possession of the gadgets of our time, *i.e.*, automobiles, household equipment, radios and now television, appear to be satisfactory.

Certainly Fairhope can take satisfaction in any comparison with Daphne and other much older communities on the eastern shore. Many of these older communities not only failed to keep pace with Fairhope but actually retrogressed for several decades after Fairhope was founded. In recent years the industrial ex-

pansion of Mobile, together with its greater accessibility by
highway from the eastern shore, has given new life to the entire
area. It would be somewhat surprising if these other areas do
not grow in population and in community income at an even
more rapid rate than Fairhope in the next few years, but this
is by no means certain.

Just as the urban community of Fairhope has outdistanced its
neighbors, that proportion of the area within the municipality
belonging to the single tax corporation has been developed
more intensively, and with greater uniformity, than has much
of the remainder of the city. The corporation owns but twenty
per cent of the land but contains over sixty per cent of the
assessed valuation.

A principal reason for both the relatively greater material
progress of Fairhope over its older and somewhat better endowed neighboring communities, and the more intensive and
better balanced development of corporation land in comparison
with other land within the municipality of Fairhope, is the
system of land tenure introduced by the original colonists.
Some of the reasons for this conclusion were given in Chapter
XVII.

In its non-material colorations Fairhope is superior to other
small, middle-class income communities of which we have personal knowledge. The population of Fairhope affords a high
diversity of interests and talents. An outstanding characteristic
of the community is a strong regard for individualism. Fairhope is well-balanced—almost cosmopolitan. The community
has a greater sympathy for, and a higher tolerance of, the occasional non-conformist, the intellectual and the artistically inclined, than is commonly found in small communities.

If Fairhope is less standardized, less tradition-bound, less
dominated by any given set of values than other small communities, major credit must go to the early colonists who were
genuinely convinced that people should be left free to think,
believe and act as they choose, up to the point where they im-
pinge upon the rights of others. Such a conviction is generally
characteristic of singletaxers although, of course, singletaxers

are not alone in their belief in freedom. Many within Fairhope might grant these assertions, but would want to add that the School of Organic Education has played an important role in forming the character and developing the talents of many local residents. We heartily agree in this but would point out that it was not mere coincidence that Mrs. Johnson located her school in Fairhope.

The nature and extent of the survival value of the Fairhope Single Tax Corporation may be determined with reference to three conditions: 1. The extent to which its future operations will result in a maximization of the lessees' material interests and a minimization of social interference with the decisions and acts of individuals. 2. The extent to which these results are in harmony with current social values. 3. The extent to which the results become generally understood by the lessees and others, both within and without Fairhope, as consequences of the corporation's land policies and procedures.

We have recorded our conviction that the past accomplishments of the corporation have been such as to lend support to a belief that the material well-being of that part of the community located on corporation land will be even further enhanced as the community grows, and that the enhancement will be greater than that achieved on non-corporation lands. Further, it seems quite probable that the municipality of Fairhope will make a more intensive use of business license taxation and other sources of revenue which will have positive effects on the decisions of individuals as producers or consumers. If so, there will be an expanded opportunity within the Fairhope community itself to demonstrate that such interferences with individual choices could be avoided, without sacrificing any public facilities or services, if the entire urban community should come under a system of appropriating land rents for community purposes.

With respect to the second point, it is reasonable to assume that people generally approve the objectives of maximum per capita output and maximum individual freedom.

Whether the corporation will be able to achieve success in

terms of point three, *i.e.,* whether people within or without Fairhope will become convinced of the causal connection between corporation policies, and an achievement of the assumed social objectives, is conjectural. Past success in this area has been meager. If the ultimate survival value depends on better results in this area, the corporation must not rely exclusively upon general discussions of, or "courses" in, the higher abstractions of the Georgian philosophy. Only a comparatively few possess the inclination and ability to evaluate the economic, ethical and psychological effects of discriminatory land taxation, in the abstract. Moreover, a tiny enclave such as Fairhope cannot possibly either experiment in, or demonstrate the assumed beneficent effects of the single tax as if it were applied internationally, nationally, or even provincially. Condition number three can be achieved by the single tax corporation only in terms of a local application, and only there if a large number of non-member lessees are brought into the counsels of the corporation in some effective and active manner *as participants in the experiment.*

Ten or twenty years from now the corporation well might be judged in accordance with the progress it has made in gaining public acceptance of the advantages of exclusive land value taxation. Although this will be difficult, the prognosis is more favorable today than formerly, for three reasons.

First, the land owned by the corporation is now supermarginal, and is steadily becoming more so.

Second, there are many evidences that society is countenancing an ever increasing variety of interferences with the terms on which land may be utilized by individual owners. The current vogue of municipal zoning laws, the acceptance of acreage controls, the increasing concern over water rights and water polution, and an awakened interest in the conservation of other natural resources—all these are manifestations of the determination of present day society to restrict the individual landlord in the interest of overriding social objectives. The issue no longer is one of whether land is to be used solely according to the judgment of individual owners; it has become one of choosing among alternative social controls. Since discriminatory (con-fiscatory) land value taxation basically is one of the possible alternative social control devices, it should be possible to obtain for it a more sympathetic hearing than could have been ob-tained twenty or more years ago.

A third reason for an optimistic judgment of the future of the single tax corporation is that it has become *almost mature*. It is now *almost* exclusively a land owning corporation perform-ing but two functions: (1) the collection of economic rent; and (2) the disbursement of its rental revenue for the benefit of lessees. There are, to be sure, vestigial remnants of past "colo-nial" values, but these either can be removed, or are not of a nature such as to prejudice the future accomplishments of this unique corporation.

If the faith of those who believe the corporation has a posi-tive survival value is to be justified, the membership should re-examine its policies to the end that it will either reaffirm or resolve to achieve:

1. A continuous improvement of the annual rent appraise-ment, designed both to achieve equitable relative rents and a general level sufficient to absorb the entire economic rent. Obviously this would be a reaffirmation of an original policy and may not be thought necessary by some.

2. A renewal of determined and systematic attempts to in-form lessees of the rent policy, and of the methods and judg-ment criteria involved in the actual appraisement.

3. An abandonment of the executive council's practice of refusing to approve a transfer when, in its judgment, the con-sideration is excessive.[1]

---

1 Implementation of this policy recommendation probably should be preceded by a rewording of Section 6, Article 8, of the constitution. The constitutional remedy for attempts to exact "bonuses" for the transfer of leaseholds is a man-date to the executive council immediately to increase the rental charge against the land specifically included in the individual leasehold. Clearly this remedy is inconsistent with the Somers System. Equally clearly, the policy and procedure adopted in 1925 is not the one contemplated by the constitution, although the constitution does not prohibit the procedure, which has become customary. Since the customary practice is not required by the constitution, probably it could be suspended by resolution of the executive council or the membership

4. The adoption of an annual disbursement budget *based* upon the judgment of the lessees, for that margin of income which remains after the expenses of the corporation and its contractual obligations are fulfilled.

5. An explicit adoption of a policy of neutrality within the community in all areas other than the collection of economic rent and its disbursement. With respect to disbursement of rental income above contractual obligations and normal expenses, neutrality demands that the lessees, not the corporation, make the disbursement decisions.

For a procedure designed to facilitate a discussion of the suggested policies and their implementation, we suggest:

1. That the executive council schedule a series of membership meetings for the express purposes of obtaining an intramural evaluation of the corporation's accomplishments, a discussion of its logical and appropriate destiny, and an evaluation of all alternative policies and procedures which the membership might support to further the effectiveness of the experiment.

One of the more alarming trends has been the cumulative lack of interest among the members in the affairs of the single tax corporation. Without question one of the reasons for this condition is a general knowledge that the current management is competent. The high proficiency of the full-time corporation personnel has left almost no general issues and few routine questions on operations, in which the membership needs to participate. However, this situation is not a healthy one. It may presage stagnation, not growth. If the corporation is to fulfill even the more moderate objectives of its founders the membership must be encouraged to take a more active part. Many members would be willing to give more freely of their time if they felt there was a substantive role in which they were needed, or could be useful.

2. That the corporation seek competent outside professional services to make an independent study of the current effective-

---

and there would be no attempt to mandamus the executive council to comply with Section 6, Article 8. Nonetheless this section should be amended to bring it into conformity with the Somers System of land valuation.

ness of the annual rent appraisement. It has been forty years since Mr. Somers established his system in Fairhope. In the meantime there have been a large number of changes in relative values and it is entirely possible that those now in effect are grossly out of line. Also it is by no means certain that the multiplier is at the proper level, or even that the corporation officials are considering the proper evidences of value in making their annual appraisements.

3. That a series of lessees' meetings be held for the purpose of (a) explaining the methods of determining rents, and (b) deciding how a predetermined portion of the anticipated receipts will be expended. These lessees' meetings should be postponed until recommendations are received by the outside appraisers and until the membership has thoroughly thrashed out policy issues. Further, as Mr. Lemon so ably pointed out, the educational process should not be one of dealing in the higher abstractions of single tax philosophy but it should be a process dealing with concrete problems of rent determination and disbursements. It should be understood that the lessees cannot be permitted either to change the underlying rent policy or to vote themselves rent refunds.

If we are correct in our understanding of the nature of the survival value of the Fairhope Single Tax Corporation, and if our suggestions are adopted, the result should be a renewed viability of the experiment. And with this new life should come renewed community interest, and a widespread conviction that the Fairhope colony can demonstrate certain beneficent effects resulting from a community expropriation of economic rent in lieu of other taxes and charges for the financing of the community household.

One of the difficult dilemmas which has embarrassed the colony from its inception has been how to bring non-member lessees into the counsels of the corporation without endangering its basic integrity as a single tax experiment. The corporation can permit the lessees neither to control the rent policy nor to vote for officers who are charged with the implementation of the basic rent policy. With these exceptions lessees should be

fully integrated into the corporation, *i.e.,* they should participate in the implementation of the rent policy to the extent that
their advice and counsel is constructive and not directed at a
weakening of the policy itself. Further, they should be permitted both responsibility and authority in deciding how rental
incomes should be disbursed after contractual obligations and
expenses are met.

If the lessees are permitted an authoritative but limited role,
and if the corporation repeals the December 21, 1925, application for land, it will attain maturity in the sense that it will
become completely objective, impersonal and neutral. In our
judgment at least three important by-products might result.

First, the entire community might develop the habit of looking to the integrity of the corporation, *per se,* rather than to the
behavior of individual members. For example, the question
whether officers or other members of the corporation live off
colony land is immaterial to the success or failure of the experiment. Actually, it is irrelevant whether members own land in
or about Fairhope. Members should (a) believe in the net
benefits of discriminatory land taxation, and (b) give freely of
their time, talents and moral support to the single tax corporation as a vehicle attempting to demonstrate these benefits. Individually and collectively they might choose to propagandize
in favor of a single tax system. There is, however, no sound
reason for condemning them as individuals for private ownership of land, and the private receipt of economic rent. The
single tax doctrine is a social doctrine; it is designed to change
a social institution and is not directed at the behavior of individuals within the existing institutional framework. Singletaxers do not condemn the individual land owner but only the
system which permits private receipt of socially created increments, and which penalizes the industrious by taxing individ-
ually-created wealth and income. There is nothing either inconsistent or morally reprehensible in the behavior of an
individual who owns and profits from land under our present
system, and who joins in an organized attempt to test the super-

iority of another system designed to remove all economic gain from private ownership of land.

The above judgment applies only to the single tax corporation as a mature instrumentality. In the formative years of the "colony," both survival and growth depended upon the existence of a hard core of dedicated, enthusiastic singletaxers filled with something akin to a missionary spirit, never permitting themselves to deviate from the letter of the gospel, and impelled to make occasional invidious distinctions as between local members who acquired land for future colony use, and those who refused to option their local landholdings to the colony. If the early colonists had behaved otherwise they would have confirmed the suspicions of some outsiders that the underlying motive was private gain rather than the purpose which they professed. These early conditions have passed; the time has arrived when attention should be focused on the sincerity, integrity and efficacy of the corporation rather than upon the personal behavior of the members.

Second, intra-community relations might be improved. Gains which might reasonably be expected from an *announced policy of neutrality* would include: (a) a diminution of community demands that the colony donate more of its lands for governmental or general social usage; and (b) a diminution of the frequency with which some local residents "blame the colony" for their failure to get general local support for certain pet projects. Although not universal, expressed sentiments either to "let the colony do it" or "the colony is retarding the progress of Fairhope," frequently are heard in Fairhope.

Actually there is little rationality behind such sentiments. The single tax corporation long since has taken the position that the disposition of its lands rests with the membership, and the membership for two decades has taken the position that the entire community should contribute to community facilities. Before this position was taken the single tax corporation made many generous—perhaps overly generous—contributions of its lands for the benefit of the entire community.

Those who attach blame to the colony and tend to charge that it now is a handicap to the future development of Fairhope fall into several categories of which only three will be given brief mention.

1. Individuals who have a different ideology contend that if the corporation were dissolved and title to its lands passed to individuals, the community would prosper at a more rapid rate. The existence and views of this group should be welcomed. Such people provide the opposition and tension so necessary to the strengthening of any organism or institution. Without such opposition the single tax corporation might become flaccid. Unfortunately, too many within this group are merely offering an opposing faith or gospel; few bother to think their opposition through to the point of offering a bill of particulars, each item of which could be examined on its merits. Until they do sharpen their objections and exceptions, they will contribute little that is useful to a balanced interpretation of the experiment; the results will be merely an endless repetition of " 't'is" and " 't'aint."

2. A second group professes to believe that the single tax corporation carries too much weight in the community—that some of its past actions have handicapped community growth and development. Illustrations offered by individuals so classified range all the way from assertions of colony domination of the town council to the restrictive clauses embodied in the deeds of streets and parks. Actually, it has been a long time since the corporation or its governing body has taken official positions on local issues not directly involving the corporation; members who have been elected to the town council are in no sense official representatives of the colony. In point of fact, the single tax corporation reasonably could be criticized for its weak official opposition to the recent municipal licensing code —an action diametrically opposed to a fundamental tenet of its creed. The fact that the official opposition was weak, and the further fact that the code was adopted, offer eloquent testimony to the relative impotence of the corporation within municipal Fairhope. There can, however, be little doubt but that the

conviction of the early colonists with respect to public ownership of utilities is a major reason why the municipality of Fairhope owns all local utilities except the telephone. It is also evident that the prohibition against any private commercial
concession obtaining a franchise for more than a year, has
affected the commercial development of the beach parks. Upon
occasion corporation spokesmen have called attention to this
restriction in the park deed and thereby have frustrated certain
individuals. But deeds may be amended and any reasonable,
responsible proposal to do so quite likely would be received by
the corporation with an open mind and a decision could be
reached on the merits of the case.

3. A third group includes all those who believe that their
individual pocketbooks have been adversely affected by the
presence of the single tax corporation. Prominent within this
group are private land speculators. Some of these have been
hurt both by the quite evident local preference for leased lands
and by the pressure caused by the corporation's practice of
investing a large part of its income in public improvements.
Some (but by no means all) of the real estate brokers feel that
their business has been adversely affected by the existence of the
single tax corporation. It is difficult to evaluate such attitudes
in view of the fact that an appreciable proportion of the sales
of Fairhope realtors has been of improvements on colony lands,
and that corporation officials have been quite co-operative in
explaining to prospective purchasers the principles and procedures of single tax corporation leaseholds. While we have
not made a determined effort to get to the bottom of these attitudes we do offer as a tentative suggestion that the usual attitude of Fairhope realtors is rooted in one or more of the following: a traditional mode of thinking about land; an imperfect
understanding of corporation policies and procedures; and an
anticipation of private gain to those on the ground if the corporation should be dissolved.

Implicit in the suggestion that an announced policy of neutrality would remove most irrational and unresolved conflicts
among the corporation, its lessees and the community, is the

assumption that the majority of Fairhopers are sufficiently mature to analyze and to resolve specific issues on their merits. And of course this includes a consensus as to the criteria used in determining what is meritorious. Much depends on the soundness of this assumption, because the ultimate judgment of the Fairhope venture as a social experiment depends on the social understanding and acceptance of its effects, not on the effects alone. The authors are neither social psychologists nor skilled personal opinion analysts; hence, they cannot test the assumption. Perhaps the corporation might benefit from the services of trained public opinion analysts.

A third by-product of an acceptance of the recommendations we have made might be a solution of the membership and continuity of leadership problems. For at least thirty years the membership has shown concern over the difficulty of keeping its ranks filled with young, sincere and capable newcomers. Yet despite this explicit concern the membership has continued to shrink, and to increase in average age. Why has this been so?

A partial explanation is the $100 membership fee which in no sense is an investment on which interest or dividends are paid or any other material gain received.

Another part of the explanation is that only a few individuals would be acceptable to the corporation as members; prospective members must both understand and believe in discriminatory land taxation. The corporation long ago learned that it had to screen individuals applying for membership in order to protect itself against those who might desire to dissolve it for their own gain, or who might sabotage the underlying rent policy.

But the most fundamental cause of the continuing membership problem lies in the fact that the corporation does not appear to need the money, time or talents of those who otherwise might qualify. As the present secretary has stated, the only reason an individual would have for applying for membership today would be a sincere desire to help the corporation carry on its experiment. If this is so, few will apply until the corporation adopts some revitalizing program that will provide challenging opportunities for new blood. If it does not succeed in this it will fail as a positive force.

Our general conclusion is that although the single tax colony has been a principal instrumentality in the transformation of "an indifferent cow pasture" into an attractive, thriving and generally sound community, it has not yet achieved its ultimate long-range objective. As Mr. Bellangee put it over sixty years ago, the underlying purpose of the colony should be "to educate the public to demand local option in taxation." We do not, however, regard this failure as a final one. There is yet time for the single tax corporation to grasp the nature of its survival value and, by adopting consistent policies and procedures, achieve its educational objective just as it has achieved many material goals. The corporation need not, and we believe it will not, suffer the fate of so many "old" institutions and organizations, and become merely tired, overly-conservative and resigned.

Appendices

Appendix A

PREAMBLE

Believing that the economic conditions under which we now live and labor are unnatural and unjust, in violation of natural rights, at war with the nobler impulses of humanity, and opposed to its highest development; and believing that it is possible by intelligent association, under existing laws, to free ourselves from the greater part of the evils of which we complain, we whose names are hereunto subscribed do associate ourselves together and mutually pledge ourselves to the principles set forth in the following constitution:

ARTICLE I.   NAME

The name of this organization shall be Fairhope Industrial Association.

ARTICLE II.   PURPOSE

Its purpose shall be to establish and conduct a model community or colony, free from all forms of private monopoly, and to secure to its members therein, equality of opportunity, the full reward of individual efforts, and the benefits of co-operation in matters of general concern.

ARTICLE III.   CAPITAL STOCK

Sec. 1. The capital stock shall be one million dollars ($1,000,000), divided into five thousand (5,000) shares, of two hundred dollars ($200) each to be paid in under the direction of the executive council.

Sec. 2. Stock shall be transferable only on the books of the association, and to persons acceptable to the association as members.

ARTICLE IV.   MEMBERSHIP

Sec. 1.   Any person over eighteen years of age who shall subscribe for at least one share of capital stock, whose application shall be approved by the executive council, shall be a member of the association; provided that ten per cent of the membership may reject any applicant by filing with the secretary their written protest within thirty days after approval of application by the executive council.

Sec. 2.   The husband or wife of a member shall, upon signing the constitution, also be considered a member and entitled to a vote in the government of the association, while such relation exists in fact.

Sec. 3.   Any member against whom complaint of violation of the spirit and purpose of the association, or invasion of the rights of any of its members is preferred in writing by ten per cent of the membershp, may be expelled by the executive council, after full investigation of the charges preferred. Such investigation shall be public and the accused shall be entitled to be represented by counsel.

Sec. 4.   In case of expulsion of a member the association shall return to him in lawful money of the United States, the amount contributed by him to the capital stock, and the actual value of any improvements made by him on lands of the association, to be determined by three appraisers, one to be chosen by the trustees, one by the expelled member, and the third by these two.

ARTICLE V.   SUPREME AUTHORITY

Sec. 1.   Supreme authority shall be vested equally in the membership, to be exercised through the initiative and referendum as hereinafter provided.

Sec. 2.   Each member not in arrears to the association shall be entitled to one vote and one only, at all elections.

ARTICLE VI.   OFFICERS

Sec. 1.   The officers of the association shall be: a president; a vice president; a secretary; a treasurer, who shall be superintendent of the department of Finance and Insurance; three trustees; and a superintendent of each of the following departments: Lands and Highways; Public Services; Merchandising; Industries; Public Health.

Sec. 2.   The six superintendents of departments shall constitute the executive council of the association.

Sec. 3.   The president, vice president, and secretary shall serve for terms of one year. The trustees shall serve for three years, one being elected each year. The superintendents of departments shall serve for terms of two years, the first named three being elected on the odd numbered years and the last named three on even numbered years.

Sec. 4.   The president shall be the chief executive officer of the association; shall preside over meetings of the executive council and have the deciding vote in case of a tie. He shall countersign all warrants drawn upon the funds of the association under authority of the executive council, and perform such other duties as may herein or hereafter be provided.

Sec. 5.   The vice president shall, in case of the death, absence or inability of the president, perform his duties.

Sec. 6.   The secretary shall have charge of the records of the association; act as clerk of the executive council; draw and attest all warrants upon the treasurer authorized by the executive council; have charge of the correspondence relating to membership; and prepare annually, and at other times when requested by the board of trustees, full statements of the condition of the association in its various departments.

Sec. 7.   The treasurer shall be the custodian of the funds of the association, shall prepare and issue, under direction of the executive council, the association's non-interest bearing obligations hereinafter provided for; and shall have general charge of the financial affairs of the association, including the collection of revenues and the department of insurance. He shall give good and sufficient bond for the faithful accounting of all moneys coming into his hands.

Sec. 8.   The trustees shall have general oversight of all affairs of the association; shall have charge of all elections, canvass the votes cast and declare the results thereof; shall act as a committee to audit all accounts and review all reports of officers and employees; and shall annually, and at other times in their discretion, submit reports advising the members fully of the condition and needs of the association's business in all departments. They shall have access to the books and accounts of all officers and all employees at all times. They shall receive compensation only for time actively employed, and shall hold no other office, either by election or appointment.

Sec. 9.   The superintendents of departments provided for in section two of this article, shall have special supervision of the affairs of the association in their respective departments, and may employ such assistants as they shall deem necessary. They shall present to the executive council annually, and at such other times as requested by it, reports of the condition of the association's business in their departments, and suggest such changes therein as will in their judgment, best promote the interest of the association.

Sec. 10.   The executive council shall have general charge of the administration of the affairs of the association, and to that end may make such rules and regulations not inconsistent with its laws as they may deem necessary; may select and employ such agents and assistants not otherwise provided for as they may deem necessary to conduct the association's business; shall fix the compensation of all officers and employees of the association, which compensation shall not, however, exceed the earnings of like ability and energy in productive industry within its limits; shall make an annual appraisal of the rental value of all lands held for lease by the association; and shall perform all other duties necessary to the carrying out of the principles and purposes herein set forth.

ARTICLE VII.   INITIATIVE AND REFERENDUM

Sec. 1.   Upon petition of ten per cent of the membership any act of the executive council, legislative or administrative, or any measure set forth in said petition, shall be submitted to a vote of the membership.

Sec. 2.   No measure of general legislation passed by the executive council shall be in force until thirty days have elapsed after its passage without the filing of a petition for its submission to the membership; provided, that nothing in this section shall be construed to prevent the immediate taking effect of any order of the executive council necessary to the execution of the measures already in force.

Sec. 3.   Upon petition of twenty per cent of the membership the question of the dismissal of any officer, however elected or appointed, must be submitted to a popular vote.

ARTICLE VIII.   ELECTIONS

Sec. 1.   The regular annual election shall be held on the first Thursday of February of each year.

Sec. 2.   Special elections may be held at any time, at the discretion of the executive council, or on petition of ten per cent of the membership, after thirty days notice.

Sec. 3. At all elections printed official ballots shall be prepared,
under the direction of the board of trustees, on which shall appear
in full any measure to be voted upon, and the names of all candidates who may be placed in nomination in manner hereinafter
provided.

Sec. 4. Nominations for office may be made by petition of five
per cent of the membership filed with the secretary ten days before
election.

Sec. 5. The name of any officer whose term of office expires at
any election shall appear on the official ballot as a candidate for
re-election unless he shall have become disqualified to fill the
position, or his declination in writing be filed with the secretary
ten days before said election.

Sec. 6. All voting shall be by secret ballot.

Sec. 7. The affirmative votes of three-fourths of the members
shall be necessary to amend or repeal any part of this constitution.

Sec. 8. In the election of officers or on the passage of any
measure not conflicting with this constitution, the decision of a
majority of those voting shall be final.

Sec. 9. Should no candidate for any office receive a majority of
the votes cast at any election the trustees shall order a second election to be held two weeks thereafter for such officer, but only the
names of the three candidates receiving the highest number of votes
shall appear on the official ballot at said second election. If at the
second election no candidate receives a majority, a third election
shall be held two weeks thereafter, but only the two names receiving
the highest number of votes at said election shall appear on the
official ballot.

ARTICLE IX.   LAND

Sec. 1. There shall be no individual ownership of land within
the jurisdiction of the association, but the association shall hold as
trustee for its entire membership, the title to all lands upon which
its community shall be maintained.

Sec. 2. Its lands shall be equitably divided and leased to members at an annually appraised rental which shall equalize the varying advantages of location and natural qualities of different tracts,
and convert into the treasury of the association for the common
benefit of all of its members, all values attaching to such lands not
arising from the efforts and expenditures thereon of the lessees.

Sec. 3. Land leases shall convey full and absolute right to the
use and control of lands so leased, and to the ownership and disposi-

tion of all improvements made or products produced thereon so long as the lessee shall pay the annually appraised rentals provided in the foregoing section, and may be terminated by the lessee after six months' notice in writing to the association and the payment of all rents due thereon.

Sec. 4.   Leaseholds may be assignable but only to members of the association. Such assignments must be filed for record in the office of the secretary and the person to whom the same is assigned thereby becomes the tenant of the association.

Sec. 5.   The association shall have a prior lien on all property held by any lessee upon lands of the association, for all arrearages of rent.

Sec. 6.   If any lessee shall exact or attempt to exact from another a greater value for the use of land, exclusive of improvements, than the rent paid by him to the association, the executive council shall, immediately on proof of such fact, increase the rental charge against such land to the amount so charged or sought to be charged.

Sec. 7.   Nothing shall be construed to invalidate the association's right of eminent domain. In all leases of lands the association shall reserve the right to resume the possession of the same for public purposes, on payment of all damages sustained by the lessee thereby, to be determined by three appraisers, one to be chosen by the board of trustees, one by the lessee and the third by these two.

ARTICLE X.   FINANCIAL

Sec. 1.   To provide its members with a safe, adequate, and independent medium for effecting exchanges of property and services, the association may issue its non-interest bearing obligations, which shall be receivable by it at face value in full payment of all its demands.

Sec. 2.   These obligations may be issued for the purchase and handling of all merchandise; for advances on goods stored in the association's warehouses to a safe percentage of their values; and for all expenses of the public services; but no more shall be issued for such public service during any year than the estimated revenue available during said year for such purpose.

ARTICLE XI.   PUBLIC UTILITIES

No private franchise for the supplying of its members with such public necessities as water, light, heat, power, transportation facilities, irrigating systems, etc., shall ever be granted by the association, but it shall as soon as practicable, erect and maintain the necessary plants, and perform such services, converting all revenues therefrom into the general treasury of the association.

ARTICLE XII.   DISTRIBUTION AND PRODUCTION

Sec. 1.   To effect in distribution the efficiency and economy demanded in the interests alike of producers and consumers, the association shall establish a store or stores at which shall be kept for sale all articles of merchandise for which there shall be sufficient demand.

Sec. 2.   Such merchandise shall be sold to members and non-members alike, at prices approximately those prevailing in the locality where the association's community may be located, and from the profits arising therefrom, the executive council may at its discretion set aside a portion to be paid into the general treasury of the association and a portion to be used as additional capital in said stores. The remainder shall be divided among the members trading at said stores, in proportion to their other purchases.

Sec. 3.   For the purpose of accumulating capital with which to purchase stock for such stores the executive council may at its discretion require of each member before taking residence upon its lands the payment of a sum not to exceed one hundred dollars for which shall be issued its non-interest bearing obligations described in article ten.

Sec. 4.   A department shall also be established to assist the association's members in the disposition of their surplus products to the greatest advantage. To this end stable products may be purchased at the market price by the management, or handled on commission as desired. Convenient and safe storage shall also be provided.

Sec. 5.   Believing that the free competition of free men in productive industry is natural and beneficent, and that therefrom will arise a natural and just co-operation in enterprises requiring the associated labor and capital of individuals, it is the declared general policy of this association to leave production free to individual enterprise. It reserves the right, however, to establish and conduct manufactories and industries of any kind.

Sec. 6.   Nothing in this article shall be construed to give the association the authority to establish a monopoly in any of the departments herein mentioned; and the same shall be maintained on a self-supporting basis, so far as possible.

ARTICLE XIII.   INSURANCE

Recognizing insurance as a proper department of public business the association will provide for the insurance of its members and their property when desired, at approximate cost of the service.

ARTICLE XIV.   PARKS, LIBRARIES, ETC.

Ample provision shall be made in platting the lands of the association for land for parks and all other public purposes; and as rapidly as may be, lands thus intended shall be improved and beautified; and schools, libraries, public halls, natatoriums, etc., established and maintained at the expense of the association for the free use and enjoyment of the members and their families.

ARTICLE XV.   NO TAXATION

No taxes or charges of any kind other than hereinbefore provided for shall be levied by the association upon the property or persons of its members.

ARTICLE XVI.   PAYMENT OF TAXES

All taxes levied by the state, county or township on the property of the association or any of its members held within its jurisdiction, credits excepted, shall be paid out of the general fund of the association.

ARTICLE XVII.   MAY DEAL WITH NON-MEMBERS

Lands not desired for use by members may be leased to non-members, and any services which the association may undertake to perform for its members may be performed also for non-members, at the discretion of the executive council, on such terms as it may provide.

ARTICLE XVIII.   INDIVIDUAL FREEDOM

The natural rights of its members to absolute freedom in production, exchange, associations, beliefs, and worships shall never be abrogated or impaired by the association, and the only limit to the exercise of the will of individuals shall be the equal rights of all others.

Appendix B

PRESENT CONSTITUTION OF THE
FAIRHOPE SINGLE TAX CORPORATION

PREAMBLE

Believing that the economic conditions under which we now live and labor are unnatural and unjust, in violation of natural rights, at war with the nobler impulses of humanity and opposed to its highest development; and believing that it is possible by intelligent association, under existing laws, to free ourselves from the greater part of the evils of which we complain, we, whose names are hereunto subscribed, do associate ourselves together and mutually pledge ourselves to the principles set forth in the following constitution.

ARTICLE I. NAME

The name of this organization shall be FAIRHOPE SINGLE TAX CORPORATION.

ARTICLE II. PURPOSE

Its purpose shall be to establish and conduct a model community or colony, free from all forms of private monopoly, and to secure to its members therein, equality of opportunity, the full reward of individual efforts, and the benefits of co-operation in matters of general concern.

ARTICLE III. MEMBERSHIP

Sec. 1. Any person over the age of eighteen years whose application shall be approved by the Executive Council and who shall contribute to the Corporation one hundred dollars, shall be a mem-

ber of the Corporation; provided that on petition of ten per cent
of the qualified membership filed with the secretary within thirty
days after action on any application by the Executive Council, such
application shall be submitted to a vote of that membership.

Sec. 2.   The husband or wife of a member shall, upon signing
the constitution, also be considered a member and entitled to vote
in the government of the Corporation, while such relation exists in
fact; but only while such member remains in good standing.

Sec. 3.   Any member against whom complaint of violation of the
spirit and purpose of the Corporation, or invasion of the rights of
its members, is preferred in writing by ten per cent of the membership, may be expelled by the Executive Council, after full investigation of the charges preferred.   Such investigation shall be public,
and the accused shall be entitled to be represented by counsel.

Sec. 4.   In case of the expulsion of a member the Corporation
shall return to him in lawful money of the United States, the
amount contributed by him to the Corporation.

Sec. 5.   Certificates of membership shall be transferable only on
the books of the Corporation, to persons acceptable as members.

ARTICLE IV.   SUPREME AUTHORITY

Sec. 1.   Supreme authority shall be vested equally in the membership, to be exercised through the initiative and referendum as
hereinafter provided.

Sec. 2.   Each member not in arrears to the Corporation shall be
entitled to one vote, and one only, at all elections involving changes
in this constitution; but on elections of officers and questions concerning local administration of affairs, only those shall be entitled
to vote who are in person on the Corporation grounds on the day
of election and who are not in arrears.

ARTICLE V.   OFFICERS

Sec. 1.   The officers of the Corporation shall be: a president, a
vice-president, a secretary, a treasurer, who shall be superintendent
of Finance and Insurance, three trustees, and a superintendent of
each of the following departments, Lands and Highways, Public
Service, Industries, and Public Health.

Sec. 2.   The superintendents of the departments shall constitute
the Executive Council of the Corporation.

Sec. 3.   The president, vice-president and secretary shall serve for
terms of one year. The trustees shall serve for terms of three years—
one being elected each year. The superintendents of departments
shall serve for terms of two years—the first named three being

elected on the odd numbered years and the last named two on even numbered years.

Sec. 4.   The president shall be the chief executive officer of the Corporation, shall preside over the meetings of the Executive Council and have the deciding vote in case of a tie. He shall countersign all warrants drawn upon the funds of the Corporation under authority of the Executive Council, and perform such other duties as may herein or hereafter be provided.

Sec. 5.   The vice-president shall, in case of the death, absence or inability of the president, perform his duties.

Sec. 6.   The secretary shall have charge of the records of the Corporation, act as clerk of the Executive Council, draw and attest all warrants upon the treasurer authorized by the Executive Council, have charge of the correspondence relating to membership, and prepare annually, and at other times when requested by the board of trustees, full statements of the condition of the Corporation in its various departments.

Sec. 7.   The treasurer shall be the custodian of the funds of the Corporation, shall prepare and issue, under the direction of the Executive Council, the Corporation's non-interest-bearing obligations hereinafter provided for; and shall have general charge of the financial affairs of the Corporation, including the collection of revenues and department of insurance. He shall give good and sufficient bond for the faithful accounting of all monies coming into his hands.

Sec. 8.   The trustees shall have general oversight of all affairs of the Corporation, shall have charge of all elections, canvass the votes cast and declare the result thereof, shall act as committee to audit all accounts and review all reports of officers and employees, and shall annually and at other times in their discretion, submit reports advising the members of the condition and needs of the Corporation's business in all departments. They shall have access to the books and accounts of all officers and employees at all times. They shall receive compensation only for time actively employed, and shall hold no other office, either by election or by appointment.

Sec. 9.   The Superintendents of departments provided for in Sec. 2 of this article shall have special supervision of the affairs of the Corporation in their respective departments and may employ such assistance as they deem necessary. They shall present to the Executive Council annually, and at such other times as requested by it, reports of the condition of the Corporation's business in their departments, and suggest such changes therein as will in their judgment best promote the interests of the Corporation.

Sec. 10.   The Executive Council shall have general charge of the administration of the affairs of the Corporation, and to that end may make such rules and regulations not inconsistent with its laws as they may deem necessary; may select and employ such agents and assistants not otherwise provided for as they may deem necessary to conduct the Corporation's business; shall fix the compensation of all officers and employees of the Corporation, which compensation shall not however, exceed the earnings of like ability and energy in productive industry within its limits; shall make an annual appraisal of the rental value of all land held for lease by the corporation; and shall perform all other duties necessary to the carrying out of the principles and purposes herein set forth.

ARTICLE VI.   INITIATIVE AND REFERENDUM

Sec. 1.   Upon petition of ten per cent of the qualified membership any act of the Executive Council, legislative or administrative, or any measure proposed by the petitioners, shall be submitted to a vote of that membership at the time set in said petition; provided that where amendments to this constitution are proposed, thirty days' notice must be given, and on other matters at least twenty-four hours' notice.

Sec. 2.   No measure of general legislation passed by the Executive Council shall be in force until thirty days have elapsed after its passage without the filing of a petition for its submission to the membership; provided, that nothing in this section shall be construed to prevent the immediate taking effect of any order of the Executive Council necessary to the execution of measures already in force.

Sec. 3.   Upon petition of twenty per cent of the membership entitled to vote upon election of officers, the question of the dismissal of any officer, however elected, or appointed, must be submitted to a popular vote.

ARTICLE VII.   ELECTIONS

Sec. 1.   The regular annual election shall be held on the first Thursday of February of each year.

Sec. 2.   Special elections may be held at any time, at the discretion of the Executive Council, or on petition of ten per cent of the membership, provided, that the notice provided in Article VI be given.

Sec. 3.   At all elections printed official ballots shall be prepared, under direction of the board of trustees, on which shall appear in full any measure to be voted upon and the names of all candidates who may be placed in nomination in the manner hereinafter provided.

Sec. 4. Nominations for office may be made by petition of five per cent of the membership filed with the secretary ten days before the election.

Sec. 5. The name of any officer whose term of office expires at any election shall appear on the official ballot as a candidate for re-election unless he shall become disqualified to fill the position, or his declination in writing be filed with the secretary ten days before said election.

Sec. 6. All voting shall be by secret ballot.

Sec. 7. The affirmative votes of three-fourths of the members shall be necessary to amend or repeal any part of this constitution. Providing that notice of every such election shall be sent by registered mail with return card, to every non-resident member at his last given place of address, and if the postoffice reports inability to deliver mail to any such member and no ballot shall be received from him at said election he shall not be counted as a member in determining the result thereof.

Sec. 8. In the election of officers or on the passage of any measure not conflicting with this constitution, the decision of a majority of those voting shall be final.

Sec. 9. Should no candidate for an office receive a majority of the votes cast at any election, the trustees shall order a second election to be held two weeks thereafter for such officer, but only the names of the three candidates receiving the highest number of votes shall appear on the official ballot at said second election. If at the second election no candidate receives a majority, a third election shall be held two weeks thereafter; but only the two names receiving the highest number of votes at said election shall appear on the official ballot.

ARTICLE VIII.   LAND

Sec. 1. There shall be no individual ownership of land within the jurisdiction of the Corporation, but the Corporation shall hold as trustee for its entire membership, the title to all lands upon which its community shall be maintained.

Sec. 2. Its lands shall be equitably divided and leased to members at an annually appraised rental which shall equalize the varying advantages of location and natural qualities of different tracts and convert into the treasury of the Corporation for the common benefit of its members, all values attaching to such lands, not arising from the efforts and expenditures of the lessees.

Sec. 3. Land leases shall convey full and absolute right to the use and control of lands so leased and to the ownership and disposition of all improvements made or products produced thereon as long as the lessee shall pay the annually appraised rentals provided in the foregoing section, and may be terminated by the lessee after six months notice in writing to the Corporation and the payment of all rent due thereon.

Sec. 4. Leaseholds shall be assignable but only to members of the Corporation. Such assignments must be filed for record in the office of the Secretary, and the person to whom the same is assigned thereby becomes the tenant of the Corporation.

Sec. 5. The Corporation shall have a prior lien on all property held by any lessee upon lands of the Corporation for all arrearages of rent.

Sec. 6. If any lessee shall exact or attempt to exact from another a greater value for the use of land, exclusive of improvements, than the rent paid by him to the Corporation, the Executive Council shall immediately, upon proof of such fact, increase the rental charge against such land to the amount so charged or sought to be charged.

Sec. 7. Nothing shall be construed to invalidate the Corporation's right of eminent domain. In all leases of land the Corporation shall reserve the right to resume the possession of the same for public purposes, on payment of all damage sustained by the lessee thereby, to be determined by the appraisers, one to be chosen by the board of trustees, one by the lessee and the third by these two.

ARTICLE IX.   FINANCIAL

Sec. 1. To provide its members with a safe, adequate and independent medium for effecting exchanges of property and services, the Corporation may issue its non-interest-bearing obligations which shall be receivable by it at their face value in full payments of all its demands.

Sec. 2. These obligations may be issued for all expenses of the public service, but no more shall be issued for such public services during any year than the estimated revenue available during said year for such purpose.

ARTICLE X.   PUBLIC UTILITIES

No private franchise for the supplying of its members with such public necessities as water, light, heat, power, transportation facilities, irrigating systems, etc. shall ever be granted by the Corporation, but it shall as soon as practicable, erect and maintain the necessary plants, and perform such services, converting all revenues therefrom into the general treasury of the Corporation.

ARTICLE XI.   INSURANCE

Recognizing insurance as a proper department of public business, the Corporation will provide for the insurance of its members and their property when desired at approximate cost of service.

ARTICLE XII.   PARKS, LIBRARIES, ETC.

Ample provision shall be made in platting the lands of the corporation for land for parks and all other public purposes, and as rapidly as may be, lands thus intended shall be improved and beautified, and schools, libraries, public halls, natatoriums, etc., established and maintained at the expense of the Corporation for the free use and enjoyment of the members and their families.

ARTICLE XIII.   NO TAXATION

No taxes or charges of any kind other than heretofore provided for shall be levied by the corporation upon the property or persons of its members.

ARTICLE XIV.   PAYMENT OF TAXES

Sec. 1.   All taxes assessed against the Corporation shall be paid from the Corporation Treasury.

Sec. 2.   Receipts for taxes paid by any lessee to state, county, town or school district, upon his improvements and personal property held upon any leasehold, (moneys and credits excepted) shall be applicable upon the rent of such leasehold; provided that the corporation shall not be bound to accept such tax receipts to a greater amount for any year than the rent for that year on the ground on which such improvements and personal property are held.

ARTICLE XV.   MAY DEAL WITH NON-MEMBERS

Lands not desired for use by members may be leased to non-members, and any services which the Corporation may undertake to perform for its members may be performed also for non-members, at the discretion of the Executive Council, on such terms as it may provide.

ARTICLE XVI.   INDIVIDUAL FREEDOM

The natural rights of its members to absolute freedom in production, exchange, associations, beliefs, and worship, shall never be abrogated or impaired by the Corporation, and the only limit to the exercise of the will of individuals shall be the equal rights of all others.

ARTICLE XVII.   NO INDEBTEDNESS

No bonds or mortgages, or interest-bearing indebtedness of any kind shall ever be given or assumed by the corporation.

Appendix C

APPLICATION FOR LAND OF
FAIRHOPE SINGLE TAX CORPORATION

Fairhope, Ala.,_____195__

TO THE EXECUTIVE COUNCIL, FAIRHOPE SINGLE TAX CORPORATION

I, the undersigned, hereby make application for lease of

_____

_____

upon the terms and conditions set forth in the leases given by you, and the further stipulations set forth in this application, which are hereby made a part of my lease contract as fully as if printed in the lease.

I make this application with the full knowledge that I will be required to pay your Corporation the full rental value of the land exclusive of my improvements thereon. I understand that the rental value will increase as demand for the land increases, whatever the cause; that said value will be determined by the Corporation in the manner set forth in its constitution and lease contracts; that the corporation will pay all taxes on the land, and will accept from lessees on rent, receipts for taxes paid to state, county, town, or school district, on improvements and personal property (moneys and credits excepted) held upon leaseholds but not to an amount greater for any year than the rent for such year on the land on which such improvements and personal property are held; and that the balance will be spent for the public good as provided in its constitution.

I further particularly state that I understand the purpose of the Single Tax Corporation to be to prevent anyone profiting from the holding of its land, other than by the bona fide *use of the same,* and respecting this purpose, of which I am beneficiary, in the Corporation making land available to me without any purchase price and recognizing further that it is to my interest that what is commonly known as "land speculation" shall be kept out of the "Single Tax Colony" conducted by the Corporation, so that rents assessed against me shall not be affected by an artificial demand for land not for use, but for resale at a profit. I agree that I will neither ask nor accept a "bonus" for transfer of an unimproved leasehold and that the proved attempt to do so shall be cause for forfeiture of my lease to such unimproved land; nor will I charge an excessive price, out of any fair relation to the value of my improvements for transfer of an improved leasehold; and, recognizing that in the transfer of an improved leasehold there are necessarily two factors of value, one the improvements which are my property and the other the land upon which the same stand, which is not my property but the property of the Corporation, I agree to advise the Corporation, before a transfer of an improved leasehold shall be effective, of the exact consideration for the transaction and that the Corporation, if it believes the consideration to include in fact a profit for the transfer of the land which belongs to it, shall be entitled to examine me and the prospective purchaser as to the elements of value in the consideration and if satisfied that the consideration is in part for the possession of the land above the value of the improvements, may refuse approval of the transfer; in which event I shall be entitled to call for an appraisal of the value of my improvements by three disinterested persons, myself and the Corporation each choosing one out of three persons named by the other and the third being selected by the two; and the Corporation shall be required to approve the transfer at such consideration as the arbitrators shall find to be the real value of my property, if accepted by me; it being understood and agreed that every factor of value attaching to the premises proposed to be transferred due to my efforts or expenditures, or in any way to my initiative which is transferable, such as the good will of a going business, the exercise of taste in planning improvements or the making of grounds attractive, or the element of time and care in growing an orchard or shade trees, or making land more productive by improved methods of farming, or increment of value due to increasing cost of building, shall be held to inure to me as fully as tangible structures upon the land; the purpose being to protect the user and improver of land in the full ownership and right of transference of everything due to him, but to preserve to the Corporation all value due to demand for the land exclusive of improvements.

I have read your constitution and pledge myself that while I hold lease of Fairhope land I will not oppose the full application of the principles set forth therein.

Respectfully yours,

_____

Appendix D

THIS LEASE, made this_____day of_____, 19__, by and between Fairhope Single Tax Corporation, of Fairhope, Baldwin County, Alabama, and

_____

of_____, hereinafter designated as the lessee.

WITNESSETH: that the said Fairhope Single Tax Corporation; for and in consideration of the annual rentals and covenants hereinafter mentioned, has this day leased to and said Lessee taken possession of the following described portion of land to wit

_____

_____

Section_____, Township 6 South, Range 2 East, Baldwin County, Alabama, for the term of ninety-nine years from this date subject to the conditions herein stated and the representations and agreements of the Lessee in his application for said land hereto attached and a part of this lease contract as fully as if printed herein.

(1) The said lessee, his heirs, or successors, shall pay to the said Fairhope Single Tax Corporation, its successors or assigns, in equal payments, on the first days of January and July of each year, the annual rental value of said land, exclusive of his improvements thereon, to be determined by the said Corporation through its Executive Council or Board of Directors, under its avowed principle of so fixing the rentals of its lands as to equalize the varying advantage of location and natural qualities of different tracts and convert into the treasury of the Corporation for the common benefit of its lessees, all values attaching to such lands, exclusive of improvements thereon. And the said lessee, for himself and his heirs,

hereby expressly agrees that the said annual rent shall be determined by the said Corporation upon the principle just stated, and shall be expended by said Corporation, subject to the conditions hereinafter stated.

(2) The land herein leased shall be used for such purposes only as may not be physically or morally offensive to a majority of the resident members of the Fairhope Single Tax Corporation, and the lessee shall be subject to such reasonable sanitary regulations as may be imposed by the Executive Council or Superintendent of Public Health of said Corporation.

(3) In consideration of the agreement of said lessee to pay the rentals herein provided for, the Fairhope Single Tax Corporation will pay all taxes upon the land leased and will accept from the lessee on rent receipts of the County Tax Collector or Clerk of Town of Fairhope, for taxes paid to State, County, School District, or Town, upon the improvements and personal property (moneys and credits excepted) held by lessee upon the land herein leased; or, if all rent due be paid, will give him a certificate in amount equal to such acceptable tax receipts remaining, receivable from bearer at face value on rent, or in discharge of any indebtedness to the Corporation; provided that said lessee will appoint whomsoever may be designated by the Corporation as his agent to return his property for taxation where permitted by law so to do; that in no event shall the Corporation be bound to accept tax receipts on more than a fair assessed valuation of the property, on the basis required by law, or to a greater amount for any year than the rent for that year on the land on which such improvements and personal property are held.

(4) And the said Fairhope Single Tax Corporation further agrees in consideration of the covenants of the said lessee herewith evidenced, that no part of the rents paid by him upon the land herewith leased, shall be appropriated as dividends to its members or any other persons, but that all shall be administered as a trust fund for the equal benefit of those leasing its lands.

(5) And the said Corporation still further agrees, that in the distribution of the benefits which its purpose is to secure for residents upon its lands, no distinction shall be made between individuals, whether members of the corporation or not, but that with the exception of the right of members as participants in the government of the Corporation, all shall be treated with strict equality.

(6) It is agreed by the parties hereto, that time is of the essence of this contract. All rents not paid within ninety days of the time

the same become due, shall be subject to interest at eight per cent per annum until paid; and the lessor shall have a prior lien on all improvements upon the land herein leased, to secure the payment of the rent and for the payment of all other indebtedness of any description whatsoever, by the lessee to the lessor. If the land leased be unimproved, or in the judgment of the Corporation the improvements thereon are not of sufficient value to secure the payment of the rent and cost of collecting same, then, in such event, all rights under this lease shall be subject to forfeiture without notice, after the rents shall have been due and unpaid for ninety days; and the improvements, if any, shall revert to the lessor. Upon failure to pay the rents, or any portion thereof, for six months after the same become due, the lessor is hereby authorized to sell at public sale the improvements on any leasehold, for satisfaction of the amount due, after first giving ten days' notice by one publication in some paper published at Fairhope, Alabama, the cost of such publication and the making of such sale to be paid with the rent out of the proceeds of such sale, and the remainder, if any, to be returned to the lessee or such other person as may be authorized to receive the same. The lessor, its agent or attorney, may conduct such sale; and the party so conducting the sale is authorized to make, in the name of the lessee, proper conveyance of the property so sold. The lessee hereby waives all right of exemption of any property as against the collection of any debt due under this contract. The sale of the improvements under legal process shall work a forfeiture of all rights under this lease.

(7) The Fairhope Single Tax Corporation agrees that in case of its dissolution, either by voluntary act of its members or otherwise, and the division of its assets among its members, the said lessee, if a member, shall be entitled to have the land herein described and leased—or so much of it as he may designate—included in his portion, at its actual value at the time, exclusive of improvements thereon, and if it exceed in value such portion, to purchase the excess at such valuation. If not a member, the lessee may at such time acquire title to the land herein leased by paying to the Corporation its actual value exclusive of improvements upon it.

(8) The Fairhope Single Tax Corporation believes its title to the land herein leased to be good, and will use every proper means in its power to maintain the same; but it is distinctly understood that the Corporation, acting only with the benevolent purpose to secure land and administer it for the benefit of those who may desire its use, shall not be held liable for any losses resulting from defects in its title.

(9) The right is reserved by the Fairhope Single Tax Corporation to resume possession of all or any portion of the land herein described, for public purposes only, on payment of the appraised value of the improvements thereon.

(10) Should it become necessary to determine the value of said land, or of the improvements thereon, in compliance with the provisions of clauses 3, 7, or 9, of this lease, the same shall be determined by three disinterested persons, to be selected as follows: the Corporation and the Lessee each choosing one of three persons named by the other and the third to be selected by the two. Should any Lessee fail to name his arbitrators within thirty days after written notice by registered mail to do so, the Corporation may name an arbitrator for him.

(11) This lease is assignable only to members of the Fairhope Single Tax Corporation, or to persons acceptable to it. The original lease must be returned to the Corporation with any proposed transfer endorsed thereon and, if approved, a new lease will be issued to the transferee.

(12) Surface rights only are hereby leased. All mineral rights are reserved by lessor.

(13) This lease may be terminated by the lessee after six months notice in writing to the Corporation and the payment of all rent due to the end of such six months period. A lessee having filed the required notice of desire to surrender, may dispose of any improvements thereon, (subject to the Corporation's lien for rent) but if not so disposed of, the land shall come to the Corporation, together with any improvements remaining thereon, without any claim of the surrendering lessee on account of such improvements, and the Corporation may decline to accept a partial surrender of a leasehold where the portion surrendered or retained, would not, in its opinion, be desirable to other lessees.

In witness whereof, the parties hereunto have set their hands in duplicate.

FAIRHOPE SINGLE TAX CORPORATION

This_____day of_____ 19_____

By order Ex. Council_____19_____

_____ Lessee

_____ Lessee

By _____President

_____Secretary

Appendix E

APPLICATION FOR MEMBERSHIP

TO EXECUTIVE COUNCIL
FAIRHOPE SINGLE TAX CORPORATION:

Having carefully read your constitution, heartily approving same and desiring to participate in the work you are doing, I hereby make application for membership in your corporation.

I particularly state that I understand and approve of your policy of collecting from holders of your land the full rental value of their holdings and, in consideration thereof assuming the payment of all taxes assessed against their improvements and personal property thereon, (moneys and credits excepted), except that no more shall be paid out in such taxes than is paid in in rent.

That I understand and agree that the certificate of membership I will receive if accepted, will not entitle me to any dividends or profits from the operation of the corporation, and will be transferable only with the consent of the corporation and to persons acceptable to it as members.

Further, I hereby pledge on my honor that I will not if a lessee charge or accept from any one a "bonus" for transfer of my leasehold if in unimproved condition, nor an excessive price out of any fair relation to the value of the improvements, for the transfer of the same with improvements thereon. Also, that I will not, while a member, buy any land for purpose of sale at a profit, in the near vicinity of the Colony. And I agree that the establishment of the fact of my violation of these conditions shall be cause for the forfeiture of my membership, on repayment to me of the membership fee.

MEMORANDA

Member of what trade or reform organization?_____
_____

Read Henry George's works?_____Which?_____
_____

References as to my standing as a Man   and a Singletaxer:
                                       Woman
_____

Date_____ Date accepted_____

Payment with application $_____. Final payment_____

Appendix F

This list consists of:

(a) The official membership record of the Fairhope Single Tax Corporation as of May 15, 1955, arranged by certificate number. Missing certificate numbers may be accounted for either because they were spoiled, transferred to an individual acceptable to the corporation as a member (and to whom a new certificate was issued), or surrendered for cancellation. Deceased members are carried on the Official record unless an acceptable transfer has been effected or the certificate has been surrendered by the estate for cancellation.

(b) An alphabetical list of sometime members either of the Fairhope Industrial Association or the Fairhope Single Tax Corporation. These individuals either failed to surrender the share of stock in the Fairhope Industrial Association, have transferred their certificates to individuals obtaining membership in their own rights, or have surrendered the certificates for cancellation.

The list does *not* include spouses of members who have, or have had, membership privileges by signing the constitution, but who have never held a certificate in their own names. The voting membership always is larger than the surviving certificate holders.

MAY 15, 1955

MEMBERSHIP RECORD FAIRHOPE SINGLE TAX CORPORATION

DECEASED

1	Ernest B. Gaston	99	L. C. Mann
2	Bolton Smith	101	Daniel Kiefer
6	L. G. Bostedo	108	W. S. Sumner
9	Joseph Fels	111	C. L. Rockwell
12	A. White	115	M. A. Bowen
15	C. L. Coleman	116	Geo. L. Hopping
16	Wm. Stimpson	120	Mrs. Kath. I. du Choine
18	S. S. Mann	121	Nelson Rockwell
28	M. V. Watros	122	J. G. Lorenzen
30	Wm. Call	124	Harry H. Parker
33	Jacob Reitz	125	Mrs. Hettie B. Wilmans
37	Richard L. Atkinson	126	Mrs. Anne B. Call
38	Wm. Schemenour	129	Fiske Warren
41	Bolton Hall	130	Daphne L. E. Curtis
45	Jacob W. Braam	133	Eloise L. Cross
49	George L. Rusby	141	C. F. Nesbit
50	Townsend P. Lyon	142	Emil Knips
52	Mrs. Ada Graham Wolf	146	Lawrence Winberg
63	John A. Patterson	149	V. S. McClintock
64	J. McDermaid	151	F. L. Higgins
70	Thomas P. Craig	159	Hartley Dennett
75	Miss N. Clements	161	Mrs. David K. Tone
78	J. F. Johnson	162	Delia K. Bancroft
81	Alex. J. Melville	163	Henry C. Littlefield
85	Jennie L. Monroe	164	Emma F. Connolly
86	J. J. Pastoriza	165	Laura A. Powell
88	Geo. H. Thornton	174	V. M. Reynolds
93	Dewey Wheeler	178	Fred Chapin, Sr.
95	A. N. Whittier		

NON-RESIDENT
(some of whom may be deceased)

27	George Hastings Wood	112	E. R. Williams
44	Fred Mathison	117	Thos. H. Bowen
48	Lona Ingham Robinson	131	O. F. E. Winberg
57	John B. Howarth	138	Frank Hemley Mallory
60	Joseph C. Campbell	143	C. D. Van Vechten
62	Charles C. Eckert	144	J. T. Worcester
65	Jas. S. Paton	147	Albert E. Schalkenbach
69	Arthur K. Trenholme	153	Thomas E. Mann
71	Walter Coates	154	Floy Mann Schermerhorn
73	Mary D. Hussey	157	Raymond Clegg Dyson
91	Dr. Hans Schmidt	158	Irene Lucier Buell
96	S. E. Mann	160	Abe D. Waldauer
97	Marie B. Moore	167	J. Francis Lemon
107	A. M. Troyer	179	Laird W. Snell
109	H. W. Noren	186	Caroline Ann McConnel

RESIDENT

5	A. H. Mershon	172	Sam Dyson
35	Ivy Powell Norton	173	Elof M. Tuveson
90	J. E. Gaston	175	R. Lucier Rockwell
100	Reuben L. Rockwell	176	Ronald B. Mershon
113	Helen Call	177	Lucien T. Wilcox
114	Marmaduke Dyson	180	Marvin Nichols
134	Isabella G. Payne	181	Lillian B. Totten
136	Don E. Andrews	182	Alexis C. Ferm
137	E. J. Roberts	183	Henry W. Rowe
140	Axil Johnson	184	Daphne B. Anderson
152	Jesse O. Stimpson	185	Oliver M. Rockwell
156	C. A. Gaston	187	Lenore M. Wolcott
168	Frances G. Crawford	188	Claude W. Arnold
169	Ethel O. Darrow	189	Marvin O. Berglin
170	R. H. Brown		

SOMETIME MEMBERS WHOSE CERTIFICATES
HAVE BEEN TRANSFERRED OR CANCELED

P. Y. Albright
Gilbert Anderson
David Gibson Armitage
Dr. Clara E. Atkinson
William A. Baldwin
George Bancroft
J. M. Beckner
Mrs. Lizzie Beckner
James Bellangee
A. O. Berglin
W. E. Brokaw
C. K. Brown
Frank L. Brown
Mrs. H. N. Brown
William Brown
Miss Altoona A. Chapman
E. Yancey Cohen
Mrs. L. J. N. Comings
Samuel H. Comings
R. E. L. Connolly
M. M. Cope
A. A. Corbett
Henry Creswell
John S. Crosby
A. J. Cullen
Mrs. Lenora Curtis
C. A. Darrow
Henry W. Davenport
J. N. Dixon
James W. Eden
William Edgerton
William Hemingway Edwards
Fred C. Foord
C. C. Ford
R. A. Hail
J. A. Haggstrom
Mrs. Anna Brown Hail
Charles A. Hall
Ida May Hall
William L. Heller

Mrs. Marie Howland
J. P. Hunnel
W. W. Kile
George Knowles
Dr. A. Lamon (Mrs.)
Capt. George A. R. Lawrence
S. Howard Leech
August Lewis
Charles E. Littlefield
John McCarthy
Mary A. McCarthy
G. M. McConnel
W. G. McConnel
Mary E. Mead (Mann)
Nathaniel Mershon
Annabell Douglas Mogg
J. J. Mogg
Clarence S. Moore
Paul Nichols
P. A. Parker
Selanah R. Patterson
William R. Pickering
George M. Pilcher
George Pollay
Robert F. Powell
H. F. Ring
Robert Ring
Franklin Rockwell
E. W. Rose
Edwin S. Ross
W. L. Ross
H. C. Schakel
C. F. Shandrew
Carrie P. Sykes
Marion Smith
Alice Christopher Snell
Mrs. Louisa Southworth
J. H. Springer
G. J. Stemerdink
Herman J. Stemerdink

William Stimpson
George Q. Thornton
Robert Tyson
Mrs. Levia Vander-Meulen
Charles Wilson

George W. Wood
E. C. Woolcott
S. D. Yarnelle
F. R. Young

Appendix G

TO THE PRESIDENT AND EXECUTIVE OFFICERS
OF THE FAIRHOPE SINGLE TAX CORPORATION:

At a meeting of the leaseholders of your corporation held at Masonic Hall on the evening of January 14, certain resolutions and memorials to your body were presented and unanimously adopted and the undersigned committee appointed to present the same to your honorable body. Said resolutions and memorials are as follows:

WHEREAS: Article 6, Section 10 of the Constitution of the Fairhope Single Tax Corporation confers exclusive power on the Executive Council to fix their own salaries as officers of each department, and

WHEREAS: This same Article and Section clothes them with exclusive arbitrary power to fix the rates of rents upon the leaseholders from year to year, therefore,

BE IT RESOLVED: That we do hereby memorialize said Council to immediately take the necessary steps to submit the question as to whether or not any officer constituting the Executive Council and receiving a salary, or in any manner in the pay of the Corporation is eligible to be a member of the rating board having power to fix the rent from year to year. Secondly,

WHEREAS: The Constitution has left the limit of taxation or fixing of rents to the caprices of the will of that Council to arbitrarily and with incentive to raise the rents so as to increase salaries, and thus annually unsettle conditions at the most unpropituous season of the year when the greater part of our visitors come from the

North and carry back with them the detrimental news of our disturbed conditions; also resulting in the great discouragement of the great majority of the leaseholders, all their plans being frustrated, their calculations upset, and as many have expressed the situation, 'I don't know what to do.' Many of them are quite disheartened, they do not know whether to pull up stakes and move off or to give someone one-half the lowest cash estimate of their improvements to get them to buy the other half, or to stoutly refuse to pay such unreasonable annually increased rents, and by so doing force a legal issue that will by law fix a limit to this excess to which there is now no limit: Therefore be it

RESOLVED: That it is the sense of this body of leaseholders, that we memorialize the said Executive Council of the Fairhope Single Tax Corporation to take such steps with as little delay as possible, to fix a legal limit beyond which the rating board cannot annually raise the rents to double and triple, quadruple and even quintuple the rents of the year previous. This body is assured that there will be no peace until there is a limit fixed to this non-ending and excessive taxation. We believe that a limit can easily and understandably be fixed on a percentage of the actual cash value of the land leased, say not to exceed 5 per cent of such valuation on all agricultural lands, and when it is found imperative that a public improvement is found necessary and is demanded and to accomplish this it is necessary to raise the rents over this limit, let the leaseholders say by their votes that they are willing to be taxed for it.

Appendix H

TO THE MEMBERS OF THE FAIRHOPE SINGLE TAX CORPORATION:

We, the tenants of your Corporation, also your neighbors and friends, respectfully present the following for your consideration:

We understand that the Fairhope Colony was established that the rental value of its lands might be used in lieu of moneys raised annually by taxation.

We believe that "the intention of the parties is the marrow of the contract."

That taxes should only be collected to provide for the necessities, welfare and prosperity of a community.

When collected and expended for any other purpose the community becomes a landlord in the most objectionable sense of the word.

That when these needs and desires have been determined the assessment of taxes becomes a matter of simple arithmetic.

That the needs and desires of a community can be best determined by the whole people.

That no satisfactory method of separating the wise and virtuous from the unwise and unscrupulous has ever been discovered.

That the rental value of land depends to some extent upon its natural location, but to a much greater extent in towns and cities upon its location in a community.

That if a community becomes desirable to live in its values will go up and adjoining values will go down; reverse conditions produce reverse results; the values in either case must be inverse to each other.

That the experience of those places where government by the people has been tried, proves that the people's desires keep pace with the rental value of land, if indeed they are not the cause of it.

That any system of taxation that cannot be safely trusted with the whole people is not worthy of consideration.

If the people who have made their homes in a community and put their all into it are not fit to be trusted with its management, who is?

We believe that citizenship is a duty and not a privilege, and conveys responsibility, and we believe it to be unsafe to make further improvements in a community that is governed by any less than all its people.

We ask you to consider these matters and take such action at an early date as will definitely determine the future policy of the Fairhope Single Tax Corporation.

The following motion was unanimously carried: "That it is the sense of this meeting of leaseholders, that in order that the business of this Colony shall not come to a standstill for the want of funds, that the rentals for the year 1905 be fixed at the sum total for the year 1904, with 10 per cent added thereto."

Respectfully submitted,

J. W. Lawrence
W. A. Baldwin
Henry M. Ewald
Leaseholders' Committee

Appendix I

REPLY OF THE TRUSTEES TO
THE MEMORIAL OF C. L. COLEMAN,
H. S. GREENO, AND OTHERS,
DECEMBER 1, 1905 (Paraphrased)

AMONG the questions asked of the trustees by the Coleman memorial were the following:

(1) Why, at the recent special election, was the resolution requiring thirty days residence on colony lands as a prerequisite to voting disregarded?

The trustees answered that there was no such resolution. They stated that under the authority of the constitution the corporation declared qualified to vote all members whose vote had been challenged.

(2) Does the corporation recognize boat certificates as equivalent to cash, and if so, are the same taken at par and by what authority?

The trustees replied that the corporation has been following a policy of accepting boat certificates at par on donations to its land fund. The corporation does not purchase or redeem these certificates at the present time. The owners of the boat have provided that its net earnings shall be donated to the corporation from time to time to provide a fund with which to make such purchases or redemptions.

(3) Why was a voucher for $212 issued to the steamer *Fairhope* in return for a loan of $200 when the charter forbids the corporation to incur interest-bearing obligations?

The trustees answered that the $12 was a bonus, not interest, that no time had been fixed for its payment and that a delay of payment would cause no additional expense to the corporation. The trustees argued that interest-bearing obligations increase with the lapse of time. They further stated: "The design of the constitution in forbidding interest-bearing obligations was to create a condition under which any lenders would be discouraged from trying to exploit the corporation through bonds and mortgages."

(4) What is the financial standing of the corporation at this time? Please give its assets and liabilities in detail.

The trustees replied that the assets consisted of unpaid rents and various items of property. They made the general statement that the improvements which belong to the corporation are worth many times all its liabilities, not to mention the value of corporation lands.

The total amount of script issued was $540. The corporation has records of the destruction of not less than $284 and the retirement of an additional $20. The balance outstanding is $236, some of which has been carried away as souvenirs, and some has been lost or destroyed.

This (the script) constitutes a liability of the corporation which we do not believe has been enumerated in former statements. "We have also included some items that have likewise been overlooked, owing to the fact that until recently the treasurer has only kept a cash account, and these items are recorded only in the minutes of the secretary. These [previously omitted items] include $100 lent by A. White, Vallejo, California, toward the expenses of the well and a like sum by our fellow townsman, George Knowles, and $50 from D. D. Chichester of Philadelphia. All of these loans are interest free. Rents charged to Knowles have been applied in payment until his claim is reduced to $14, making the total unpaid loans $164. Currently the unpaid rent is sufficient to pay the outstanding warrants and the debt on the well and leave a balance of $31.95. This added to the $31.20 cash in the treasury, plus the receipts from the wharf for the two remaining months of this year, ought to cover the land tax of the association and leave a small amount for corporation running expenses. The corporation, therefore, should begin the new year with a small debt, if any. There is no compelling need for the immediate retirement of the script. This is simply outstanding warrants held by our own people. But the debt on the well should be paid as soon as possible since it has been standing for several years. That it does not draw interest is all the more reason why it should be promptly discharged."

The trustees reconstructed entries made in the stub books of the treasurer and presented the following statement of assets.

ASSETS

Land—in section 18 between the windmill and the bay		
(with the bay frontage of 2,000 feet)	221	acres
in section 17, next east	280	"
in section 16, next east	320	"
in section 15, next east	400	"
in section 14, next east	160	"
in section 22, south of section 15	160	"

Total   1,541 acres

Wharf, 1,800 feet long, warehouse, and bathhouse
Well, windmill, and tank
Schoolhouse, new and complete, with two rooms
Telephone system
Town hall, well lighted and seated

Equity in the White tract		$ 600.00
In the hands of a representative to pay Mr. White		74.97
Boat certificates, face value		911.75
Unpaid rents for 1905		681.09
Cash on hand in the treasury:		
Script	$20.50	
Wharf certificates	1.15	
Checks	9.55	$ 31.20

LIABILITIES

Outstanding warrants	$ 485.14
Outstanding script	236.00
Taxes for 1905	254.88
Debt on the well	164.00

(The trustees emphasize that none of these liabilities draw interest.)

(5) What amount of script has been issued by the corporation, to whom, and for what purpose?

The trustees replied that the Fairhope Industrial Association had issued $440 and the Fairhope Single Tax Corporation, $100. The script was issued partly to individuals for service rendered in lieu of warrants or orders. The late issue was made to the treasurer and by him transferred, if desired, to creditors of the corporation.

(6) By what authority was this done?

By the article of the constitution entitled "Financial."

(7) Where is the record of this issue of script kept?

It is kept in the books of the treasurer, the records of the secretary, stub book, the cash book, and the minutes.

(8) Give detailed statements of the amount of collections made by Bellangee, showing the names of donors and the amount of each contribution.

The trustees complied with this in detail. There were 170 donations ranging from $.50 to $200. The total collections by Mr. Bellangee amounted to $3,240.70. Disbursements from this sum were:

Mr. Bellangee's expenses on the first trip	$ 435.80
His salary at $1.00 per day	212.00
Expenses for the second trip	278.69
His salary at $1.00 per day	148.50
Postage and stationery, spent by Mr. Bellangee	4.91
Mr. Bellangee's time in corresponding	5.00
Paid for the Morphy tract	799.76
Paid on the White tract	600.00
Cash in hands of special representative for transfer to Mr. White	74.97
Covered into the corporation treasury, not withdrawn	135.32
Boat certificates in the hands of the treasurer	540.75
Wharf certificates canceled by the treasurer	5.00
Total	$3,240.70

(9) It was inquired as to why the donations collected by Mr.
Bellangee had not been turned over to the treasurer.

In reply, the trustees pointed out that these were in the custody
of the treasurer and special representative until his successor was
elected in February. Since he (Mr. Bellangee) ceased to be treasurer, he has continued to collect the funds and apply them to the
specific purpose for which he was appointed special representative
"to which he considers himself bound both to the corporation and
to the donors who have entrusted their funds to his hands." Reference to the statement herewith will show that over $130 of dona-
tions left by him in the treasury last year has been temporarily
diverted from its purpose.

(10) These special collections not having been covered into the
treasury, by what authority can receipts given for the same be
accepted as cash for membership fees?

The trustees answered by the authority of Section 1, Article 3,
of the constitution and by the further authority of the Council
which made them expressly so receivable from anyone accepted as
a member. "Besides, they have been covered into the treasury by
proper entries in its books for the money received in 1903 and have
been fully reported to the Council as contributions by its special
representative since that time."

(11) What amount of the receipts for donations have been received on membership fees, whose receipts, and for what members?

On the membership of J. A. Hagstrom, receipts of donations by
C. W. Darby—$10, J. H. Blakey—$18, Mary C. Richard—$17; on

the membership of Jacob W. Braam, receipts from L. G. Bostedo—
$37.50, and Mrs. Jenny L. Monroe—$55.30. All others have donated
on their individual memberships either cash, boat certificates, land,
or receipts given them for cash. Transferred receipts amount to
$137.80 in the two above cases, the parties using the receipts con-
tracted to make good to the parties furnishing them by future payments to the land fund. (Mr. Bellangee stated that "Mr. Braam
has already paid into my hands $80.30 for this purpose.") "These
receipts were purposely made receivable on membership account
from anyone acceptable as a member since they represent actual
contributions to the land fund, add to membership, and facilitate
the work of the special representative. We believe the corporation
would do itself great discredit were it to refuse to receive contributions of boat certificates on the membership account because the
boat was built in the interest of the community. The entire cost of
the boat would not cover the benefits which it has brought to us."

Signed: C. E. Littlefield
           Marie Howland
           J. Bellangee

Index